FEUDALISM

F. L. Ganshof

Professor Emeritus of Medieval History
in the University of Ghent

TRANSLATED BY PHILIP GRIERSON, F.B.A.
WITH A FOREWORD BY SIR F. M. STENTON, F.B.A.

Third English Edition

Longman

To the memory of
FRANÇOIS OLIVIER-MARTIN
Membre de l'Institut
Professor of Legal History in the University of Paris

LONGMAN GROUP LIMITED
London
Associated companies, branches and representatives
throughout the world

© *F. L. Ganshof 1961 and 1964*

First English Edition 1952
Second English Edition (Harper Torchbooks) 1961
Third English Edition 1964
Seventh impression 1977
ISBN 0 582 48216 X

Permission has been given to the
National Library for the Blind for this book
to be transcribed into Braille

"Qu'est-ce que la féodalité" was first published
in 1944. (Second edition 1947, Third edition
1957). It has been translated into Portuguese
(Que è o Feudalismo, 1959), German (Was ist
das Lehnswesen? 1961), and Spanish (El
Feudalismo, 1963).

Printed in Hong Kong by
Commonwealth Printing Press Ltd

FEUDALISM

Frontispiece: see Note, page viii.

CONTENTS

PART ONE
ORIGINS

PART TWO
CAROLINGIAN FEUDALISM

PART THREE

THE CLASSICAL AGE OF FEUDALISM
(Tenth to Thirteenth Centuries)

ABBREVIATIONS

M.G.H. stands for the great German collection of sources entitled *Monumenta Germaniae Historica*. Its various parts are referred to as follows:

Constitutiones
Epistolae
Leges
Leges Nat(ionum) Germ(anicarum)
SS. = *Scriptores*
S.R.M. = *Scriptores rerum Merovingicarum*

NOTE ON THE FRONTISPIECE

The illustrations are from the Heidelberg manuscript of the *Sachsenspiegel*, which dates from the beginning of the fourteenth century. The upper one shows the rite of homage (below, p. 72). The lord, seated and in the presence of his feudal court, takes his vassal's hands between his own. The vassal is provided symbolically with three additional hands; with one he points to himself and with the other two he points to the fief, represented by corn stalks, in return for which he does homage. This is the 'monstrée de fief' (p. 128).

The lower illustration shows investiture with various types of fief. A king seated on his throne invests a bishop and an abbess with a sceptre, and three laymen by handing them each a standard.

The illustrations are on fos. 6v. nd 21r. of the Heidelberg MS., Cod. Pal. germ. 164, and represent respectively the Lehnrecht, 24, 2, and the Landrecht, iii. 60, 1. A selection of other illustrations reproduced in colour from the same manuscript has been published by E. von Künszberg, *Der Sachsenspiegel. Bilder aus der Heidelberger Handschrift* (Leipzig, Insel Verlag, 1937). A complete facsimile of the equally remarkable Dresden manuscript was published by K. von Amira, *Die Dresdener Bilderhandschrift des Sachsenspiegels: Facsimile Band* (2 Parts. Leipzig, 1902); a commentary on this in English is available in an article by Mr. M. Letts, 'The Sachsenspiegel and its Illustrators', *Law Quarterly Review*, xlix (1933), 555–74.

FOREWORD

It is now six years since the first appearance of Professor Ganshof's *Qu'est-ce que la féodalité?* During this interval, historians have come to realize that they possess in this book a survey of the essential feudal order which in breadth of view, wealth of learning, and sureness of judgment is a model among works of its scale. It is firmly based on recorded facts, and in spite of its title it should be regarded, not as the exposition of a theory, but as a synthesis of evidence. It is a tribute to Professor Ganshof's skill as a writer that the reader is never conscious of a break in continuity as the survey passes from the obscurities of the Dark Ages, where the origins of feudalism lie, to the highly developed organization of the twelfth and thirteenth centuries, for which the sources of information embarrass the historian through their sheer volume.

It should be added that the book makes much of its effect through the limitations which its author imposes upon himself. In his Introduction, Professor Ganshof writes: 'I propose . . . to concentrate on the regions lying between the Loire and the Rhine, which were the heart of the Carolingian state and the original home of feudalism. Further afield, in the south of France and in Germany beyond the Rhine, the institutions that grew up are often far from typical of feudalism as a whole. I shall deal less fully with England, and scarcely at all with Italy.' In the past, the student of feudalism has repeatedly been led astray by the mirage of an ideal type of social order, dominant throughout western Europe, displaying everywhere the same essential characteristics and resting everywhere upon identical postulates. Professor Ganshof's study is founded upon a realist's sense that social arrangements, arising from the instinctive search for a tolerable life, vary indefinitely with varieties of time and circumstance. In place of an ideal, everywhere in mind but nowhere achieved, Professor Ganshof's readers are shown, within a wide but central region, the development of what may justly be called 'classical feudalism' from its Carolingian origins.

Although Professor Ganshof gives little space to England, his work should be considered closely by all students of English feudalism. They will find many suggestions which throw light on English problems, and much material which invites comparison with the English evidence. They will continually be reminded of the many occasions at which, in the comparative study of societies, differences are as significant as resemblances. Above all, after following his survey of the manner in which the feudal order arose in northern France, the Low Countries, and the Rhineland, they will be delivered from the insidious temptation to regard the peculiarities of the English system as deviations from a continental model. They will realize that English feudalism is the product of English history.

Professor Ganshof's work, revised in the light of recent research, is now made easily available to English readers in a translation by Mr. Philip Grierson. It would be pointless to add anything to this statement in commending this edition most sincerely to all who are interested in the structure and development of medieval society.

1950   F. M. STENTON

AUTHOR'S PREFACE TO THE FIRST ENGLISH EDITION

The first edition of this volume appeared at Brussels, in the autumn of 1944, in the Collection Lebègue (published by the Office de Publicité) and went out of print in a few months. In the second (French) edition, published in February 1947, I attempted to repair certain omissions, to correct some errors of fact, and to take into account work published during the war in England and America and articles and studies published between the autumn of 1944 and the spring of 1946.

In this first (English) edition I have been able to take account of recently published studies and of the reviews of the two previous editions. I have also taken the opportunity of making further corrections in the text, of expanding certain sections which seemed to me to be inadequate, and of bringing the bibliography up to date. In both revisions I have been able to profit by the comments and criticisms of several of my friends and colleagues, and I wish particularly to express my gratitude to Dr. Cécile Seresia, to Professors J. Dhondt, E. I. Strubbe and C. Verlinden of the University of Ghent, to Professor F. Vercauteren of the University of Liége, to Dr. L. Voet, curator of the Plantin-Moretus Museum at Antwerp, to Dr. T. Luykx of the Higher Institute of Commercial Studies at Antwerp, and to Mr. P. Grierson of the University of Cambridge. To the last of these, who is also my translator, I should also like to express my appreciation of the pains he has taken and the success he has achieved in presenting my ideas as precisely as possible in an English form. Dr. Lipstein, of the University of Cambridge, has been kind enough to give his advice on the most suitable English renderings of certain continental legal terms, and Professor T. F. T. Plucknett, of the University of London, has read the translation in manuscript and given his advice on many points. To both of these I am sincerely grateful.

F. L. GANSHOF

BRUSSELS, 7 *February* 1950.

AUTHOR'S PREFACE TO THE TORCHBOOK EDITION

The text of this second English edition is basically the same as that of the first, but it has been revised in the light of the changes that were made in the third French edition, some further emendations have been inserted, and the bibliography has been brought up to date.

In addition to the scholars mentioned in the preface to the first edition, the author would like to express his gratitude to Professors F. Beyerle, J. Rubió-Lois, and R. Van Caenegem, of the Universities of Freiburg i. Br., Barcelona, and Ghent respectively, for the comments and suggestions they have been kind enough to make.

F. L. GANSHOF

BRUSSELS, 5 June 1961.

AUTHOR'S PREFACE TO THE THIRD
ENGLISH EDITION

The text of this third English edition is basically the same as that of the second one (published by Harper Torchbooks in 1961). It has, however, been revised in the light of the changes that were made in the German edition, of recent historical and legal literature and of the result of the author's own research. The bibliography has been brought up to date.

F. L. GANSHOF

BERKELEY (CALIFORNIA)
1 *March* 1964

INTRODUCTION

The word 'feudalism' (Germ. *Lehnswesen* or *Feudalismus*; Fr. *féodalité*) is one to which many different meanings have been attached. During the French Revolution, it was virtually adopted as a generic description covering the many abuses of the *Ancien Régime*, and it is still in popular use in this sense today. Even if this quite illegitimate extension of its meaning be ignored, there exist many attempts at its analysis and definition which do not seem to be very closely related to one another. But if we limit ourselves to essentials it will be found that the word is used by historians in two more or less distinct senses.[1]

Feudalism may be conceived of as a form of society possessing well-marked features which can be defined without difficulty. They may be summarized as follows: a development pushed to extremes of the element of personal dependence in society, with a specialized military class occupying the higher levels in the social scale; an extreme subdivision of the rights of real property; a graded system of rights over land created by this subdivision and corresponding in broad outline to the grades of personal dependence just referred to; and a dispersal of political authority amongst a hierarchy of persons who exercise in their own interest powers normally attributed to the State and which are often, in fact, derived from its break-up.

This type of society, whether one calls it 'feudalism' or the 'feudal régime', was that of western Europe in the tenth, eleventh and twelfth centuries. It came into existence in France, Germany, the kingdom of Burgundy-Arles and Italy, all of them states deriving from the Carolingian empire, and in other countries—England, certain of the Christian kingdoms of Spain, the Latin principalities of the Near East—which passed under their influence. In other places and at other times, types of society have existed

---

[1] The way in which the word is commonly used by historians in Soviet Russia and in other countries behind the Iron Curtain seems to me to be absolutely irrelevant.

which show many analogies with the feudalism which one finds in France, Germany, the kingdom of Burgundy-Arles and Italy during the Middle Ages, so that scholars have been led to speak of 'feudalism' in ancient Egypt, in India, in the Byzantine empire, in the Arab world, in the Turkish empire, in Russia, in Japan, and elsewhere. In making these comparisons, historians have sometimes drawn parallels which a closer examination of the sources has failed to justify, though in some instances, as in that of Japan, the parallelism is very close.[1]

The late Professor Calmette and the late Marc Bloch, in writing on feudalism in this sense, preferred to speak of 'feudal society'. Such a practice, if it were generally accepted, would have the advantage of allowing one to use the word 'feudalism' only in the second sense that can be attached to it.

In this second sense of the word, 'feudalism' may be regarded as a body of institutions creating and regulating the obligations of obedience and service—mainly military service—on the part of a free man (the vassal) towards another free man (the lord), and the obligations of protection and maintenance on the part of the lord with regard to his vassal. The obligation of maintenance had usually as one of its effects the grant by the lord to his vassal of a unit of real property known as a fief. This sense of the word feudalism is obviously more restricted and more technical than the other. We can perhaps regard it as the legal sense of the word, while the first use covers mainly the social and political senses.

These two meanings of the word feudalism are not unrelated to each other, since the society which we have described above is known as feudal because in it the fief, if not the corner-stone, was at least the most important element in the graded system of rights over land which this type of society involved.

Feudalism in its narrow sense, meaning the system of feudal and vassal institutions, was also, and to an even greater degree than

[1] See particularly O. Hintze, 'Wesen und Verbreitung des Feudalismus', in *Sitzungsberichte der Preuss:schen Akademie der Wissenschaften, Phil.-Hist. Klasse* (1929), pp. 321-47, M. Bloch, *La Société féodale. Les classes et le gouvernement des hommes* (Paris, 1940), pp. 241 ff. and *Studien zum mittelalterlichen Lehenswesen*, edited by T. Mayer (Lindau, 1960). See also the articles on 'Feudalism' in the sixth volume of the *Encyclopaedia of Social Sciences* (sections by K. Asakawa on Japan, O. Franke on China, and A. H. Lybyer on the Islamic world), and for Japan the work of F. Joüon des Longrais, *L'Est et L'Ouest* (Tokyo and Paris, 1958).

feudalism in its broad sense, proper to the states born of the break-up of the Carolingian empire and the countries influenced by them. Once again, however, we find in other historical environments certain institutions which bear a remarkable resemblance to those of the feudalism of the western middle ages. The 'daimios' and the 'bushi' or 'samurai' of Japan can be compared to vassals, and land which was granted to them is comparable to the fief. The same is true of the Arab and Turkish 'iqta'. Russia, between the thirteenth and sixteenth centuries, knew institutions very close to that of vassalage, and the 'conditional ownership' which is met with at the same period and which in the fifteenth century came to be known as 'pomestie' has many analogies with the fief.[1]

In the pages that follow, I intend to deal with feudalism only in the narrow, technical, legal sense of the word. The structure of society or the state will appear only in so far as it exercised a direct action over feudal institutions or was acted upon by them. It would be impossible in a sketch as brief as this to give even a superficial account of the characteristics of feudal society. But the student will be better prepared to understand the characteristics of such a society if he has first grasped the significance of certain of its legal forms: the meaning of the words 'lord' and 'vassal', and the legal relationship which existed between the persons whom they described.

In this short sketch I propose to study feudalism mainly as it existed in France, in the kingdom of Burgundy-Arles and in Germany, since in these countries its characteristics were essentially the same, and to concentrate on the regions lying between the Loire and the Rhine, which were the heart of the Carolingian state and the original home of feudalism. Further afield, in the south of France and in Germany beyond the Rhine, the institutions that grew up are often far from typical of feudalism as a whole. I shall deal less fully with England, and scarcely at all with Italy. These are the limitations in space. As for the limitations of time, I shall be mainly concerned with the tenth, eleventh and

---

[1] Hintze, *op. cit.*, pp. 338 ff.; Bloch, *op. cit.*, pp. 249–52; on Japan, Joüon des Longrais, *op. cit.*; on Russia, see also A. Eck, *Le moyen âge russe* (Paris, 1933), pp. 195–212, 219–24 and M. Hellmann, *Probleme des Feudalismus in Russland*, in *Studien* (see above, pp. xx, note 1), p. 235 ff.

twelfth centuries, though also, to some extent, with the thirteenth century. These formed the classical age of feudalism, when its institutions were full of vigorous life and activity. But in order to understand them, it will be necessary to see how this system of institutions came into existence within the framework of the Carolingian monarchy in the eighth and ninth centuries, and this I deal with in an introductory section. The period after the classical age I shall scarcely refer to at all.

In my analysis and description of feudal institutions, I have endeavoured to bring out as clearly as possible their essential features, since, once these are grasped, it is easy for the student to disentangle the elements that can properly be described as feudal in the institutions of the period or country with which he is primarily concerned. The illustrations of their working which are given, and which are intended to make them at once more real and more intelligible to the modern reader, are largely taken from the Low Countries: from Flanders, which was part of the medieval kingdom of France, and from the Lotharingian principalities (Brabant, Cambrai, Guelders, Hainault, Holland, Liége, Looz, Luxemburg, Namur, etc.) which were part of the medieval kingdom of Germany. There are, in fact, few regions in western Europe for which contemporary sources relating to feudal institutions between the tenth and thirteenth centuries are more detailed and revealing than for these 'middle lands'.

This volume necessarily owes much to the work of scholars who have studied or are studying the institutions of feudalism, but some of the ideas put forward are my own and derive from my independent researches. Since my aim is to place at the disposal of the educated public a general outline of one of the great institutions of European history, as it appears in the light of the most recent research, I have refrained from elaborate and controversial annotation; the only notes are the references to contemporary documents cited in the text.[1] A brief bibliography is given for the benefit of the reader who desires to push his studies further.

[1] In this I follow the example of Marc Bloch; see his *La société féodale. La formation des liens de dépendance* (Paris, 1939), p. 8, n. 1. In order to render the documents more generally intelligible, they have been translated into English, but the Latin originals have been left in the text, instead of being relegated to the footnotes, in the hope that they may not be ignored by the student.

BIBLIOGRAPHY

This bibliography is only intended to provide readers with some suggestions for further reading, and makes no claims to completeness. It does not include the original authorities referred to in the notes.

1. FEUDALISM IN THE FRAMEWORK OF INSTITUTIONAL HISTORY

Hintze, O. 'Wesen und Verbreitung des Feudalismus' in *Sitzungsberichte der Preussischen Akademie der Wissenschaften, Phil.-Hist. Klasse* (Berlin 1929), pp. 321–47. (General sketch, remarkable for its range and grasp of essentials.)
Studien zum mittelalterlichen Lehenswesen, Lindau and Konstanz, 1960 (Vorträge und Forschungen herausgegeben von . . . Theodor Mayer, V).
Les liens de vassalité et les immunités. (Recueils de la Société Jean Bodin, vol. i) 2nd ed. Brussels, 1958.
Encyclopaedia of the Social Sciences (ed. E. R. A. Seligman and A. Johnson), articles in vol. vi (London, 1932) on 'Feudalism' by Marc Bloch (European), A. H. Lybyer (Saracen and Ottoman), O. Franke (Chinese) and K. Asakawa (Japanese).
Coulborn, Rushton (ed.) *Feudalism in History.* Princeton, 1956.
Joüon des Longrais, F. *L'Est et l'Ouest. Institutions du Japon et de l'Occident comparées.* Tokio and Paris, 1958.

II. FEUDALISM IN GENERAL

Calmette, J. *La société féodale.* 4th ed. Paris, 1938. (Clear and reliable summary.)
Mitteis, H. *Lehnrecht und Staatsgewalt.* Weimar, 1933. (The best work on feudal institutions in western and central Europe. See the comments and addenda of W. Kienast, 'Lehnrecht und Staatsgewalt im Mittelalter', in *Historische Zeitschrift,* clviii (1938), pp. 3–51.)
Bloch, Marc. *La société féodale. I. La formation des liens de dépendance. II. Les classes et le gouvernement des hommes.* 2 vols. Paris, 1939–40. English translation by L. A. Manyon: *Feudal Society.* New York and London, 1961. (One of the outstanding historical works of modern times. Feudalism is studied in the general framework of contemporary society. Based on a profound study of sources of the most varied descriptions. Excellent bibliography.)
Stephenson, C. *Medieval Feudalism.* Ithaca, 1942. (Popular sketch.)
IXᵉ Congrès International des Sciences Historiques, Paris, 1950. I. Rapports. (Section on medieval institutions by R. Boutruche, C. Cahen, P. Dollinger and Y. Dollinger-Leonard, pp. 417–71, especially pp. 440–7 on feudalism and the problems raised in recent works.)
Boutruche, R. *Seigneurie et féodalité. I. Le premier âge des liens d'homme à homme.* Paris, 1959. (Very well informed.)

III. THE ORIGINS AND THE FRANKISH PERIOD

Dopsch, A. 'Beneficialwesen und Feudalität', in *Mitteilungen des Oester-reichischen Instituts für Geschichtsforschung*, xlvi (1932), pp. 1-36.

Lot, F., Pfister, C., and Ganshof, F. L. *Les destinées de l'Empire en Occident de 395 à 888* (Vol. I of the *Histoire du Moyen Age* in the *Histoire Générale* of G. Glotz). 2nd ed. Paris, 1940-41. (Chapter 25, by F. Lot on 'Les transformations de la société franque: Avenement du régime vassalique'.)

Cronne, H. A. 'Historical Revisions, xci. The origins of feudalism', in *History*, xxiv (1940), pp. 251-9. (Critical summary.)

Stephenson, C. 'The origin and significance of feudalism', in *American Historical Review*, xlvi (1941), pp. 788-812, and in the author's selected essays, *Medieval Institutions*. Ithaca, 1954, pp. 205-33.

Sánchez-Albornoz, C. *En torno a los orígenes del feudalismo.* 3 vols. Mendoza (Argentine), 1942.

Sánchez-Albornoz, C. *El 'stipendium' hispano-godo y los orígenes del beneficio prefeudal.* Buenos Aires, 1947.

Sánchez-Albornoz, C. 'España y el feudalismo Carolingio', in *I problemi della civiltà Carolingia.* Spoleto, 1954. (Settimane di Studi del Centro Italiano di Studi sull'Alto Medioevo, i, 1953.)

Merea, P. 'Precarium e Stipendium', in *Boletin de Faculdade de Dirieto, Coimbra,* XXXV (1960).

Leicht, P. S. 'Gasindi e Vassali', in *Rendiconti della Reale Accademia Nazionale dei Lincei. Classe di Scienze morali, storiche e filologiche,* 6a serie, iii (1927), pp. 291-307.

Leicht, P. S. 'L'introduzione del feudo nell'Italia franca e normanna', in *Rivista di storia del diritto italiano,* xii (1939), pp. 421-37.

Leicht, P. S. 'Il feudo in Italia nell'età Carolingia', in *I problemi della civiltà Carolingia.* Spoleto, 1954. (Settimane di Studi del Centro Italiano di Studi sull'Alto Medioevo, i, 1953.)

Lesne, E. *Histoire de la propriété ecclésiastique en France,* Paris and Lille, 1910-43. Six vols. in 8 parts. (Vol. i and parts 1-3 of vol. ii are important for the part played by ecclesiastical property in the development of feudal institutions.)

Schur, J. *Königtum und Kirche im ostfränkischen Reiche vom Tode Ludwigs des Deutschen bis Konrad I.* Paderborn, 1931.

Lot, F. 'Origine et nature du bénéfice', in *Anuario de historia del derecho Español,* x, 1933, pp. 174-85.

Krawinkel, H. *Untersuchungen zum fränkischen Benefizialrecht.* Weimar, 1936.

Ganshof, F. L. 'Note sur les origines de l'union du bénéfice avec la vassalité', in *Etudes d'histoire dédiées a la mémoire de Henri Pirenne* (Brussels, 1937), pp. 173-89.

Ganshof, F. L. 'Benefice and vassalage in the age of Charlemagne', in *Cambridge Historical Journal,* vi (1939), pp. 149-75.

Ganshof, F. L. 'La juridiction du seigneur sur son vassal à l'époque carolingienne', in *Revue de l'Université de Bruxelles,* (1922), pp. 566-75.

Ganshof, F. L. 'L'origine des rapports féodo-vassaliques. Les rapports féodo-vassaliques dans la monarchie franque au nord des Alpes à l'époque carolingienne', in *I problemi della civiltà Carolingia.* Spoleto, 1954. (Settimane di Studi del Centro Italiano di Studi sull'Alto Medioevo, i, 1953.)

Ganshof, F. L. 'Les liens de vassalité dans la monarchie franque', in *Les liens de vassalité et les immunités* (above, p. xxv).

Ganshof, F. L. 'Das Lehnswesen im fränkischen Reich. Lehnswesen und Reichsgewalt in karolingischer Zeit', in *Studien zum mittelalterlichen Lehenswesen* (above, p. xxv).

Ganshof, F. L. 'Charlemagne et le serment', in *Mélanges d'histoire du Moyen Age dédiés à la mémoire de Louis Halphen*. Paris, 1951.

Lot, F. 'Le serment de fidélité à l'époque franque', in *Revue belge de philologie et d'histoire*, xii (1933), pp. 569–82.

Odegaard, C. E. 'Carolingian oaths of fidelity', in *Speculum*, xvi (1941), pp. 284-96.

Odegaard, C. E. *Vassi and fideles in the Carolingian Empire*. Cambridge (Mass.), 1945.

IV. FEUDALISM IN DIFFERENT COUNTRIES [1]

A. GERMANY

Waitz, G. *Deutsche Verfassungsgeschichte*. Vols. II, pt. i (3rd ed., Kiel, 1882), IV (2nd ed., Berlin, 1885), VI (2nd ed., revised by G. Seeliger, Berlin, 1896). (Particularly valuable on account of the number of texts cited in the notes.)

Brunner, H. *Deutsche Rechtsgeschichte*. Vol. II. 2nd ed., revised by C. Freiherr von Schwerin. Munich-Leipzig, 1928. (Excellent account of feudal institutions in the Frankish period.)

Schroeder, R. *Lehrbuch der deutschen Rechtsgeschichte*. 7th ed., revised by E. Freiherr von Künszberg. Berlin-Leipzig, 1932. (Particularly valuable for German feudalism at the period of the 'Rechtsbücher'.)

Huebner, R. *Grundzüge des deutschen Privatrechts*. 5th ed. Leipzig, 1930.

Tellenbach, G. (ed.) *Studien und Vorarbeiten zur Geschichte des gross-fränkischen und frühdeutschen Adels*. Freiburg i. B., 1957.

Ebel, W. Über den Leihegedanken in der deutschen Rechtsgeschichte', in *Studien zum mittelalterlichen Lehenswesen* (see above, p. xxv).

Bosl, K. 'Dienstrecht und Lehnrecht im deutschen Mittelalter', in *Studien zum mittelalterlichen Lehenswesen* (see above, p. xxv).

Klebel, E. 'Territorialstaat und Lehen', in *Studien zum mittelalterlichen Lehenswesen* (see above, p. xxv).

B. ENGLAND

Petit-Dutaillis, C. *La monarchie féodale en France et en Angleterre, Xᵉ–XIIIᵉ siècle*. Paris, 1933. English translation by E. D. Hurst under the title *The Feudal Monarchy in France and England from the 10th to the 13th*

---

[1] Since the feudalism of the Latin Orient did not fall within the scope of this book, no attempt has been made to deal with it in the bibliography. An excellent statement of the problem will be found in J. Prawer, 'Les premiers temps de la féodalité dans le royaume latin de Jérusalem' (*Tijdschrift voor Rechtsgeschiedenis*, xxii, 1954), and 'La noblesse et le régime féodal du royaume latin de Jérusalem' (*Le Moyen Age*, 1959). The author re-examines the position in the light of the feudalism of western Europe.

century. London, 1936. (Particularly valuable for its account of feudal institutions in England.)

Pollock, F., and Maitland, F. W. *The history of English law before the time of Edward I.* 2 vols. 2nd ed. Cambridge, 1898. (Feudal institutions at a fairly advanced stage of development.)

Plucknett, T. F. T. *A concise history of the Common Law.* 5th ed. London, 1956.

Jolliffe, J. E. A. *The constitutional history of medieval England from the English settlement to* 1485. 2nd ed. London, 1947. (Also the important review of the first ed. by Dr. H. M. Cam in the *English Historical Review,* liv (1939), pp. 483–9.)

Round, J. H. *Feudal England.* London, 1895. (A work which began a thoroughgoing revision of traditional views.)

Stenton, F. M. *The first century of English feudalism.* 2nd ed., Oxford, 1961. (An original and penetrating study, placing our knowledge of feudal institutions in England on a firm basis.)

Stenton, F. M. *Anglo-Saxon England.* ('The Oxford History of England.') 2nd ed., Oxford, 1947. (Fundamental for the transition from late Anglo-Saxon society to the feudal institutions of the Anglo-Norman period.)

Stenton, D. M. *English Society in the early Middle Ages* (The Pelican History of England), 2nd ed., Harmondsworth, 1952 (the chapter on 'Barons and Knights' is very important).

Stephenson, C. 'Feudalism and its antecedents in England', in *American Historical Review,* xlviii (1943), pp. 245–65; and in the author's selected essays, *Medieval Institutions* (see above, p. xxvi), pp. 234–60.

Joüon des Longrais, F. *La conception anglaise de la saisine du XIIe au XIVe siècle.* Paris, 1925.

Joüon des Longrais, F. 'La tenure en Angleterre au moyen âge', in *Recueils de la Société Jean Bodin. III. La tenure.* Brussels, 1938, pp. 165–210.

Douglas, D. C. 'The Norman Conquest and English Feudalism', in *Economic History Review,* ix (1939), pp. 128–43.

Plucknett, T. F. T. *The Legislation of Edward I.* Oxford, 1949.

Warren Hollister, C. *The Norman Conquest and the genesis of English feudalism,* in *The American Historical Review,* LXVI, 1961, pp. 641–663.

H. G. Richardson and G. O. Sayles, *The governance of mediaeval England from the Conquest to Magna Carta.* Edinburgh, 1963.

C. BELGIUM

Didier, N. *Le droit des fiefs dans la coutume de Hainaut au moyen âge.* Lille-Paris, 1945. (A monograph which might well serve as a model for similar local studies.) See also the important review by R. Latouche in *Revue du moyen âge latin,* i (1945), pp. 423–8.

Genicot, L. *L'économie rurale namuroise au bas moyen âge* (1190-1429). 2 vol. Namur, 1943. Louvain, 1960.

D. SCOTLAND

Barrow, G. W. S. 'The beginnings of feudalism in Scotland', *Bulletin of the Institute of Historical Research,* xxix, 1956.

E. FRANCE

Guilhiermoz, P. *Essai sur les origines de la noblesse en France au moyen âge.* Paris, 1902. (A penetrating and highly individual study, based on very wide knowledge of the sources.)

Luchaire, A. *Manuel des institutions françaises. Période des Capétiens directs.* Paris, 1892.

Esmein, A. *Cours élémentaire d'histoire du droit français.* 15th ed., revised by R. Génestal. Paris, 1925.

Declareuil, J. *Histoire générale du droit français des origines à 1789.* Paris, 1925.

Chénon, E. *Histoire générale du droit français public et privé des origines à 1815.* Vols. I and II (i), the latter edited by F. Olivier-Martin. Paris, 1926–29.

Olivier-Martin, F. *Histoire du droit français des origines à la Révolution.* Paris, 1948.

Olivier-Martin, F. *Histoire de la coutume de la prévôté et vicomté de Paris.* 2 vols. in 3 parts. Paris. 1922–30. (Substantial and carefully considered account of the historical development of feudal institutions as shown in a particular regional framework.)

Olivier-Martin, F. 'Les liens de vassalité dans la France médiévale', in *Société Jean Bodin. I. Les liens de vassalité et les immunités*, 2d ed. Brussels, 1958, pp. 217–222.

Lagouelle, H. *Essai sur la conception féodale de la propriété foncière.* Caen, 1902. (Dealing with Normandy.)

Carabie, R. *La propriété foncière dans le très ancien droit normand. I. La propriété domaniale.* Caen, 1943.

Navel, H. 'Recherches sur les institutions féodales en Normandie', *Bulletin de la Société des Antiquaires de Normandie*, li, 1948–51.

Duby, G. *La Société aux XIe et XIIe siècles dans la région mâconnaise.* Paris, 1953.

Portejoie, P. *Le régime des fiefs d'après la coutume de Poitou*, 2nd ed., (Mémoires de la Société des Antiquaires de l'Ouest, 4th série, III, 1959). (Excellent monograph.)

F. ITALY

Leicht, P. S. *Storia del diritto pubblico italiano. Lezioni.* Milan, 1938.

Cahen, C. *Le régime féodal de l'Italie normande.* Paris, 1940.

Mor, C. G. *L'età feudale.* (Storia Politica d'Italia.) 2 vols. Milan, 1952.

Fasoli, G. 'La feudalità siciliana nell'età di Federico II', in *Rivista di Storia del Diritto Italiano*, XXIV, 1951, pp. 47–68.

Fasoli, G. 'Lineamenti di politica e di legislazione feudale veneziana in terraferma', in *Rivista di Storia del Diritto Italiano*, XXV, 1952.

G. NETHERLAND

Blécourt, A. S. de. *Kort begrip van het oud-vaderlandsch burgerlijk recht.* 5th ed. Groningen, 1939.

V. STUDIES ON PARTICULAR TOPICS

A. TERMINOLOGY

Hollyman, K. J. *Le développement du vocabulaire féodal en France pendant le haut Moyen Âge.* Geneva, 1957.

Binué, E. Rodon. *El lenguaje tecnico del feudalismo en el siglo X en Cataluña.* Barcelona, 1957.

Niermeyer, J. F. 'De semantiek van "honor" en de oorsprong van het heerlijk gezag', in *Dancwerc. Opstellen aangeboden aan Prof. Dr. D. Th. Enklaar.* Groningen, 1959.

A. VASSALAGE AND FIEFS

Krawinkel, H. *Feodum*. Weimar, 1938.

Ganshof, F. L. 'Les relations féodo-vassaliques aux temps post-carolingiens', in *I problemi communi dell'Europa post-carolingia*. Spoleto, 1955. (Settimane di Studi del Centro Italiano di Studi sull'Alto Medioevo, ii, 1954.)

Ganshof, F. L. 'Note sur l'apparition du nom de l'hommage particulièrement en France', in *Aus Mittelalter und Neuzeit. Festschrift für Gerhard Kallen*. Bonn, 1957.

Kienast, W. 'Rechtsnatur und Anwendung der Mannschaft (*homagium*) in Deutschland während des Mittelalters', in *Deutsche Landesreferate zum IX. Internationalen Kongress für Rechtsvergleichung in Paris 1954*, ed. E. Wolff, Dusseldorf, 1955.

David, M. *Le serment du sacre du IXe au XVe siècle*. Strasbourg, 1951.

Bloch, M. 'Les formes de la rupture de l'hommage dans l'ancien droit féodal', in *Nouvelle revue historique de droit français et étranger*, xxxvi (1912), pp. 141–77.

Bloch, M. 'Un problème d'histoire comparée: la ministérialité en France et en Allemagne', in *Revue historique de droit français et étranger*, 4e série, vii (1928), pp. 46-91.

Petot, P. 'L'hommage servile: essai sur la nature juridique de l'hommage', in *Revue historique de droit français et étranger*, 4e série, vi (1927), pp. 68-107.

Lemarignier, J. F. *Recherches sur l'hommage en marche et les frontières féodales*. Lille, 1945.

Chénon, E. 'Le rôle juridique de l'osculum dans l'ancien droit français', in *Mémoires de la Société nationale des Antiquaires de France*, 8e série, vi (1924), pp. 124-55.

Esmein, A. *Nouvelles théories sur les origines féodales*', in *Nouvelle revue historique de droit français et étranger*, xviii (1894), pp. 523-44.

Meynial, E. 'Notes sur la formation de la théorie du domaine divisé du XIIe au XIVe siècle chez les romanistes', in *Mélanges H. Fitting*, ii (Montpellier, 1908), pp. 409-61.

Dillay, M. 'Le "service" annuel en deniers des fiefs de la région angevine', in *Mélanges Paul Fournier* (Paris, 1929), pp. 143-51.

Richardot, H. 'Le fief roturier à Toulouse aux XIIe et XIIIe siècles', in *Revue historique de droit français et étranger*, 4e série, xiv (1935), pp. 307-59, 495-569.

Richardot, H. 'Francs-fiefs. Essai sur l'exemption totale ou partielle des services de fief', in *ibid.*, xxvii (1949), pp. 28-63, 229-73.

Richardot, H. 'Quelques textes sur la reprise de censive en fief', in *ibid.*, xxviii (1950), pp. 338-50.

Richardot, H. 'A propos des personnes et des terres féodales. Conversions, dissociations, interférences', in *Etudes d'histoire du droit privé offertes à Pierre Petot*. Paris, 1959.

Richardot, H. 'L'hommage. Sa nature et ses applications dans l'ancien droit français', in *Etudes de droit contemporain. Contributions françaises aux IIIe et IVe Congrès internationaux de droit comparé*. Paris, 1959.

C. MONEY FIEFS

Sczaniecki, M. *Essai sur les fiefs-rentes*. Paris, 1946. (Also the review of this work by F. L. Ganshof in the *Revue belge de Philologie et d'Histoire*, xxvii (1949), pp. 237-43.)

Lyon, B. D. 'The Money Fief under the English Kings, 1066-1485', *English Historical Review*, lxvi (1951), pp. 161–93.

Lyon, B. D. 'Le fief-rente aux Pays-Bas: sa terminologie et son aspect financier', *Revue du Nord*, xxxv, 1953.

Lyon, B. D. 'The fief-rente in the Low Countries. An evaluation', *Revue belge de Philologie et d'Histoire*, xxxii, 1954.

Lyon, B. D. *From fief to indenture*. Cambridge (Mass.), 1957.

Didier, N. 'Les rentes inféodées dans le comté de Hainaut du XIIe au XVe siècle', *Revue du Nord*, xvii, 1931.

D. LIEGEANCY AND THE PLURALITY OF VASSAL ENGAGEMENTS

Ganshof, F. Ł. 'Depuis quand a-t-on pu en France être vassal de plusieurs seigneurs?', in *Mélanges Paul Fournier* (Paris, 1929), pp. 261–70.

Zeglin, D. *Der 'homo ligius' und die französische Ministerialität*. Leipzig, 1915.

E. SUCCESSIONS, MINORITIES AND ALIENATIONS

Génestal, R. *Le parage normand*. Caen, 1911.

Ganshof, F. L. 'Armatura', in *Archivum latinitatis medii aevi* (Bulletin Du Cange), xv (1941), pp. 179–93.

Didier, N. 'Le droit de liget dans la coutume de Hainaut,' *Revue historique de droit français et étranger*, 1936, pp. 476–522.

Mitteis, H. 'Zur Geschichte der Lehnsvormundschaft', in *Festschrift Alfred Schultze* (Weimar, 1934), pp. 129–74. Reprinted in H. Mitteis, *Die Rechtsidee in der Geschichte*, Weimar, 1957.

Faletti, L. *Le retrait lignager*, Paris, 1923.

Goez, W. *Der Leihezwang. Eine Untersuchung zur Geschichte des deutschen Lehnrechtes*. Tübingen, 1962 (extremely important).

F. STUDIES ON SOME FEUDAL RELATIONSHIPS

Ganshof, F. L. 'Note sur le rattachement féodal du comté de Hainaut à l'église de Liége', in *Miscellanea Gessleriana* (Antwerp, 1948), pp. 508–21.

Ganshof, F. L., Van Caenegem, R., and Verhulst, A., 'Note sur le premier traité anglo-flamand de Douvres', *Revue du Nord*, xl, 1958. This volume has also been published as *Mélanges dédiés à la mémoire de Raymond Monier*. Paris and Lille, 1958.

Ganshof, F. L. 'Le roi de France en Flandre en 1127 et 1128', in *Revue historique de droit français et étranger*, 4e série, xxvii (1949), pp. 204–28.

Mitteis, H. 'Politische Prozesse des früheren Mittelalters in Deutschland und Frankreich', in *Sitzungsberichte der Heidelberger Akademie der Wissenschaften, Phil.-Hist. Klasse*, Band xvii, Dritte Abhandlung (1927).

G. FEUDALISM AND THE STATE

Halphen, L. 'La place de la royauté dans le système féodal', in *Anuario de historia del derecho Español*, ix (1933), pp. 313–21.

Ganshof, F. L. 'Contribution à l'étude des origines des cours féodales en France', in *Revue historique de droit français et étranger*, 4e série, vii (1928), pp. 644–65.

Keeney, B. C. *Judgement by Peers*. Cambridge (Mass.), 1949.

Lot, F. *Fidèles ou vassaux?* Paris, 1904.

Dumas, A. 'Encore la question "Fidèles ou Vassaux?" ', in *Nouvelle revue historique de droit français et étranger*, xliv (1920), pp. 159–229, 346–90.

Dhondt, J. *Etudes sur la naissance des principautés territoriales en France.* Bruges, 1948.

Mitteis, H. *Der Staat des hohen Mittelalters.* 4th ed. Weimar, 1953.

Lousse, E. *La société d'Ancien Régime.* I. Louvain-Paris, 1943.

Meyer, B. 'Das Lehen in Recht und Staat des Mittelalters', in *Zeitschrift für Schweizerische Geschichte*, xxvi (1946), pp. 161–78.

Kienast, W. *Die deutschen Fürsten im Dienste der Westmächte bis zum Tode Philipps des Schönen von Frankreich.* Vols. I and II (i). Utrecht-Leipzig, 1924–31.

Kienast, W. *Untertaneneid und Treuvorbehalt in Frankreich und England.* Weimar, 1952.

Kienast, W. 'Untertaneneid und Treuvorbehalt', in *Zeitschrift der Savigny-Stiftung für Rechtsgeschichte*, lxvi (1948), *Germanistische Abteilung*, pp. 111–47.

Stengel, E. E. 'Land- und Lehnrechtliche Grundlagen des Reichsfürstenstandes', in *ibid.*, pp. 294–342.

Mayer, T. *Fürsten und Staat.* Weimar, 1950.

Lemarignier, J. F. 'Les fidèles du roi de France', in *Recueil de travaux offerts à M. C. Brunel.* Paris, 1955.

H. WESTERN FEUDAL INSTITUTIONS IN
CONTACT WITH THE BYZANTINE EMPIRE

Ganshof, F. L. 'Robert le Frison et Alexis Comnène', *Byzantion*, xxxi, 1961, pp. 57–74.

Hill, J. H. and Hill L. L. 'The Convention of Alexius Comnenus and Raymond of Saint-Gilles', *The American Historical Review*, LVIII, 1953, pp. 322–327.

Ganshof, F. L. 'Recherche sur le lien juridique qui unissait les chefs de la Première Croisade à l'empereur byzantin', *Mélanges offerts à M. Paul E. Martin*, Genève, 1961, pp. 49–63.

PART ONE
ORIGINS

Chapter One

THE ORIGINS OF FEUDALISM

I. The Development of Retainers in the Merovingian Period

The origins of medieval feudalism must be looked for in the Frankish kingdom of the Merovingians, and more particularly in the heart of the kingdom between the Loire and the Rhine.

Under the Merovingians, Gaul was rarely united or at peace, and it frequently lapsed into a state of almost complete anarchy. The main cause of this, a cause which was renewed every few years, lay in the family feuds occasioned by the custom which required that on the death of a king his inheritance should be divided between his sons. Later, after repeated partitions had given birth to the kingdoms of Austrasia, Neustria and Burgundy, there was added to this the bitter rivalries between the regional aristocracies. The quarrels between the sons and grandsons of Clovis in the sixth century resembled nothing so much as the fighting of wild beasts, and in the succeeding period the conflicts between the kings and the magnates increased steadily in violence and ferocity as the seventh century drew to its close. Even apart from the political struggle for power, the state was quite unable to maintain the public peace or secure the safety of its inhabitants. Its structure was too primitive, the officials in its service too few in number and too unreliable, for it to carry out successfully this elementary function of government.

Such a society formed an ideal medium for the growth of bodies of retainers, and particularly of bodies of armed retainers. Those who felt the need of protection would look for it to their more powerful neighbours, and such protection would involve in return the acceptance of some form of service. The magnates on their side, whether from a desire to play a conspicuous part in political affairs or from the hope of profiting by the political disorder and of establishing or increasing their own power and wealth, needed the services of men who were personally attached

3

to them and whom they could use in private warfare. In ex⁺reme cases, free men might be prepared to become the slaves of powerful protectors, or the latter might create their own soldiery by arming their slaves. Neither of these proceedings, however, could be regarded as typical. A more general custom was that by which a free man placed himself under the protection and at the service of another free man, while maintaining his own free status. Contemporaries called such persons *ingenui in obsequio*, free men in dependence.[1]

The phenomenon itself was not new; the novelty lay in its wider diffusion. Like other parts of the *Orbis Romanus*, Gaul under the later empire was accustomed to the existence of private bands of soldiers, often called *buccellarii*, who formed the bodyguards of prominent men. The practice survived the barbarian invasions, at least south of the Loire, as we learn from the laws of the Visigothic king Euric towards the end of the fifth century.[2] The Franks on their side had the institution known as the *comitatus*, the *Gefolgschaft* of German historians, which is already described in a celebrated passage of Tacitus at the end of the first century.[3] The *comitatus* consisted of a group of free warriors who had taken service of their own free will under a chieftain, and fought with him and on his behalf as a band of close comrades. The bodies of armed retainers whom we meet with during the Merovingian period had thus a double origin, and it is not possible to say whether they owed more to their Róman or to their Germanic predecessors.

The *ingenui in obsequio* of the sixth and seventh centuries included persons of very varied status. Amongst the free men who placed themselves under the personal protection and at the personal service of the king were the *antrustiones*, the members of the *trustis*. The *trustis*—the word is a Frankish one, with a Latin ending—appears to have corresponded to the *comitatus*, so that the *antrustiones* may be regarded as armed companions of the king. The *antrustio* enjoyed a triple wergeld; that is to say, if he was killed, the murderer had to pay to the victim's family a sum three

---

[1] The term occurs in the Ripuarian Law (e.g. *Lex Ribuaria*, ed. F. Beyerle and R. Buchner, M.G.H., *Leges Nat. Germ.*, iii [2]), 35 (31), 1.

[2] *Codex Eurici*, cccx (*Leges Visigothorum*, ed. K. Zeumer in M.G.H., *Leges Nat. Germ.*, i. 18).

[3] Tacitus, *Germania*, xiii–xiv.

times as large as that normally due for the death of any other free man. It was his direct relationship with the king that assured to the *antrustio* this special mark of protection. He was a picked fighting man, and whatever might have been his origin he was treated as if he belonged to one of the highest social ranks in the population.

Only the king and the queen had *antrustiones*. But by the side of this superior category of retainer there were many other free men *in obsequio regis*, in direct dependence on the king, or in dependence on other powerful or important personages whom contemporary texts term *optimates* or *proceres*. They generally seem to have been given the name of *gasindi*,—once more the latinized form of a German word—, at any rate when they were armed retainers. The word was used to cover all men of this type, whatever might be their social position, and since this was frequently a humble one we find applied to them words like *puer* (probably) and *vassus* (certainly) which were properly used of slaves.

It was the word *vassus* that was to have a great future. Its origin was the Celtic *gwas*, meaning a young boy or a servant, and it was latinized very early as *vassus*. The form *vassallus* seems to have been formed from the adjective *gwassawl*, meaning one who serves. During the whole Merovingian period, *vassus* meant a slave, and this meaning, attested already by the Salic Law at the beginning of the sixth century, had not entirely disappeared in the eighth century.[1] But towards the beginning of this century the term was also applied to free men who were dependent on a lord. The earliest known texts are passages in the *Lex Alamannorum* and in the *Lex Baiuuariorum*.[2] The use is no doubt older and dates from before the year 700.

II. *Commendation*

The protective relationship set up by one free man over another was called in Latin *patrocinium*; in latinized German it was *mundium* or *mundeburdis*, whence *maimbour* in medieval French.

---

[1] *Lex Salica*, xxxv. 9 (ed. K. A. Eckhardt, *Pactus legis Salicae*, ii. 1. 65 *Titel Text*, Göttingen, 1955, p. 236); C. Wampach, *Geschichte der Grundherrschaft Echternach*, i. 2 (Luxemburg, 1930), no. 17.
[2] *Lex Alamannorum*, xxxvi. 3 (ed. K. Lehmann in M.G.H., *Leges Nat. Germ.*, v [i]. 96). *Lex Bauuariorum*, ii. 14 (ed. E. von Schwind in M.G.H., *Leges Nat. Germ.*, v [2], 308).

In either case the word carried with it an implication of superior authority as well as of protection. The legal act by which one free man placed himself in the *patrocinium* or the *mundeburdis* of another was known as *commendatio*, commendation. The substantive itself is not used in any of our existing sources before the Carolingian period, but the verb *se commendare*, in the sense of placing oneself under the authority of another, is frequently found. The phrase bore this meaning even in classical times,[1] and it appears in Gaul in the fifth century in the laws of the Visigothic king Euric, and in the sixth century in the *Historia Francorum* of Gregory of Tours.[2]

A Merovingian formula in a collection known from its place of origin, Tours, as the *Formulae Turonenses* gives us some useful information on the subject of commendation. The one which concerns us, no. 43 in the collection, dates from the second quarter of the eighth century, but both in form and content it looks back to an earlier epoch. It is so important that it is worth reproducing and translating in its entirety.[3]

'He who commends himself to the power of another man.

To the magnificent Lord (A.), I (B.). Inasmuch as it is known to all and sundry that I lack the wherewithal to feed and clothe myself, I have asked of your pity, and your goodwill has granted to me, permission to deliver and commend myself into your *mundoburdus*. This I have therefore done, in such fashion that, you have undertaken to aid and sustain me in food and clothing, while I have undertaken to serve you and deserve well of you so far as lies in my power. And for as long as I shall live, I am bound to serve you and respect you as a free man ought, and during my lifetime I shall not have the right to withdraw myself from your authority and *mundoburdus*; I must on the contrary be for the remainder of my days under your power and protection. And in virtue of this action, if one of us tries to alter the terms of the

---

[1] E.g. Terence, *Eunuchus*, 1039; Caesar, *De bello gallico*, iv. 27, 7.

[2] *Codex Eurici*, cccx (p. 18); Gregory of Tours, *Historia Francorum*, iv. 46, vii. 20 (ed. B. Krusch and W. Levison, in M.G.H., S.R.M., I², p. 181, 339).

[3] *Formulae Merowingici et Karolini Aevi* (ed. K. Zeumer in M.G.H.), p. 158. These 'formulae' are specimen charters from which the concrete elements—the names of the parties, indications of date and place, etc.—are omitted; they were collected into 'formularies' which were used to provide models for all kinds of legal documents.

agreement, he will have to pay [a fine of] x *solidi* to the other, but the agreement itself shall remain in force. Whence it has seemed good to us that the two parties concerned should draw up and confirm two documents of the same tenor, and this they have done. (*Qui se in alterius potestate commendat. Domino magnifico illo ego enim ille. Dum et omnibus habetur percognitum, qualiter ego minime habeo, unde me pascere vel vestire debeam, ideo petii pietati vestrae, et mihi decrevit voluntas, ut me in vestrum mundoburdum tradere vel commendare deberem; quod ita et feci; eo videlicet modo, ut me tam de victu quam et de vestimento, iuxta quod vobis servire et promereri potuero, adiuvare vel consolare debeas, et dum ego in capud advixero, ingenuili ordine tibi servicium vel obsequium inpendere debeam et de vestra potestate vel mundoburdo tempore vitae meae potestatem non habeam subtrahendi, nisi sub vestra potestate vel defensione diebus vitae meae debeam permanere. Unde convenit ut, si unus ex nobis de has convenntiis se emutare voluerit, solidos tantos pari suo conponat, et ipsa convenentia firma permaneat; unde convenit, ut duas epistolas uno tenore conscriptas ex hoc inter se facere vel adfirmare deberent; quod ita et fecerunt.*)

Before commenting on this document, it is important to observe that it is not a charter intended to serve as evidence of the fact that one person has commended himself to another; still less is it a charter whose drafting, confirmation and handing over (*traditio*) form in themselves the act of commendation. The dispositive clause (*dispositio*), the essential part of the act, that by which its author expresses his will and which is here introduced by the word *unde*, only creates an accessory obligation, i.e. a penal clause providing a sanction for the obligations inherent in the act of commendation itself. The latter is known to us only from the terms of the exposition (*narratio*), the narrative portion of the act, which is intended simply to explain and justify the dispositive clause.

The legal effects of the act of commendation, as they are described in the *narratio*, are a series of obligations binding on both parties. The person who commends himself assumes the obligation of serving and respecting his superior, whom he calls his *dominus*, his lord, but with the reservation that this service and respect shall be limited to what is compatible with the maintenance of his status as a free man. The lord on his part assumes the obligation of aiding and supporting, in the matter of food and clothing, the man who commends himself to him. In other words, he agrees to assure him the maintenance and protection which are implied in the words *mundoburdus* and *defensio*. The phrase *iuxta quod vobis servire et promereri potuero* makes the execution by the lord of his obligations conditional on the vassal carrying out his share of the agreement.

Commendation, then, at least in the shape in which it is presented in the Tours formula, is in the fullest sense a mutual contract. The document itself declares that the contract ceases to operate on the death of the vassal, and it must be presumed that the death of the lord would have the same effect. Commendation was in its essence a contract concluded by each partner in consideration of some quality possessed by the other; it may be described as being concluded *intuitu personae*.

The Tours formula does not inform us of the mode by which the contract was concluded, but in the much older formulary of Marculf, which was probably composed in the Paris region towards the middle of the seventh century, there is the model of an act by which the king admits a certain person to the number of his *antrustiones*.[1] This document describes a formal oath of fealty taken 'in the king's hand' (*in manu nostra*), presumably in the literal sense of the expression: the *antrustio* would actually place his hand in the king's while repeating the words of the oath. But the *antrustiones* were the king's protégés in a very special sense, and it would not be safe to conclude from this that every free man commending himself to another free man would do so by a similar gesture of the hand (in German, *Handgebärde*) and by taking an oath of fealty. It is quite possible that he would, and from what we know of the later history of fealty it may even be regarded as probable, but in the absence of direct evidence it is best to admit our ignorance. We can at least be certain that the contract must have been a verbal one and must have been accompanied by certain ritual acts, for this would be in keeping with the general custom of the time.

It should finally be noted that the contract of commendation is

[1] 'De regis antrustione', in *Marculfi Formulae*, i. 18 (ed. Zeumer, *Formulae*, p. 55).

of a quite general character, which could be adapted to many different circumstances. The nature of the services required from the vassal in the Tours formula is not laid down in precise terms; they might be domestic, economic, military, or all three. Free men at all social levels might commend themselves to a lord. The *narratio* of the Tours formula introduces us to a poor man who lacks the means to clothe and feed himself, and this is evidently the most frequent type, the *id quod plerumque fit*. But it is not the only one.

If the form of service due from the *gasindus* or *vassus*, the person commending himself, might vary greatly, the lord on his side had the choice of various possibilities in providing for the maintenance of the person who had placed himself under his protection. The most common form was certainly direct maintenance by the lord, either in his own household or by means of allowances. The Tours formula with which we have had to do seems to have had in mind some kind of maintenance of this character. But it might also be done by a grant of land.

III. Benefice

In a society in which agriculture was the chief form of economic activity and the most important source of wealth, it might often be convenient to bestow on the vassal sufficient land to assure his proper maintenance. This land might be given in full ownership (*proprietas*), but there is no text for the Merovingian period which proves indisputably that it was ever in fact done in this way. For there was another alternative. The lord might make a grant of land to his vassal as a tenement.

A tenement (Fr. *tenure*, Germ. *Leihe*) was a piece of land, great or small, the use and enjoyment of which for a prolonged period were granted by the owner to another person, the tenant, in such a fashion that the tenant exercised over the land immediate and direct control, what we would call nowadays a real right. The tenant had thus acquired what in Roman Law was called a *ius in re aliena*, a right over a thing belonging to another. The existence of tenements was very widespread in the Frankish kingdom, as it had already been in the Roman empire during the last centuries of its history. Such tenements were those fractions (*mansi*) of great estates (*villae*) which were cultivated not by the

owners themselves but by *coloni* or *laeti* or slaves for their own
profit, in return for the payment of certain fixed rents *(census)*
and the performance of certain labour dues. These tenements were
nearly always held for life, and were in practice normally hereditary.

This type of tenement, which was the commonest, may be described as onerous, since the rent and the labour dues owed by the
tenant were directly related to the value of the land he held and
weighed heavily upon him. But by the side of these were other
types of tenement, the particular feature of which was that from
the point of view of the tenant they were held by him on very
favourable terms. They carried with them no labour dues, and
their rent was an extremely moderate one. Sometimes there might
even be no rent at all, the owner having for some particular reason
granted a tenement to another person while demanding no payment in return.

The favourable terms on which these tenements were held explains the word *beneficium*, 'benefice' or 'benefit', by which they
are described in contemporary texts. We hear of them frequently
in the formularies and charters of the Merovingian period.

For example, we find in one case the grantor of a tenement declaring that the grantee will exploit it *per nostro benefitio*, which
in the context can only mean 'as a benefit from us'. Or again, the
grantee who is the author of the charter declares that the grantor
has conferred a 'benefit' on him in transferring to him the land in
question *(fecistis mihi beneficium de rem vestra)*. Sometimes the
expression is clearer still. The author of a charter declares to a
grantor: *locello aliquo ecclesiae vestrae . . . nobis ad beneficium
. . . excolere permisistis*, 'you have permitted us to exploit to our
benefit a small estate belonging to your church'. Or still more
explicitly: *ipsa villa . . . nobis ad beneficium usufructuario ordine
colendum tenere permisistis*, 'you have permitted us to hold this
estate to our benefit, in order to cultivate it with the right of
usufruct'. We hear also that land will be exploited *sub usu benefitio* or *in usum beneficii ecclesie*, that is to say, in using it as a
'benefit'.[1]

[1] *Marculfi Formulae*, ii. 40 (ed. Zeumer, pp. 99–100); *Formulae Ande-
cavenses*, 7 (*ibid.*, p. 7); *Marc. Form.* ii. 39 (*ibid.*, pp. 98–99), ii. 5, 6, (pp.
77, 79); a charter of 736 for Murbach in J. M. Pardessus, *Diplomata*, ii
(Paris, 1849), no. 558.

The *beneficium* or benefice may thus be defined as a tenement held on easy terms or even gratuitously, and which the tenant owes to the generosity of the grantor.

The benefices of the Merovingian period about which we are best informed are those whose grant was the object of a contract known as a *precaria*. This was an institution of vulgar Roman law which had come into existence in the late imperial times and had applied to it the name (*precarium*) of an institution of classical Roman law which had fallen into desuetude. In this period it conferred on the beneficiary of the grant the right of usufruct over the land in question. The contract was created by a request on the part of the would-be beneficiary, and an indication on the part of the owner that the request was acceded to. Two charters would be drawn up to serve as title-deeds, and would be held respectively by the owner making the grant and by the tenant receiving it. The name *precaria* was applied both to the contract itself and to the charters in which it was embodied, and more particularly to the one emanating from the tenant; the word *prestaria* was sometimes used to describe the charter emanating from the grantor.

The *precaria* gave rise to a form of tenement, generally of some size and normally granted for life, held in return for the payment of a low rent and sometimes for no rent at all. Precarial grants were made principally by the Church, though sometimes also by the king or great lay landowners; they frequently involved entire estates or even groups of estates. There were many possible reasons for their creation. They might be intended to stimulate the cultivation of land which was still waste or which was only in process of being brought under the plough; they might be intended to induce the tenant to give another estate to the grantor, which would then be granted back on precarial tenure, so that the precarist thus surrendered one estate and got back two; they might be intended to win the goodwill of some important personage; they might be intended to recognize an existing usurpation while reserving rights of ownership for the future; and so on.

The tenement created by a precarial contract forms a particularly important type of the larger group of beneficial tenements. We do not know exactly how other forms of beneficial grants were made, but we would probably not be far wrong in assuming a legal act in which a form of words was accompanied by some form of

symbolic gesture, such as was customary in the legal procedure of
the time.

What we would like to know is whether, during the Merovingian period, beneficial tenements were ever in fact granted by
lords to those who commended themselves to them, in order to
assure them the maintenance that was their due. There seems
little doubt that it must sometimes have been done, at least in the
seventh century, though we have no direct evidence of the fact.
When Eberhard, son of Duke Adalbert of Alsace, declares in a
charter of 735/37 to the abbey of Murbach that he has made a
grant of a certain estate as a benefice (*inbeneficiatum habuimus*),
and when in this same charter, at the end of a list of his property,
he groups together all those estates which he has granted in benefice to his vassals (*ad vassos nostros beneficiatum habui*), he is evidently alluding to a well-known practice, and even probably to an
old-established one.[1] But the examples of this practice provided
by our texts are not numerous enough to justify us in regarding it
as a very widespread one, at any rate before the middle of the
eighth century.

[1] Pardessus, *Diplomata*, ii, no. 544 (pp. 355–7). Cf. W. Levison, 'Kleine
Beiträge zu Quellen der fränkischen Geschichte', in *Neues Archiv der Gesell-
schaft für ältere Deutsche Geschichtskunde*, xxvii (1902), pp. 373–88.

PART TWO
CAROLINGIAN FEUDALISM

INTRODUCTION

As we have seen in the last chapter, vassalage, an institution involving relationships of subordination and service on the part of one person with regard to another, and the benefice, a form of tenement held for life on very easy terms by the tenant, existed together in Merovingian society. A lord could indeed grant a benefice to his vassal in order to provide the latter with the maintenance due to him in return for service, but such a union of the two institutions was quite exceptional. There is nothing to suggest that it was as yet a normal or widespread practice, and there is certainly no evidence of the 'government'—kings or mayors of the palace—granting such benefices to its vassals or *antrustiones*.

During the Carolingian period a change gradually came about. The two institutions of vassalage and benefice, which up to this time had been quite independent of each other, now began to combine so as to constitute a new system of institutions. It is this that justifies us in using such an expression as 'Carolingian feudalism'. The union of benefice and vassalage, however, and the interaction of these two institutions upon each other, are things which only develop by degrees. We must therefore distinguish, in what follows, two distinct periods: that of the first Carolingians, and that of Charlemagne and his successors.

Chapter One

FEUDALISM UNDER THE EARLIEST CAROLINGIANS

I. The Union and Spread of Vassalage and Benefice

The normal (though not the necessary) union of vassalage and benefice dates from the period of the early Carolingians: Charles Martel, mayor of the palace (716–41), Carloman, mayor of the palace (741–47), and Pepin III, mayor of the palace (741–51) and king (751–68). This at least is true if one considers the union simply as a matter of fact, leaving the legal question on one side.

The end of the seventh and the first half of the eighth century saw the Frankish monarchy involved in almost continuous warfare. The rise to power of Pepin II (Pepin 'of Herstal') and of his illegitimate son Charles Martel was in each case accompanied by several years of civil war. Military action was repeatedly required against Alamanni, Bavarians, Aquitanians and Provençals, who enjoyed a high degree of regional autonomy and were always on the verge of becoming completely independent. Campaigns had to be undertaken against such foreign enemies as Frisians, Saxons, and Saracens. In order to create a sufficiency of well-armed warriors on whom they could depend, Pepin II and still more Charles Martel greatly increased the number of their vassals. They gave them landed estates not merely to secure them the maintenance to which they had a right, but in order to make it possible for them to provide themselves with the necessary military equipment, more expensive now that cavalry had begun to be the decisive arm, and a following of other soldiers dependent on themselves. In the majority of cases, these estates were no doubt granted in full ownership. Some of them had probably formed part of the family inheritance of Pepin II and Charles Martel, and some may also have been royal estates (*fisci*), but it is quite certain that the major part had been the property of the churches, cathedrals and abbeys of the kingdom. The landed wealth of the Frankish

Church was surprisingly large, and even in earlier times the kings had frequently called upon it to satisfy similar needs in similar emergencies.

The seizure of ecclesiastical estates by Pepin II and to a greater degree by Charles Martel deprived the Church of its most important source of income, and rendered still more serious the lamentable state of disorder in which it found itself by the middle of the century. Everywhere there were complaints of the decline in ecclesiastical discipline, the moral failings of the clergy, the irregularities of public worship, the invasion of dogma and liturgy by superstitions and pagan practices, the disorganization of the ecclesiastical hierarchy. When Carloman and Pepin III (Pepin 'the Short'), the sons and successors of Charles Martel, set to work under the inspiration of St. Boniface to find some remedy for a state of affairs so harmful to the spiritual life of their subjects, they were obliged to provide some solution for the problem of the confiscated lands of the Church.

The remedy was worked out in three Frankish councils which met in 743 and 744, the first (743) at some place unknown, the second (744) at Les Estinnes in Hainault, and the third (744) at Soissons.[1] In theory, all secularized property was to be restored, but in fact the Church only recovered a small fraction of what it had lost. The external dangers which still threatened the state made it quite impossible for it to deprive the military class of so much wealth, and in any case this class would be little disposed to give it up. It was therefore decided that the ruler—the mayor of the palace at that particular moment, but in later times the king—should hold this property, and should grant it out in benefice on life tenure to those vassals who held it already. If, on the vassal's death, the situation was still such that the ruler had need of soldiers—*si necessitas cogat*, says the edict promulgated by Carloman at the council of Les Estinnes—he would have the right to regrant the property in benefice to another of his vassals. The vassal was to pay the prince, his lord, no rent for the occupation of the benefice: his only obligation to him was the

[1] *Capitularia regum Francorum* (ed. A. Boretius in *M.G.H.*), i, nos. 10, 11, 12. We accept the dates arrived at by T. Schieffer, *Angelsachsen und Franken* (Akad. d. Wissensch. zu Mainz, Abhandl. d. Geistes und Sozialwissenschaftl. Kl., 1950, no. 2) and *Winfrid-Bonifatins* (Freiburg, i. B, 1954), pp. 208–22, 306–7.

service which he owed in virtue of his status as vassal. But in order to ensure that the proprietary rights of the Church over its former property should be maintained, it was agreed that these estates held in benefice of the ruler by his vassals should be at the same time held on precarial tenure from the church to which the estates belonged. The occupant should pay a rent to the church, and an agreement of *precaria* should be drawn up. Thirty-five years later, precarial grants of this nature were called *precariae verbo regis*, precarial grants made by the king's order,[1] to distinguish them from those created by the Church for reasons of its own.

The essential features of the new situation of the mid eighth century were that there was now throughout the Frankish state, and more particularly in the region between the Loire and the Rhine, a much greater number of vassals than in the past; that amongst these there was a growing proportion of vassals of the mayor of the palace, soon to be vassals of the king; and finally that the vassals of the mayor, the king, and other personages were more and more frequently receiving from their lords, grants of land in the form of life-benefices for which they paid no rent. The custom of disposing of the Church's property in this way underwent a further development when, towards the middle of the century, Pepin III imposed on all the churches of Francia a *divisio*, a formal partition of their patrimony.[2] Only a part of the latter remained henceforward in their effective possession; the remaining part, sometimes much the larger of the two, was granted by the king to his vassals in the form of life-benefices on the conditions that we have just described. In order to give the Frankish Church some sort of compensation for its losses, Pepin III made obligatory the payment of tithes by all the inhabitants of the kingdom.

Another stage in this development was reached when the mayor of the palace or the king began to grant not merely the secularized estates of the Church but estates which formed part of his family inheritance as life-benefices to his vassals. Such an arrangement

---

[1] Capitulary of Herstal of 779 (Boretius, *Capitularia*, i, no. 20), c. 13.
[2] *Annales Alamannici, Guelferbytani, Nazariani*, a° 751 (ed. G. H. Pertz, M.G.H., SS. I, pp. 26–27): *Pippinus rex elevatus. Res eclesiarum descriptas atque divisas.*

was clearer and entailed fewer complications, for it did not involve the condition that such estates should also be held on precarial tenure from the Church.

Thus during the half-century between the death of Pepin II (714) and the accession of Charlemagne (768) a great change had taken place. In the last years of Pepin II's government, the grant of benefices to vassals seems to have been only occasional, and was not practised at all by the mayor of the palace or the king. By the accession of Charlemagne, the king, like other members of the ruling class—dukes, counts, great landowners or *potentes*, bishops and abbots—was granting benefices on a large scale to many, though not to all, of his vassals. Although there was no necessary connection between them, the actual union of benefice and vassalage had become an everyday affair.

II. *The Rise of Vassals in the Social Scale*

This transformation in the structure of society went hand in hand with another phenomenon. In the seventh century, a man who commended himself to a lord and became his *vassus* was no doubt free in law, but no man of any social consequence would accept such a position. The early Carolingians, by distributing as benefices to their vassals the wealth of the Church, and subsequently great estates of their own, attracted members of higher social levels into the ranks of their vassals. A steadily growing proportion of members of the aristocracy, including also such local representatives of the central government as the counts, were now prepared to become vassals of the king. The landed wealth which was in this way placed at the disposal of the members of the aristocracy permitted these in their turn to create vassals for themselves. The consequence was a general rise in the social status of vassals. Vassalage now became a coveted status, a mark of honour, at any rate where direct vassalage to the king was concerned and where the vassal obtained a benefice in return. This is perhaps the explanation of the disappearance, towards the middle of the eighth century, of the class of *antrustiones*. The change in the status of vassalage meant that these had no longer anything to gain in trying to maintain a distinction between themselves and other types of royal vassals.

Chapter Two

FEUDAL INSTITUTIONS UNDER CHARLEMAGNE
AND HIS SUCCESSORS

I. Terminology

The growing importance of vassalage becomes at once apparent to anyone studying the institutions of the Frankish monarchy under Charlemagne and Louis the Pious, and of the Frankish kingdoms which arose out of its ruins in the ninth century: East Francia, which was to become Germany; West Francia, which was to become France; Lotharingia, which was in the end to be united to Germany; the kingdoms of Provence and Transjurane Burgundy, which ended by uniting as the kingdom of Burgundy; the kingdom of Italy. The royal and imperial ordinances which are known as capitularies are full of regulations dealing with vassals, and they appear with ever-growing frequency in the narrative sources and charters of the time.

Changes were already taking place in the technical vocabulary of vassalage. The word *gasindus*, which recalled too vividly the humble origins of the institution—*das Gesinde* still signifies domestic servants in modern German—practically disappeared from use. *Vassus* became the normal term, though it was not everywhere regarded as entirely satisfactory, and it was sometimes accompanied by a note of apology. It was perhaps because in southern Gaul it still recalled a condition not far removed from slavery that the Aquitanian biographer of Louis the Pious who is known to us as the 'Astronomer', writing of the royal vassals established in Aquitaine by Charlemagne, refers to them as 'many others, Franks by nationality, who in common parlance are called vassals' (*alios plurimos quos vassos vulgo vocant, ex gente Francorum*).[1] But such doubts did not seriously hinder the success of the word. It was also regularly used in the form of *vassalus* throughout the ninth century. When Pope Nicholas I wrote in 862 to

[1] *Vita Hludowici imperatoris*, c. 3 (ed. G. H. Pertz in M.G.H., SS., ii. 608).

Charles the Bald, king of West Francia, on behalf of Count
Baldwin I (later called Baldwin 'Bras de Fer'), the ancestor of the
house of Flanders, who had married the princess Judith without
her father's permission, he referred to him as *Balduinus, vassallus
vester*, and there are other texts from purely Frankish areas which
prove that the pope was not using a term confined to Italy.[1] In
the second half of the ninth century one begins also to find the
word *miles*, which emphasized the growing military character of
the institution. One may assume, for example, that it is a list of
royal vassals who are introduced by the words *de militibus* among
the guarantors of an act of Lothar II in 865.[2] There is also the
word *homo*, which could refer to anyone dependent on a lord,
and which was often used in the technical sense of vassal, as for
example in a constitution of Louis the Pious of 815 where the
emperor speaks of the *obsequium* which *nostrates homines de
simili beneficio senioribus suis exhibere solent*, 'the service which
vassals amongst us are accustomed to furnish their lords at the
charge of similar benefices'.[3]

II. Further Spread of Vassalage and Benefice

There can be no doubt that the proportion of vassals to the total
number of free men was steadily increasing during the second
half of the eighth and throughout the whole of the ninth century. This increase is manifest in several ways. In the old Frankish
territory between the Loire and the Rhine, we find a considerable
growth in the number of contracts of vassalage; elsewhere, we
find the institution spreading into Franconia, on the right bank
of the middle Rhine and in the region of the Main, and Thuringia,

[1] *Nicolai Papae Epistolae*, no. 7 (ed. E. Perels in M.G.H., *Epistolae*, vi.
273). The term appears frequently in the Charters of Charles the Bald: see
the index to the *Recueil des actes de Charles II le Chauve*, by G. Tessier
(iii, Paris, 1955), p. 414, s. v.

[2] *Annales Bertiniani*, a. 865 (ed. G. Waitz, Hanover, 1883, p. 77); they
follow the list of counts in the same act which is introduced by the words
de comitibus. Cf. the analysis of a letter (of 857/80) from Archbishop Hincmar of Rheims to Bishop Isaac of Langres in Flodoard, *Historia Remensis
Ecclesiae*, iii. 23 (ed. J. Heller and G. Waitz in M.G.H., SS., xiii. 529).

[3] *Constitutio de Hispanis Prima*, c. 6 (ed. Boretius, *Capitularia*, i, no. 132,
p. 264) and R. d'Abadal i de Vinyals, *Catalunya Carolingia, ii. Els Diplomes
Carolingis a Catalunya*, ii (Barcelona, 1952) Apéndix III. Cf. *Capitularia*,
i, no. 73 of 811, c. 7 (p. 165); ii, no. 204 (of 847), sect. iii, cc. 3 and 5
(p. 71).

and into such non-Frankish region as Aquitaine, Alamannia, and Bavaria whose autonomy had been curtailed by Charlemagne or his predecessors. Vassalage had also been introduced into Italy, where it had immediately assumed certain characteristics of its own, since the position of the vassal was there influenced by that of the Lombard *gasindus*. On the other hand, it did not penetrate very deeply into such newly conquered lands as Frisia and Saxony. There can be little doubt that its diffusion was closely connected with the spread of the system of great estates and the exploitation of the soil within the framework of the manor (*villa*). This type of property and this form of cultivation lent themselves better than any other to the distribution of benefices by a lord to his vassals, and by the latter, in many cases, to vassals of their own.

It is in fact very important to realize that vassals endowed with benefices which consisted of estates of some magnitude would normally acquire other vassals for their own service. This would often no doubt be done at their lord's express desire, since in this way they could raise a larger number of fighting men for his service. Many of these subvassals they would maintain directly in their households; at the beginning of the ninth century, perhaps most of them were still maintained in this way. But to some of them they would prefer to grant a benefice, which might consist either of some allodial property (*alodis, allodium*) which formed part of their family inheritance or of a fraction, for example some *mansi*, of the benefice which they held themselves. As the ninth century wore on, this practice by which the vassals of a lord granted further benefices to their own vassals became steadily more general.

There were a number of factors at work in the remarkable spread of vassalage in the reigns of Charlemagne and his successors. In the first place, such an extension represents a policy deliberately pursued by the Carolingians themselves. They hoped to strengthen their own authority by increasing the number of their vassals, and by imposing on such officials as counts, margraves, and dukes the obligation of entering into royal vassalage. In the latter case, they were trying to reinforce the obedience which their officials owed them in virtue of the offices they held by the fealty which was due from the vassal to his lord. The same policy, with the encouragement of the head of the state, was followed by the more important officials towards those below them, as well as by the heads of great ecclesiastical establishments with regard to the principal secular agents of their authority. Later, from the reign of Louis the Pious onwards, the magnates, who were generally invested with political offices, had a natural interest in building up their own bodies of vassals in order to increase their military power and sell their support to one or other of the political factions at the highest possible price. Finally, in a period which was incessantly troubled by civil war and by the invasions of Normans, Slavs, Arabs and Hungarians, considerable importance must be attached to the desire for security on the part of the smaller landowners. Their wish for protection conflicted with their anxiety to maintain their personal status as free men and to avoid being confounded with the ranks of those who actually tilled the soil. The simplest solution to their difficulties was to enter the caste of qualified warriors through admission as vassals of some greater lord.

The contemporary author of the *Miracula S. Bertini*, describing a Viking invasion of the region of the Aa and the upper Lys in 891, gives us a picture of a state of society which must have been true for a large part of the Carolingian world, or at any rate the western part of it, in the last decades of the ninth century. Speaking of the upper classes of society, the author contrasts the large majority, who had accepted the status of vassal and were bound to follow their lords on any type of expedition, with the much smaller number of those who possessed enough allodial property to maintain their independence and so were bound only by those obligations imposed by the king on all his subjects. *Pene nobilitas terrae ex multo iam tempore ob amorem vel dominatum carorum sibi dominorum abscesserat, nativitatis patria relicta, praeter paucos, qui ita hereditariis praediti erant patrimoniis ut non esset eis necesse subdi nisi sanctionibus publicis.*[1]

III. Royal Vassals

The last decades of the eighth and the whole of the ninth century were not only characterized by the spread of the institutions

---

[1] *Miracula S. Bertini*, c. 8 (ed. O. Holder-Egger in *M.G.H.*, *S.S.*, xv (i), 513.)

of vassalage and benefice, but also by the accentuation of another phenomenon which we have observed already under the early Carolingians. This is the rise in the social status of vassals.

This rise is naturally much more marked in the case of royal vassals than in that of others. In virtue of the close relationship existing between them and the king, and the duties which were entrusted to them, the *vassi dominici*—the phrase should literally have covered the vassals of any lord, but it was in fact only used of vassals of 'the lord king'—enjoyed particular consideration. The texts sometimes describe as *honor*[1] this title to respect and consideration which was attached to them, a sense which carried over into the English word 'honour' and the French 'honneur'. Amongst the royal vassals, those who had obtained a benefice, or to use the contemporary technical term were *casati*, enjoyed a prestige much higher than that of others. Vassals maintained by the king in his palace are termed *pauperiores vassos*, 'poorer vassals', in a tone of contempt, by an annalist of the beginning of the ninth century.[2] By the end of Charlemagne's reign it seems likely that a vassal who had carried out his services satisfactorily might normally hope sooner or later to receive a benefice in some part of the empire.

The Carolingians in fact may be said to have sown *vassi dominici* far and wide throughout their territories by endowing them with benefices. In this way, in many regions of the empire, they called into existence groups of men on whom they could depend, men whose service and support, reinforced often by that of their own vassals, were assured to the king in case of need. Pepin III and Charlemagne pursued this policy with particular thoroughness in recently conquered territories, as in Aquitaine,[3] Italy and Bavaria, where a part of the estates confiscated from former rulers or rebels was turned into benefices for royal vassals. The successors of Charlemagne followed his example. The pre-eminent po-

[1] Capitulary of Herstal of 779, c. 9 (ed. Boretius, *Capitularia*, i, no. 20, p. 48).
[2] *Annales Laureshamenses*, a⁰ 802 (ed. G. H. Pertz in M.G.H., SS., i. 38, 39).
[3] Capitulary of Pepin for Aquitaine of 768, cc. 5 and 9 (ed. Boretius, *Capitularia*, i, no. 18, p. 43). See also above, p. 20 and n. 1, the quotation from the "Astronomer".

sition accorded to these *vassi dominici* in relation to other vassals is shown by the regulations laid down for the taking of the oath of fealty to Charlemagne in 792–3. Royal vassals are to take their oath between the hands of the *missi dominici*, in company with bishops, abbots and counts, while other vassals take their oath between the hands of the counts, just as does the generality of the king's subjects.[1]

IV. Vassals of Other Lords

The vassals of other lords might be of very varied social ranks; even under Charlemagne one still finds amongst them serfs and other men who were not entirely free, though such cases are quite exceptional.[2] The *vassi casati*, the beneficed vassals, were those who occupied the most eminent position. But there were other possible criteria of rank besides that of holding a benefice; for example, a man of high rank who for some reason became a vassal of some still more powerful personage or of some ecclesiastical establishment would continue to enjoy the consideration which he owed to his personal authority or his wealth. The further one advances in the ninth century, the more frequent do cases of this type become, and they certainly contributed a great deal to the general rise in social status of the main body of vassals.

This rise in social status explains the distinction which was steadily becoming clearer between the vassal and the person who asked and obtained the protection (Fr. *maimbour*) of another in return for furnishing him services of a humbler character than those of a fighting man. The term *vassus* was no longer applied to the former type of person. The vassal, however modest might be his origins or family fortunes, disposed at least of a horse and arms—lance, sword and shield—even though the horse and the equipment might belong to his master.[3] It was in virtue of these that he now moved in a social world quite different from that of the domestic servant or the worker in the fields.

[1] *Capitulare missorum*, of 792–3, cc. 2, 4 (ed. Boretius, *Capitularia*, i, no. 25, pp. 66–7).
[2] *Ibid*, c. 4 (p. 67). On the dates of the Capitularies see the table published by A. Verhulst as an appendix to my *Recherches sur les Capitulaires* (Paris, 1958).
[3] See the text cited in the last note.

V. Legal Forms by which Vassalage was Created

The legal forms by which the relationship of lordship and vassalage was created are clearly set out in two texts which refer to the history of the reign of Louis the Pious. In 837 the emperor confided to his young son Charles the Bald the titular government of the land between Frisia and the Seine, and in the following year added to this Neustria, the land between the Seine and the Loire. The Annals of St. Bertin describe what took place on the first occasion in the following words: *episcopi, abbates, comites et vassalli dominici in memoratis locis beneficia habentes, Karolo se commendaverunt et fidelitatem sacramento firmaverunt*; 'the bishops, abbots, counts and royal vassals who had benefices in the aforesaid regions commended themselves to Charles and confirmed their fealty with an oath'. With regard to the events of 838, the biographer of Louis the Pious who is usually known as 'the Astronomer' wrote as follows: *Neustriae provintiae primores Karolo et manus dederunt et fidelitatem sacramento obstrinxerunt*, 'the magnates of the province of Neustria gave their hands to Charles and promised their fealty by oath'.[1] In the first place, then, there is an act described as commendation which involved a gesture with the hands (*se commendaverunt et manus dederunt*); in the second place, there is an oath.

VI. Commendation

A person commending himself to another did so by placing his hands between those of the man whose vassal he was about to become. The texts speak of *in vasatico se commendare per manus*, 'to commend oneself into vassalage by ones hands', *manus suas commendare*, literally 'to commend ones hands', *in manus* or *in manibus N. se commendare*, 'to commend oneself in the hands of N.'[2] The latter passages show that the hands of the future lord

[1] *Annales Bertiniani*, a. 837 (ed. G. Waitz, Hanover, 1883, p. 15); *Vita Illudowici Pii*, c. 59 (M.G.H., SS., ii. 644).

[2] *Annales regni Francorum*, (original text), a. 757 (ed. F. Kurze, Hanover, 1895, p. 14); *Capitularia*, no. 104, c. 8 (ed. Boretius, i. 215); *Ann. reg. Franc.*, a. 814 (p. 141); charter of Louis the Pious of 815 in M. Bouquet, *Recueil des historiens des Gaules et de la France*, vi. 472; letter of Dhuoda, wife of margrave Bernard of Septimania, to her son William, a. 843, at the end of the introductory sentence, E. Bondurand, *L'éducation carolingienne. Le manuel de Dhuoda*, Paris, 1887, p. 54.

were also thought of as playing an active part in the ceremony.

The most explicit description of the act of commendation itself occurs in Ermoldus Nigellus' account of the commendation of King Harald of Denmark to Louis the Pious in 826:

> Mox manibus junctis regi se tradidit ultro . . .
> Caesar ad ipse manus manibus suscepit honestis.

'Soon he delivered himself, with joined hands, to the king . . . , and the emperor himself took his hands between his own glorious ones.' The future vassal placed his joined hands between those of his future lord, who for his part placed his own outside those of his future vassal. This double gesture with the hands, *immixtio manuum*, was an essential part of the act of commendation, and was presumably accompanied by a declaration of intention on the part of the future vassal.[1]

It must be remembered, however, that commendation provided a legal framework which could cover many different forms of personal subordination. In the Tours formula cited above it is applied to the case of a poor man who could render to his lord only services of a very humble character.[2] What we are concerned with here, however, is the part played by commendation in the formation of the bond of vassalage.

VII. The Oath of Fealty

By the second half of the eighth and during the ninth century those entering into the bond of vassalage did not simply commend themselves; they took an oath of fealty as well.[3] The term used to describe what was sworn was *fidelitas*, though *fides* occurs also from time to time. Paschasius Radbert, for example, places in the mouth of Louis the Pious when he is remonstrating with his rebel sons in 833 the following words: *Mementote . . . etiam et quod mei vasalli estis mihique cum iuramento fidem firmastis*, 'remember that you are also my vassals and that you have con-

---

[1] Ermoldus Nigellus, In honorem Hludowici, iv. vv. 601, 606 (ed. E. Dümmler in M.G.H., Poetae, ii. 75; ed. E. Faral, Paris, 1932, vv. 2481, 2486, p. 188; perhaps also vv. 603-4, ed. Dümmler, 2484-5, ed. Faral).

[2] Above, pp. 6-7.

[3] Texts cited above, p. 26.

[4] *Epitaphium Arsenii*, ii. 17 (ed. E. Dümmler in *Abhandlungen d. Preussischen Akademie d. Wissensch. zu Berlin*, 1900, p. 85) - Vita Walae, c. 17 (ed. G. H. Pertz, M.G.H., SS., ii. 563).

firmed your fealty by an oath'.[4] The oath of fealty was essentially a promise of fidelity reinforced by an oath, which itself involved not merely an appeal to God but physical contact with some *res sacra*—a relic, a Gospel book or some similar object.

One may reasonably wonder why an oath of fealty should have added to an act of commendation which by itself rendered a vassal so completely subject to his lord.[1] One explanation is undoubtedly the desire of the lords to ensure in the most effective manner possible the fulfilment by the vassals of their duties. A man violating a sworn oath thereby rendered himself guilty of perjury, which was a mortal sin, and in an age of faith this would mean a good deal. A further consideration, not in the least incompatible with this, is that it was to some extent in the interests of the vassals themselves to take an oath.

It has been seen already that in the middle of the eighth century a considerable change was taking place in the social status of vassals, and that members of the aristocracy themselves were now prepared to become the vassals of others.[2] For such persons it was desirable to enhance the status of the act of commendation, thus making it clear that they were not to be confounded with persons of lower rank who might commend themselves and be bound to render services of a less honourable character. They would wish it to be generally recognized that they served as free men, *ingenuili ordine*. But the gesture of the hands in the act of commendation was that of a man handing himself over to another, and as such could be held to indicate a loss of freedom, more especially since the word *vassus* was not one well thought of and the terminology connected with it was essentially one of servitude.[3] By adding an oath to the ceremony, however, one implied an engagement continuously operative in the future and therefore a degree of freedom on the part of the person undertaking such an obligation. It is possible, indeed, that the oath was essentially that by which the old royal *antrustiones* had bound themselves to the king's service,[4] this now being transferred to the act of commendation by persons of the same social standing, for *antrustiones* disappear from the texts at about the

[1] See above, pp. 5–9.
[2] See above, pp. 19, 25 and n.g.
[3] See above, 20 and below, p. 36.
[4] See above, 4–5, 8.

same time that large numbers of magnates are found becoming vassals of the head of the Frankish state.

Confirmation of this way of thinking is to be found in the commentary on the Rule of St. Benedict ascribed to Paul the Deacon, where the obedience of the slave, inspired by the fear of physical punishment, is contrasted with that of the vassal. *Bassallus servit seniori suo propter fidem suam quam professus est illi servire, ut non inveniatur fallax*, 'the vassal serves his lord in virtue of the faith by which he has promised to serve him, so that he shall not be taken as a breaker of his word.'[1] *Fides*, 'faith', is fealty promised under oath; it is this which governs the conduct of a free man, while a slave is governed only by fear of the rod.

The oath of fealty was added to the act of commendation by 757 at the latest. It was in this year that Duke Tassilo III of Bavaria became the vassal of the Frankish king Pepin III, and the Royal Annals record the event as follows: *Ibique Tassilo venit, dux Baioariorum, in vasatico se commendans per manus, sacramenta iuravit multa et innumerabilia, reliquias sanctorum manus inponens, et fidelitatem promisit regi Pippino et supradictis filiis eius, domno Carolo et Carlomanno, sicut vassus recta mente et firma devotione per iustitiam, sicut vassus dominos suos esse deberet*, 'Tassilo, duke of the Bavarians, came there (to Compiègne) and commended himself into vassalage by his hands; he swore many and innumerable oaths, placing his hand on the relics of the saints, and he promised fealty to King Pepin and to his sons the aforementioned lords Charles and Carloman, as by law a vassal ought to do with uprightness and devotion, assuming the position a vassal ought to have in relation to his lords'.[2] We here see that the acts which create the bond of vassalage comprise commendation with *immixtio manuum* and a promise of fealty, the latter reinforced by an oath and the touching of a *res sacra*. It is possible even that the concluding section of the account incorporates a part of the oath formula itself.

The text of such an oath of fealty, taken by a royal vassal of

---

[1] *Expositio in regulam S. Benedicti*, in the *Florilegium Casinense*, iv (in Vol. iv of the *Bibliotheca Casinensis*, Monte Cassino, 1880), p. 56, col. 2. The same idea is expressed a little further on in a slightly different form.

[2] *Annales regni Francorum* (original text), a. 757 (p. 14).

the Carolingian period, has been preserved in one of the capitularies, since Charlemagne used it in 802 as the model for the
oath of fealty to the emperor which he imposed on all his subjects. It ran as follows: 'By this oath I promise to be faithful to
the lord Charles, the most pious emperor, son of King Pepin and
Bertha, as a vassal should rightfully be to his lord, for the preservation of his kingdom and of his rights. And I will keep and
hope to keep this oath which I have sworn as I know it and
understand it, from this day henceforward, with the help of God,
the creator of heaven and earth, and of these sacred relics.'[1]
(*Sacramentale qualiter repromitto ego: domno Karolo piissimo
imperatori, filio Pippini regis et Berthane fidelis sum, sicut homo
per drictum debet esse domino suo ad suum regnum et ad suum
rectum. Et illud sacramentum quod iuratum habeo custodiam et
custodire volvo, in quantum ego scio et intellego, ab isto die
inantea, si me adiuvet Deus, qui coelum et terram creavit et ista
sanctorum patrocinia.*)[2]

VIII. *Freedom of Action of the Parties Concerned*

These two acts, the *immixtio manuum*, the placing of one's
own hands between the hands of one's lord, and the *sacramentum*, the oath of fealty, created the *nexus iuris*, the legal bond
between the two parties.

Although it no doubt frequently happened that a man was
compelled by force of circumstances to become the vassal of a
lord, the contract of vassalage was in theory regarded as one freely
concluded between the two parties. Charles the Bald refers to this
principle in 847: *Volumus etiam ut unusquisque liber homo in
nostro regno seniorem qualem voluerit, in nobis et in nostris
fidelibus accipiat*, 'and we also wish that every free man in our
kingdom may choose as his lord whomsoever he will, whether it

---

[1] *Capitularia missorum specialia* of 802, *in fine* (ed. Borctius, *Capitularia*,
i, no. 34, p. 102). The taking of this oath did not of course imply that all
the subjects of the emperor thereby became his vassals.

[2] In some texts the terms *commendatio* and *se commendare* are used to
cover the whole complex of acts by which the bond of vassalage was created.
The fact that these words, applying properly to only a part, could be used
for the whole is easily explained, for it was the *immixtio manuum* which
would make the deepest impression on witnesses. See e.g. the *Capitulare
missorum* of 792–3, c. 4 (ed. Boretius, *Capitularia*, i, no. 25, p. 67) and
the *Vita Hludowici*, c. 2 (M.G.H., SS., ii. 618).

be ourself or one of our *fideles*'.[1] But once the contract had been concluded, it could not be unilaterally denounced, at any rate once it had actually come into operation. In one of his capitularies, Charlemagne lists those extreme cases in which a vassal might quit his lord. It was permissible only if the lord had tried to kill him or to strike him with a rod, or had tried to violate his wife or commit adultery with her, or had tried to violate his daughter or seduce her, or had deprived the vassal of part of his patrimony, or had tried to make him a serf, or had fallen upon him with raised sword, or had failed to defend him as he ought. The obligation laid upon the vassal of not quitting his lord without the consent of the latter is constantly repeated by Charlemagne's successors.[2] The engagement of vassalage could normally only be terminated by the death of the lord or the vassal. There was also as yet no question of contracting bonds of vassalage towards several lords. To permit this would have been to withdraw the vassal in a large measure from the personal, direct, and almost exclusive authority that the lord had over him, and would have seriously impaired the efficacy of the whole institution.

IX. The Service of Vassals

The service due from the vassal was becoming more and more specialized. It is true that the *vassi dominici* were employed on political, judicial and administrative duties, and no doubt the vassals of counts performed similar functions from time to time. They also, like the vassals of the church and private persons, would be charged with certain duties in their lord's household or in the management of his estates. But already in the reign of Charlemagne the military services due from a vassal were visibly taking precedence over all others, and the capitularies begin to be full of regulations regarding them. In theory, the vassal owed these military obligations only when his lord was serving the king, but in practice, from the time of Louis the Pious onwards, magnates in rebellion against the emperor were able to take the field at the head of their vassals.

[1] First *Conventus* of Meersen, iii. 2 (ed. A. Boretius and V. Krause, *Capitularia*, ii, no. 204, p. 71).

[2] *Capitularia*, nos. 77 (802/03), c. 16 (i. 172) and 104, c. 8 (i. 215); cf. also no. 204 (of 847), iii, c. 3 (ii. 71).

Contemporary texts describe the service of the vassal by names which are reminiscent of slavery, or rather of the serfdom which was gradually taking its place. The word most commonly used was *servitium*, servitude, and despite its implications it does not seem to have caused offence. The Uuldalrich who gave himself in 807 *in servitium* to the bishop of Freising in Bavaria may well have been a person of no consequence, but towards the end of the ninth century the chronicler Regino saw nothing inappropriate in using the word to describe the entry of Duke Tassilo of Bavaria into the vassalage of Charlemagne: *tradens se manibus ad servitium*. One even meets, though only in literary works, the expression *militiae vestrae servitutem*, 'the servitude of your vassalage', to describe, without any wish to depreciate, the service due from royal vassals.[1]

X. *The Subordination of the Vassal to his Lord*

All these things—the humiliating terms employed, the very restricted number of grounds on which a vassal could quit his lord, the prohibition against the vassal's commending himself to another lord—emphasize what one may call the 'totalitarian' character of the subordination of the vassal. An analysis of the acts which constituted the contract of vassalage—for reasons of clarity, we postpone consideration of them till we come to a later and more developed period—only confirms what we have seen already. One may go so far as to say that the lord exercised a species of sovereignty over the person of his vassal. It is therefore the more necessary to emphasize the fact that, great as the lord's authority might be, the vassal, however humble was his origin or condition, remained a free man in the eyes of the law, and as such enjoyed the most essential prerogative of freedom, that of being tried in the public courts. The lord might possess at certain times the power of compelling his vassals to perform certain actions; when they were carrying out their military obligations, he might exercise over them disciplinary functions: but he could not judge them. The vassal was amenable only to the count's tribunal, the *mallus*, unless indeed he was a royal vassal, in which

[1] T. Bitterauf, *Die Traditionen des Hochstifts Freising*, i (Munich, 1905), no. 257; Regino, *Chronicon*, a. 787 (ed. F. Kurze, Hanover, 1890, p. 56); Radbert, *Epitaphium Arsenii*, II, 17 (p. 86).

case he was amenable to the palace tribunal. But this itself was a public court, and not a private court in which the king presided as the lord of his vassals; it was indeed under the Carolingians the public tribunal *par excellence*, with the king presiding in his capacity as sovereign.

Already in the Carolingian period there existed what one may term a 'mystique' of vassalage: a spiritual compulsion which reinforced in the minds of many the idea of the absolute character of the devotion which a vassal owed to his lord. The religious character of the oath of fealty went far to nourish this conception. One may form some idea of it by reading the exhortation addressed by Dhuoda, wife of margrave Bernard of Septimania, a lady of high birth and wide culture, to her eldest son William in 843.[1] She urged on him the duty of fealty towards the lord to whom he had commended himself by the order of his father (*audivi . . . quod genitor tuus Bernardus in manus domini te commendavit Caroli regis*). Although it is true that the lord in this case was the king, it is necessary to remember that Charles's power was still disputed, and the whole context shows that the passionate attachment which Dhuoda urged her son to show towards the king was no more than the attachment which a *vassus* should display towards his *senior*, whosoever he might be.

The most characteristic passages are as follows:

'An admonition relating to your lord.

Since God, as I believe, and your father Bernard have chosen you, in the flower of your youth, to serve Charles as your lord, I urge you ever to remember the record of your family, illustrious on both sides, and not to serve your master simply to satisfy him outwardly, but to maintain towards him and his service in all things a devoted and certain fealty both of body and soul . . . That is why, my son, I exhort you to maintain faithfully all that is in your charge, with all your strength of body and soul, as long as your life shall last . . . May the madness of infidelity be ever far from you; may evil never find such a place in your heart as to render you unfaithful to your lord in any matter whatsoever . . . But I do not fear this on your part or on the part of those who serve with you . . . Therefore, my son William, you who

[1] E. Bondurand, *L'éducation carolingienne. Le manuel de Dhuoda* (Paris, 1887), pp. 54, 90-2.

are of our blood, show yourself towards your lord, as I have already urged, true, vigilant, useful and most prompt to his service. In every matter which concerns the power and welfare of the king, both within the kingdom and without, show that wisdom with which God has plentifully endowed you. Read the lives and words of the holy men of former times, and you will find there how to serve your lord and be faithful to him in all things. And when you receive his commands, apply yourself faithfully to execute them. Observe also and regard carefully those who show the greatest fidelity and assiduity in his service, and learn of them the way in which to act.' (*Admonitio erga seniorem tuum exhibenda. Seniorem quem habes K[arolum], quando Deus, ut credo, et genitor tuus B[ernardus], in tuae inchoationis iuventute florigeram vigorem tibi ad serviendum elegit, adhuc tene quod est generis ex magno utrumque nobilitatis exorto progenie, non ita serviens ut tantum placeas oculis, sed etiam sensui capax, utrumque ad corpus et animam puram et certam illi in omnibus tene utilitatis fidem . . . Quamobrem, fili, hortor te ut quod tenes corpore fideliter dum vivis tene et mente . . . Nunquam aliquando ex infidelitatis vesania improperium ex te exeat; malum non sit ortus nec in corde tuo unquam ascendens ut infidelis tuo seniori existas in ullo . . . Quod in te tuisque militantibus futurum esse non credo . . . Tu ergo, fili V[uillelme], ex illorum progenie ortus, seniori ut praedixi tuo sis verax, vigil, utilisque atque praecipuus; et in omni negotio utilitatis regiae potestatis, in quantum tibi Deus dederit vires, intus forisque prudentius te exhibere satage. Lege vitas vel dicta sanctorum praecedentium patrum et invenies qualiter vel quomodo tuo seniori debeas servire atque fidelis adesse in omnibus. Et cum inveneris studeas jussa illius complere fideliter. Considera etiam et conspice illos qui illi fidelissime militant assidue et disce ab illis documenta servitii . . .*)

XI. The Concept of Fealty

The concept of fealty is one that deserves our attention. It can be most clearly grasped with the help of a text which is concerned with the fealty due to the king by his subjects, for this is not essentially different from that due by vassals to their lord.

In the spring of 802, after becoming emperor, Charlemagne imposed a new oath of fealty on his subjects. using for the purpose the formula already employed for the oath to the king taken by the royal vassals.[1] In a capitulary which sets out in its broad lines the programme of the imperial government Charles seeks to define the precise implications of 'fealty', extending its meaning and affirming that this should not be limited to the general accepted notions as to what constitute its primary elements. This *communis opinio*, regarding the primary elements in fealty can be understood from the way in which the emperor declares that henceforward it is . . . *non ut multi usque nunc extimaverunt, tantum fidelitate domno imperatori usque in vita ipsius, et ne aliquem inimicum in suum regnum causa inimicitiae inducat, et ne alicui infidelitate illius consentiant aut retaciat,* 'not as many have thought up to now, involving simply fidelity to the lord emperor as far as his life is concerned'—i.e. the obligation of refraining from any action against him which will put his life in danger—'and the obligation of not introducing into his kingdom any enemy out of hostility towards him, and of declining to be a party to the disloyalty towards him of others or keeping silent regarding such'.[2]

The Carolingian notion of loyalty was thus essentially negative in character, consisting in nothing more than the duty of undertaking nothing against the interests of the person to whom one owes fealty. This notion is confirmed by the passage already quoted from the commentary on the Rule of St. Benedict ascribed to Paul the Deacon: a vassal should serve his lord in virtue of his *fides*, his 'faith,' *ut non inveniatur fallax,* 'so that he shall not be taken as a breaker of his word'.[3] But this essentially negative aspect of fealty was supplemented by the more positive aspect which appears in some passages already cited, notably in the Manual of Dhuoda.

The history of the ninth century, none the less, brings us frequently into contact with vassals who abandon or betray their lords. Perhaps the most frequent motive of such lapses was the desire of vassals to enrich themselves, to obtain fresh benefices. We must therefore turn now to consider the property element in Carolingian feudalism.

[1] See above, p. 29–30.

[2] *Capitulare missorum generale*, c. 2 (Boretius, *Capitularia*, i, no. 33, p. 92).

[3] See above, p. 29, n. 1.

XII. Beneficed and Unbeneficed Vassals

The very existence of this property element was, as we have seen, a necessary consequence of the obligation incumbent on the lord of maintaining his vassal. Under Charlemagne and his successors, this could be and often was done directly, in the lord's household. We have already referred to those royal vassals who lived in the palace and received directly from the king their clothing and food and arms; of such a vassal it would be said that he 'would have no benefice' (beneficium non habuerit), in the words of the Capitulary of Herstal of 779. Private persons might also have unbeneficed vassals, but these would be people in very humble circumstances. It is no doubt to such as these that allusion is made in a piece of legislation forbidding a vassal to leave his lord once he has received from him some object of the value of 1 s., postquam acciperit valente solido uno.[1] But it is certain that during the second half of the eighth and the whole of the ninth century, the custom of 'beneficing' vassals became steadily more general, and in the case of vassals who through their family connections or fortune or their official functions occupied a high rank in society, such 'beneficing' as this was the rule.

It is also true that we hear quite frequently in the ninth century of rulers giving estates to their vassals in full ownership, as allodial property (iure proprietario or ad proprium), and that sometimes the grant says explicitly that it is in recompense for the service given by the vassal, ob devotionem servitii sui. It might also happen that the king converted into allodial property an estate which the vassal had up till then held as a benefice.[2] But these were only exceptions. The normal custom was that a lord desirous of endowing his vassal granted him a benefice.

XIII. The Benefice of the Vassal

The study of the Carolingian benefice is complicated by the fact that the word beneficium, although applied by preference to the

[1] Capit. Haristallense, c. 9 (ed. Boretius, Capitularia, i, no. 20, p. 48); Capitulary of Aachen of 802/03, c. 16 (ibid., no. 77, p. 172).
[2] E.g. G. Tessier, Recueil des actes de Charles II, le Chauve, i (Paris, 1943), nos. 16 (843), 17 (843; d'Abadal, op. cit., ii (2), Preceptes per a particulars, no. 15, pp. 332-4), and 69 (845); ii (1952), nos. 275 (864), 336 (870) J. Tardif, Monuments historiques. Cartons des Rois (Paris, 1866), no. 214 (of 879/84), p. 137.

tenement of a vassal, could still bear other meanings. It could refer to an ecclesiastical benefice, the right of receiving the income from church property, which an ecclesiastical office carried with it; it could cover precarial tenure; it could be applied to tenements held by estate officials or even domestic servants. Disregarding these anomalous uses, however, there are plenty of texts from which we can form some idea of what the benefice of a vassal was like in the time of Charlemagne and his successors.

The essential features of the benefice had scarcely changed since the middle of the eighth century. As in these earlier times, its size might vary greatly. It might consist of a *villa*, that is to say a manor often as large as a modern village, or of several of these, or of only fractions of them; it might consist of only a few *mansi*, agricultural holdings whose normal size in northwestern Gaul was 10–18 hectares (25–48 acres). It appears that towards the end of the reign of Charlemagne the possession of a benefice amounting to 12 *mansi* imposed on the vassal the duty of serving on horseback with the full equipment of a heavily armed knight. In the case of royal vassals, benefices consisted of at least 30 *mansi*, but were often larger; we hear of benefices of 50, 100, 200 or even more *mansi*. Benefices held by *vassi dominici* and consisting of one or two entire manors were therefore in no way exceptional.[1] Moreover a benefice did not necessarily consist of a manor or a fraction of a manor. When Carolingian rulers granted an *abbatia*, the office of abbot of some monastery, to a layman or to a secular churchman, a thing which they frequently did, they usually gave him this lucrative post as a benefice.

A perpetual preoccupation of the Carolingians was that of ensuring that their proprietary rights over their allods, their *res proprietatis nostrae*, which they granted in benefice to their vassals should not be endangered in the process. Vassals were constantly on the look-out for opportunities of converting estates which they held in benefice into property belonging to them in a private capacity. 'We have heard', declared Charlemagne on one occasion, 'that counts and other persons who hold benefices from us treat these as if they were their own allodial possessions': *auditum habemus qualiter et comites et alii homines qui nostra*

---

[1] *Capitulare missorum* of Thionville of 805, c. 6 (ed. Boretius, *Capitularia*, i, no. 44, p. 123); *Capitulare episcoporum* of 792/3 (*ibid.*, i, no. 21, p. 52).

beneficia habere videntur comparant sibi proprietates de ipso nostro beneficio.[1] Some of these usurpations were successful, particularly in West Francia during the second half of the ninth century, when conditions were more than usually unstable. The general picture which we obtain from the texts is a confused one of constant threats and attempts at usurpation, and of measures of preservation which were not always successful, but there can be no doubt that most benefices managed to maintain their proper character. This is equally true of benefices granted by the kings to their *vassi dominici* and of benefices granted by private lords, and in particular by ecclesiastical establishments, to their own vassals. At the end of the ninth century, the rights of a vassal over his benefice still remained those of a usufructuary.

These observations hold good in the case of the vast majority of benefices, but those which were granted by the kings to their vassals out of the sequestrated property of the Church continued, as in the times of Pepin III and Carloman, to show some peculiar features. These features, however, had by now somewhat changed their character. Charlemagne had in 779[2] prescribed that the church which owned the property in question and from which it was, by the king's order, held on precarial tenure (*precaria verbo regis*) should henceforward be paid only a very small rent, but in compensation should have the right to a 'ninth' (*nona*), a second tithe in addition to the tithe due to the Church which since the reign of Pepin III had been paid by every type of land. After Charlemagne, and even more after Louis the Pious, this practice, though it did not entirely disappear, became much less common. Benefices granted in early times by the Crown out of church property were usually converted either into benefices held purely and simply of the king or into benefices or *precariae* held of the churches themselves. This at least is true of those benefices which had not been usurped by the vassals, as must frequently have happened.

Towards the middle of the ninth century, the Carolingians began again to seize the property of the Church and to distribute it in benefices to their vassals. This was particularly the case in West Francia, Lotharingia and Burgundy; it was less frequent in

---

[1] *Capitulare missorum* of Nijmegen of 806, c. 6 (*ibid.*, i, no. 46, p. 131).
[2] Capitulary of Herstal, c. 13 (*ibid.*, i, no. 20, p. 50).

East Francia, where the wealth of the Church was much less great. But the rulers no longer made use of the ancient *precaria verbo regis*; other expedients took its place. Sometimes the property of a particular church or abbey was simply bestowed by the king on the vassal as a benefice. More frequently the ruler might, in a manner that brooked no denial, require a particular church or abbey to receive into its vassalage a given number of knights, and grant to them some of its estates in benefice. These knights would become *milites* or *homines ecclesiae*, vassals of the church in question, but they would be at the disposal of the king in case of need.[1] In either case benefices consisting of church property, granted directly by the king or on his orders by the Church to his vassals, were henceforward a very common phenomenon.

A type of tenement closely related to benefice was that *per aprisionem*, which is only found in Septimania and in the Spanish March. It was applied to waste or half-cultivated land, and had the express object of securing its better cultivation. A royal vassal who held an *aprisio* exercised over the land the same rights as did the holder of a benefice, but his rights were hereditary and could only be terminated as a result of infidelity on his part. When the king from whom the grant had emanated died, his successor seems to have been bound to renew it. A tenement *per aprisionem* could naturally be converted without much difficulty into full private ownership, and this was often done.[2]

The documents of the Carolingian period give us little explicit information regarding the exact procedure by which a benefice was granted to a vassal. In conformity with the legal habits of the period, we must assume that a formal handing over or livery (*traditio*) of the benefice was necessary in order to enable the vassal to acquire rights over it, and that this *traditio* would be carried out by handing to the vassal some object which symbolized the benefice. We hear, for example, that when in 787 Duke

[1] An example of the successive application, during the century 768–876, of *precaria verbo regis* and the two methods of procedure described in the text is provided by the *villa* of Neuilly-Saint-Front (dép. Aisne). See Hincmar, *De villa Novilliaco* (ed. O. Holder-Egger in *M.G.H., SS.*, xv (ii), 1167–69).

[2] E.g. *M.G.H., Diplomata Karolinorum*, i (ed. E. Mühlbacher), no. 179 of 795 (p. 241); Bouquet, *Recueil des Historiens*, vi. 472 (815); Tessier, *Recueil des actes de Charles II, le Chauve*, i, nos. 43 (844), 94 (847), 118 (849); or d' Abadal, *op. cit.*, ii (2), *Preceptes a particulares*, nos. 1, 7, 17, 18, 19).

Tassilo III of Bavaria, after his condemnation as a rebel, had been compelled by Charlemagne to submit and to resign the duchy which he held in benefice, he did so by handing to the king *baculo in cuius capite similitudo hominis erat scultum*, 'a sceptre whose end was carved into the likeness of a man'. It was by the handing back of this same symbolic object that Tassilo subsequently recovered his duchy, once again as a benefice.[1] The actual procedure, like most legal acts of the time, was a purely oral one; it was only rarely that a charter would be drawn up as evidence of the rights of the two parties concerned.[2]

XIV. The Legal Union of Vassalage and Benefice

Having analysed separately the personal and the property elements in the system of feudal relationships under Charlemagne and his successors, it is now necessary to consider their actual union. Was it a case of a simple combination in practice, merely the general acceptance of a usage whereby the king and other lords granted benefices to their vassals? Or was there an actual legal fusion between the two?

When we come to examine the question, we find it impossible to doubt that there was some legal connection between the two institutions. This relationship must have existed in early Carolingian times, and it is clearly attested in those of Charlemagne and Louis the Pious. The circumstances attending the transfer of a particular region from one ruler to another provide us with evidence in this matter. When in 837 Louis the Pious installed his youngest son Charles as king of the country between Frisia and the Seine, we are told that bishops, counts and royal vassals 'who had benefices in these parts' (*in memoratis locis beneficia habentes*) 'commended themselves to Charles and took oaths of fealty to him' (*Karolo se commendaverunt et fidelitatem sacramento firmaverunt*). A letter of Einhard addressed to Lewis the German, king of Bavaria and ruler of other areas east of the Rhine, and written (in 834?) to ask for a vacant benefice on behalf of some personage whose name has not been preserved

[1] *Annales Guelferbytani*, a. 787 (in M.G.H., SS., i. 43); *Annales Laurissenses minores*, a. 787 (*ibid.*, i. 119).

[2] An example of 876 is in Tessier, *Recueil des actes de Charles II le Chauve*, II. n° 411.

(*aliquam consolationem ei faciatis de beneficiis*), asks specifically that it might be granted when 'he shall have commended himself to you' (*quando in vestras manus se commendaverit*).[1] The acceptance of the status of vassal is here regarded as a necessary condition for the bestowal of a benefice.

There was yet another legal tie which bound together the two institutions of vassalage and benefice. Its existence is implied in the wording of a constitution of Louis the Pious of 815 dealing with Spanish refugees who had been received into Septimania and the Spanish March. The emperor laid down that they should have the right to commend themselves to the counts administering the counties of these areas, and adds: 'and if they have received of those to whom they have commended themselves some benefice, let them know also that from it they are bound to provide their lord with the same service that the vassals of our country [i.e. of Francia] are bound to pay to their lords from similar benefices' (*ut si beneficium aliquod quisquam eorum ab eo cui se commendavit fuerit consecutus, sciat se de illo tale obsequium seniori suo exhibere debere, quale nostrates homines de simili beneficio senioribus suis exhibere solent*).[2] Vassals are evidently bound to use the resources of their benefices to furnish their lord with the services which they owe him by the terms of the contract of commendation.

The fact that the grant of a benefice lapsed not only on the death of a vassal (Germ. *Mannfall*) but also on the death of a lord (Germ. *Herrenfall* or, where the lord was the king, *Thronfall*) proves equally the existence of a legal bond between the two institutions, since it was evidently the ending of a personal relationship of vassalage which terminated the property relationship created by the grant of a benefice. We know for a fact that the termination of benefices by *Mannfall* and *Herrenfall* existed already in the time of Charlemagne and his successors. For example, we hear that a royal vassal named John, who had obtained from Charlemagne a tenement by *aprisio*—which, as we

---

[1] *Annales Bertiniani*, a. 837 (ed. Waitz, p. 15); *Einharti Epistolae*, no. 34 (ed. K. Hampe in *M.G.H., Epistolae*, v. 126, 127).

[2] *Constitutio de Hispanis prima*, c. 6 (ed. Boretius, *Capitularia*, i, no. 132, p. 262); or d'Abadal, *op. cit.*, II (2) Apèndix III).

have seen, could be regarded as a kind of benefice—in the county of Narbonne, did homage after the emperor's death to Louis the Pious, and so obtained from him a regrant of his tenement. In 832/3 we find Einhard asking that a vassal of the bishop of Würzburg whose contract of commendation had been terminated by the death of Bishop Wolfger should be allowed to remain for the moment in possession of his benefice; the right of the vassal to the benefice had come to an end, but Einhard would endeavour to obtain from the new bishop after his consecration a regrant of the benefice to its former holder. In another letter, which can be dated 833, Einhard asks a correspondent to secure from the Emperor Lothar that a certain Frumold, a royal vassal who at the moment was ill, should be left for the time being in possession of the benefice which he had held in turn of Charlemagne and Louis the Pious; after he has recovered, he will commend himself to the new emperor and can then be reinvested by him with the benefice (*ut permittat se habere beneficium, quod avus eius illi concessit et pater habere permisit, quo usque viribus receptis ad eius presentiam venerit ac se solemni more commendaverit*). There is a still more instructive text which dates from 868 and comes from the Breton abbey of Redon. Abbot Conuuoio had died and Ritcant had succeeded him. He ordered three vassals, Milo and two persons who both bore the name of Haeluuoco, who had received benefices of his predecessors (*beneficiaverat eis in fidelitate Sancti Salvatoris et abbatis*), to appear before him, and demanded that they should surrender their benefices, as there had been a change of abbot and consequently of lord (*ut redderent ipsa beneficia in manu sua, quia ipse erat electus ad abbatem post Conuuoion*). They did so, but they besought the new abbot to regrant them the same benefices, and he did so after having received them as vassals (*reddidit illis iterum ipsa beneficia . . . in fidelitate et servitio Sancti Salvatoris . . . et ut essent defensores totius abbatie . . .*)[1]

The legal union between vassalage and benefice was in fact even closer than these facts suggest. We are entitled to maintain that, by the end of Charlemagne's reign, the service due from a

---

[1] Charters of 795 and 815 cited above, p. 39, n. 2; *Einharti Epistolae*, nos. 24, 27 (pp. 122, 123); A. de Courson, *Cartulaire de l'abbaye de Redon* (Paris, 1863), no. 96, p. 72.

vassal was regarded in the eyes of the law as being the immediate consideration (in the legal sense of the word) for the grant of a benefice. If the service was neglected or rendered badly, the consideration for the grant disappeared and the grant itself might be revoked. Confiscation of a benefice would thus become the principal sanction for the failure of a vassal to fulfil his obligations of vassalage. It is to this principle that the emperor appeals in a capitulary of 802/03 when he lays down that if a royal vassal is summoned to the assistance of another *vassus dominicus* and ignores the summons, he should lose his benefice. The same principle is applied in a charter of 807, in which a bishop of Freising, when granting a benefice to a vassal, stipulates that the benefice shall be forfeited if the vassal does not punctually carry out his duties.[1] These are only the earliest of a long series of texts in which this principle is clearly and repeatedly invoked.

We must remember, however, that this close union between vassalage and benefice did not prevent a vassal from holding property other than that which he had been granted by his lord. He might possess allodial estates of his own, and he might hold property on precarial tenure from some ecclesiastical establishment. If he were a vassal of some social position, he would normally hold one or both of these types of property.

XV. *The Rights of Lord and Vassal over the Benefice*

From what we have said already, it should be clear that in the nexus of feudal and vassal relationships, the personal relationship was in Carolingian times the more important of the two. A benefice, in the technical sense of the word, would be granted only to a vassal, but it was perfectly possible to be a vassal without at the same time holding a benefice. None the less, the grant of benefices plays so prominent a part in the framework of the relationship of vassalage that by the end of the ninth century it has already begun to modify it in several important respects.

This is at once evident when we begin to consider the rights of the two parties over the benefice. That the lord retained the legal ownership of the land which he granted in benefice was never disputed. Unless he held it himself in benefice or on pre-

---

[1] Capitulary of Aachen, c. 20 (ed. Boretius, *Capitularia*, i, no. 77, p. 172); Bitterauf, *Traditionen des Hochstifts Freising*, i, no. 257.

carial tenure, it remained his allodial property: *tam ea quae nos in dominicatura habemus quam etiam ea quae vasalli nostri . . . de eodem alodo in beneficio videntur habere,* 'both the lands which we actually occupy and the portions of our allodial property which are held in benefice by our vassals', wrote Count Echard à propos of the manor of Perrecy in *c.* 876.[1] Moreover the lord was under no obligation to regrant to another vassal a benefice which had become vacant.

It is equally true, however, that the right of disposing of land granted in benefice was, in the course of the ninth century, withdrawn more and more from the control of the lord. It may be doubted if it was ever in the lord's power to deprive a vassal. who had faithfully fulfilled his requirements of service of a benefice which had been granted to him, at any rate without offering him some compensation in return. When Louis the Pious in 817 gave the canons of Tournai some land for an extension of their cloister, it included '79 perches of the royal estate which Werimfred holds there in benefice' (*in eodem loco de fisco nostro quem Werimfredus in beneficium habet, perticas xcix*), but he no doubt gave Werimfred some other land in exchange. Half a century later, Charles the Bald declared that he could not give the abbey of St. Lucien of Beauvais one half of the manor of Luchy, excusing himself on the ground that 'one of our vassals named Sigefrid held it in benefice' (*vassallus noster quidam, nomine Sigefridus, tunc in beneficium retinebat*), but he gave it to the abbey after Sigefrid's death. At about the same time, in another charter, Charles enumerated the estates which he would give to the church of St. Urban at Châlons-sur-Marne as soon as he could arrange some exchange (*per concambium*) with the royal vassals who held them in benefice, or, if he failed to do this, after the vassals' death.[2]

These limitations on the lord's control of his property were consequences resulting from the facts that the relationship of vassalage was one which was effective for life, and that the benefice was granted to the vassal in order to make it possible for him to

[1] M. Prou and A. Vidier, *Chartes de Saint-Benoît-sur-Loire* (Paris, 1907), i, no. 26, p. 70.
[2] Bouquet, *Recueil*, vi. 509 (of 817); Tessier, *Recueil des actes de Charles II le Chauve*, ii, nos. 325 (869), 248 (862).

fulfil his obligations. An exception, however, must be made in the case of *honores*, that is to say public offices, such as the office of count, and the endowments which were attached to them. These endowments were often granted to their holders as benefices, but since the public offices were revocable, the benefices attached to them were naturally revocable as well. None the less, during the second half of the ninth century, the confiscation of *honores* and their dependent benefices was becoming more and more difficult, at least in West Francia, Lotharingia, Italy and Burgundy, even when their holders were guilty of or were charged with treason. Every such attempted confiscation became a trial of strength between the king on one side and the vassal and the party to which he belonged on the other.

It was also becoming very apparent that, when a lord died, the rights of his successor to dispose of land held in benefice were becoming more and more ineffective. It does not seem, as a matter of law, to have been disputed that death terminated both the contract of vassalage and with it the grant of a benefice; we have already cited a text which dates from 860 and comes from one of the most western and the most disturbed parts of West Francia that shows this quite clearly.[1] But a vassal clearly expected that he would be permitted to commend himself to his lord's successor, and that he would receive from the new lord a regrant of the benefice which he had previously held. The effective use of the right of disposing of benefices was becoming in practice more and more difficult, if not absolutely impossible, to exercise. When Louis the Stammerer, for example, wished to exercise such a right on the death of his father Charles the Bald in 877, he was faced with the prospect of a general revolt of the magnates throughout the kingdom and had to abandon the attempt. A similar state of affairs existed in the case of benefices granted by churches to their vassals. A French ecclesiastic writing at the very beginning of the tenth century complains that the withdrawal and free disposition of benefices was no longer possible on the occasion of the death of a bishop, and he notes enviously that in this respect the German bishops of East Francia have managed to retain their powers.[2]

[1] See above, p. 42.
[2] *Annales Bertiniani*, a. 877 (p. 137); E. Dümmler, 'Über den Dialog "De Statu Sanctae Ecclesiae"', in *Sitzungsberichte der Preussischen Akademie der Wissenschaften* (Berlin, 1901), pp. 385, 386.

There can be no doubt that this diminution of the rights of the
lord over his benefice to the profit of the vassal was the consequence of the effective occupation of the benefice by the vassal
and of the latter's desire to absorb it into his family inheritance.
The same motive explains the attempts constantly made by vassals to establish by some device or other their full ownership of
estates which they held in benefice. Examples of this tendency
are already numerous in the time of Charlemagne.

XVI. The Heritability of Benefices

A second aspect of feudal relationships which was already under-
going a profound transformation in the course of the ninth century was that of the heritability of benefices.

The contract of commendation, in its strictest and simplest
form, excluded any idea of heritability. A lord received a certain
person into the number of his vassals because of some particular
qualities he possessed, and which his son would not necessarily
inherit. Consequently the grant of a benefice, which was in theory
conditioned by the prior creation of the relationship of lord and
vassal established by the act of commendation, should not in its
turn possess an hereditary character.

But from the earliest times circumstances must have frequently
arisen in which a lord would welcome the commendation of the
son of a deceased vassal and grant him the benefice held by his
father. The latter might even during his lifetime have made arrangements with his lord for his son's succession. We have evidence from quite early times of benefices being inherited, and
there is no reason to suppose that the occasions we know of were
in any way exceptional. A case in point is that of the manors of
Perrecy and Baugy, in the Autunois, which passed as benefices
from father to son in the family of the Nibelungen from the time
of Charles Martel to the late ninth century, when they ended by
being transformed into allodial property. Another example is a
manor of the church of Rheims situated at Folembray in the
neighbourhood of Laon, which was held in benefice from father to
son from the time of Charlemagne to that of Hincmar. We find
members of a single family constantly endeavouring between 768
and 876 to obtain or to keep as a benefice the manor of Neuilly-
Saint-Front on the Ourcq, in spite of being deprived of it on more
than one occasion. From a charter of Charles the Bald, we can

deduce that the grant of a benefice to a vassal was sometimes only a confirmation of an already existing state of affairs; the benefice had previously been held by the father and grandfather of the vassal, and the latter had held it provisionally up to the mo.nent at which he commended himself to the king and the king in his turn regranted him the same benefice.[1] It might even happen that in granting a benefice to a vassal, the lord would give an undertaking that the vassal's son would receive it after him.[2] Hincmar of Rheims, a man extremely jealous of the rights and interests of his church, was well aware of the fact that an estate granted in benefice and maintained for a long period of time in this condition ran the risk of never again entering the *indominicatum*, that part of the patrimony of the lord which remained under his immediate authority. But the custom by which benefices passed from father to son had become so much a matter of general acceptance that we find him stating to Charles the Bald in 868 that 'when a bishop grants a benefice to a man from the property of the church in return for military service, he is bound to give it to his sons if they are fitted to succeed their father, or else to others who are in a position to render to Caesar that which is Caesar's and to God that which is God's' (. . . *episcopus . . . cum de rebus Ecclesiae propter militiam beneficium donat, aut filiis patrum, qui eidem Ecclesiae profuerunt et patribus utiliter succedere poterunt . . . aut talibus dare debet, qui idonei sunt reddere Caesari quae sunt Caesaris et quae sunt Dei Deo . . .*).[3] Hincmar therefore admitted that it was normal for a son to receive his father's benefice if he was a suitable person, though naturally after having become a vassal of the same lord.

This custom was never formulated as a rule of law by any legislative act, but on one occasion it was made the subject of a royal decision even though this was only intended to be of a provisional character. When Charles the Bald was making his preparations in 877 for the Italian expedition from which he was never to return,

[1] L. Levillain, 'Les Nibelungen historiques', *Annales du Midi*, 1937, pp. 346, 353-57; Hincmar, Letter to Hincmar of Laon, in Migne, *Patrologia latina*, cxxvi. 538; Hincmar, *De villa Novilliaco* (see above, p. 39, n. 1); Tessier, *Recueil des actes de Charles II, le Chauve*, i, no. 34 (of 844).

[2] Tessier, *op. cit.*, ii, no. 411 (876).

[3] *Ad Carolum Calvum regem pro Ecclesiae libertatum defensione*, in Migne, *Patrol. lat.*, cxxv. 1050.

he held an assembly at Quierzy-sur-Oise at which he promulgated a series of measures to take effect during his absence. Some of these were intended to regulate the succession in the case of counts who might die while he was away. It was provided that a provisional administration should be established in cases where the son of the dead count was with the king in Italy or was still too young to succeed his father, but that subsequently the son 'should be honoured by our grant with the father's honours' (*per nostram concessionem de illius honoribus honoretur*). Then he adds: *Similiter et de vassallis nostris faciendum est*, 'and the same shall be done with regard to our vassals'. This shows that the succession of the son, not only to the honour of a count, but also to the benefice of a royal vassal, was regarded as a normal proceeding. Finally, in general, the king ordained that bishops, abbots, counts and other *fideles*—all of whom would be equally his vassals—shall act in the same manner *erga homines suos*, with regard to their own vassals.[1] If at Quierzy Charles the Bald did not, as was long supposed, give to benefices an hereditary character, the measures which he took there amounted almost to an official recognition of the fact that their hereditary character was already an established custom.

Even more than the restrictions on the lord's right of disposing freely of his benefice, the hereditary character which this had acquired in the second half of the ninth century marked the way in which the benefice was tending to pass more and more under the control of the vassal. Once more we have a consequence of the fact that it was the vassal who effectively occupied the benefice. The vassal would naturally hope that the benefice would pass after his death to one of his children, and the lord would be tempted to strengthen the loyalty of the vassal towards him by allowing him to expect that this hope would be gratified.

The growing heritability of benefices was mainly characteristic of West Francia, but it was also fairly widespread in the kingdoms of Italy[2] and Burgundy, at least in the case of important benefices held from the king. It was much less general in East Francia. Here

[1] *Capitula excerpta in conventu Carisiacensi coram populo lecta*, c. 3 (ed. Boretius Krause, *Capitularia*, ii, no. 282, p. 362); *Capitulare Carisiacense*, c. 9 (*ibid.*, no. 281, p. 358).

[2] See a characteristic case in the *Annales Fuldenses*, pars III, a. 883 (ed. F. Kurze, Hanover, 1891, p. 100).

there was less internal disorder, the royal power remained greater, and the authority of lords over their vassals was more effectively maintained.

XVII. *Multiplicity of Vassal Engagements*

There was yet a third change which we must note in feudal relationships in the course of the ninth century. The close subordination of a vassal to his lord carried with it the implication that this relationship was a unique one; a duality or a multiplicity of vassal engagements would put a strain on vassal and lord alike. The legislation of Charlemagne and Louis the Pious was directed towards preventing it, but was not wholly successful in so doing. Just as it was the desire to acquire benefices for themselves and their children that lay behind the successful efforts made by vassals to secure the permanence and hereditary character of benefices, so it was the desire of increasing to the utmost the number of benefices which a vassal might hold that explains the efforts made by vassals to render legal the multiplication of engagements of vassalage. These attempts no doubt had begun even in the reign of Charlemagne, but they were not completely successful until late in the ninth century. The earliest relevant text which we know of that refers to an actual case of plurality dates from 895. In this year, the provost and the advocate of St. Martin's of Tours lodged a number of complaints with Count Berengar of Le Mans against one of his vassals named Patericus. Berengar refused to receive them, and sent the plaintiffs to Robert, the brother of King Eudes, *quod non esset suus solummodo vasallus, quamvis ex suo beneficio aliquid haberet, sed potius vasallus Rotberti, amici sui, quia plus ab ipso beneficium tenebat:* 'since Patericus was not simply his vassal and held of him a benefice, but because he was much more the vassal of his friend Robert since he held of the latter a much larger benefice'.[1] The text implies that by this time the custom of double vassalage was fairly generally admitted, at least in West Francia. No change could have more profoundly altered the primitive character of feudal relationships. In East Francia the practice was at this date much less common.

A fourth aspect of feudal relationships which had been modified by the union of benefice and vassalage was the actual connec-

[1] *Gallia Christiana*, xiv (ed. B. Hauréau), Instrumenta, no. 37, col. 53.

tion between the personal and the property elements in them. Louis the Pious in 815 referred to the rule whereby a vassal was bound to use all the resources of his benefice for the service due to his lord.[1] The contract of vassalage which created the obligation of service was the essential feature in the relationship. It was in virtue of it that the benefice itself existed, for the intention behind the grant of a benefice was that of rendering the service due as efficient as possible. But in 868, Hincmar, referring to the service owed by its vassals to a church and through the church to the king, declared that it was the vassals' duty to render this service *secundum quantitatem et qualitatem beneficii*, 'according to the size and nature of their benefices'.[2] He admitted, in fact, that the service of the vassal and the importance of the benefice which he held were related to one another, and that the value of the benefice was the measure and almost the condition of the service due. Cause and effect are now reversed, with service being rendered in return for a benefice instead of the other way round.

---

[1] See above, p. 41, n. 2.
[2] *Ad Carolum Calvum regem pro Ecclesiae libertatum defensione*, in Migne, *Patrol. lat.*, cxxv. 1050.

Chapter Three

FEUDALISM AND THE CAROLINGIAN STATE

I. The Place of Vassalage in the Carolingian State

The development of vassalage and the granting of benefices to vassals were in part, as we have seen, the consequences of a policy deliberately pursued by the Carolingians, who hoped in this way to increase their own authority and the power of the Frankish realm. They were prepared to go even further than this, and incorporate feudal institutions in the structure of the state itself. This policy was begun by Pepin III, but it represents in the main the work of Charlemagne and Louis the Pious.

The Frankish monarchy, partly as a consequence of the immense territorial expansion which it underwent during the reign of Charlemagne, lacked an efficient administration, and the structure of the state was inadequate to the tasks which it had to fulfil. Charlemagne and his advisers had to take account of this, and they hoped to find in vassalage a means of remedying this defect. A body of trained soldiers, consisting of royal vassals and the vassals of bishops, abbots, and counts, and even in some cases of their sub-vassals, would impart new strength to the old general levy, which from the point of view of numbers, armament and military efficiency was extremely ineffective. The duty imposed on royal vassals and on those of the counts of assisting at judicial assemblies would render more efficient the working of the courts.

Furthermore, in the hope of making the agents of his authority more effectively subordinate to him, Charlemagne did something more important than simply increase the number of royal vassals. He extended the practice, already occasionally applied by his father, of requiring the counts and other high officials in the public service to become his vassals. This practice became the general custom under Louis the Pious, and it remained in force in the kingdoms which arose after the Partition of Verdun in 843. The subordinates of the chief officials became in their turn the vassals of their immediate superiors; in West Francia, for example, the viscounts became the vassals of the counts.

It is reasonable to enquire whether the counts, the court officials and other highly placed individuals who had commended themselves to the king and taken an oath of fealty to him should really be regarded as 'vassals' in the ordinary sense of the word. Would it not be better to reserve for them the term *fidelis*, and use that of *vassus* only for persons of more limited means and of a lower social grade, whether they were vassals of the king or of other lords? Such a distinction, however, finds no justification in the texts. These simply show that *vassi dominici* were sometimes persons of ample means and that even the highest officials were freely termed *vassi* or *vassalli*; in other words, that *fidelis* was the name of the genus of which *vassus* was simply a species.[1]

II. *The Benefice and the 'Honour'* [2]

The counts, and still more the margraves and dukes who controlled several counties, often held from the king benefices which were situated sometimes within their spheres of territorial jurisdiction, sometimes outside them. They were normally also in occupation of estates which formed the endowment of their office. These were the *res de comitatu*, the property attached to the office of count; their connection with this was so close that they were sometimes simply called *comitatus* or *ministerium*, as if they were the office themselves. An example of this occurs in a charter of 817 by which Louis the Pious gave to the cathedral of Tournai a part of the royal estate (*fiscus*) which belonged to the endowment of the

---

[1] For very wealthy *vassi dominici* see above, p. 37, n. 1. For the general significance of the words *vassus* and *vassallus*, see the *Epitaphium Arsenii*, ii. 17 (above, p. 27, n. 4) and the *placitum* of Louis the Pious of 838, *Gesta domni Aldrici Cenomannicae urbis episcopi*, c. 47 (ed. R. Charles and L. Froger, Mamers, 1889, pp. 147–8). For *fidelis* as genus and *vassus* as species, see the *placitum* of Charles the Bald of 861 (Tessier, *op. cit.*, ii, no. 228). The texts of the *Epitaphium Arsenii* and of the *placitum* of 838 cited in the present note, as well as those of the *Annales Bertiniani* of 837 and the Astronomer for 838 cited above, p. 26 and n. 1, all bring before us high officials who are described as royal vassals. For a viscount who was the vassal of a count, see Agobard, *Epistolae*, no. 10 (to Matfrid) of c. 818/28 (ed. E. Dümmler, *M.G.H.*, *Epistolae*, v. 201–3).

[2] It should be noted that in Carolingian times, the continental 'honour' is an office, and must be distinguished from the English use of the term 'honour' for a great feudal lordship.

local count.¹ These *fisci* or *villae* were technically 'benefices' from at least the time of Charlemagne onwards. In consequence, the counts and other higher officials, who were vassals of the king and held from him in benefice these estates whose income represented the chief attraction of their office, must frequently have been led to regard their office itself, which in technical language was called their honour (*honor*), as held in benefice likewise. This point of view was accepted by the sovereign. It is even probable that the king invested his officials with their offices by handing to them some object symbolizing their authority. This ceremony was essentially the same as that used by a lord in placing his vassal in possession of a benefice, and this coincidence would tend to familiarize men's minds with the idea that the 'benefice' covered not only the *res de comitatu*, the actual landed estates attached to the office of count, but also the *honor*, the office to which these estates were only accessory. So when in the second half of the ninth century the texts refer to *honores* granted to or confiscated from some personage, as for example when we are told that in 868 Charles the Bald deprived Eudes, the son of Robert the Strong, and the sons of Count Rainulf of Poitiers of the *honores* held by their fathers,² we must understand by this term a complex of offices as well as landed property held in benefice from the king. The *honor* might involve one or more counties, one or more lay abbacies, and a varying number of estates. Hincmar, in the last section of the Annals of St. Bertin to which this account belongs, habitually applies the term *honor* to both the endowments and the functions of counts and bishops, and even to the benefices of royal vassals. This has become general.³

The 'beneficial' character gradually assumed by public offices

---

¹ E.g. *comitatus:* charter of Charles the Bald of 864 (Tessier, *op. cit.*, ii, no. 263); *ministerium:* Bouquet, vi, 509.

² *Annales Bertiniani*, a. 868 (ed. Waitz, p. 91).

³ *Ann. Bert.*, a. 866, 869, 872, 877, 878 (pp. 81, 98 and 107, 121, 137, 140). Prudentius of Troyes, in the earlier part of these annals of which he was the author, still employs the transitional term *beneficiarii honores* (a. 839, p. 20). See also *Tertium missaticum ad Aquitanos et Francos directum*, a. 856; the *Conventus* of Koblenz, a. 860, *Adnuntiatio Karoli, Capitula*, c. 7 and final *Admonitio* of Charles the Bald in the romance tongue; and the Capitulary of Quierzy, a. 877, c. 10 (Boretius-Krause, *Capitularia*, ii, nos. 265, 242, 281; pp. 285, 156 and 158, 358). In all these texts, *honor* has the same meaning as in the last section of the Annals of St. Bertin.

goes far to explain the ease with which *honores* became in fact generally heritable in the course of the ninth century. Just as ordinary vassals devoted their energies to ensuring that their benefices should pass to one of their sons after their death, so the holders of *honores* were anxious to add to their family inheritance the estates attached to their offices. The assimilation of *honor* and *beneficium* was already an established fact by 877, as we can see from the measures taken at Quierzy in this year by Charles the Bald on the eve of his departure to Italy.[1] The same regulations were made for the *comitatus*, that is to say for the *honores* of a count, as for the *beneficia* of royal vassals, in the event of a vacancy caused by the death of their holder. In the one case as in the other, it was assumed that a son would normally succeed his father. The hereditary character of both public office and benefice was clearly recognized, at least in fact.

This assimilation of the 'honour' to the benefice appears in East as well as in West Francia in the second half of the ninth century, but in East Francia the heritability of *honores*, as of *beneficia*, was much less completely accepted.

It was not only the secular representatives of the royal authority who in the ninth century entered the ranks of royal vassals and held their offices as benefices from the king. From the reign of Louis the Pious onwards, it is clear that bishops and abbots, who in any case were regarded as royal officials, were required to commend themselves to the king, and their office, whether *episcopatus* or *abbatia*, was regarded as a benefice. When Bishop Prudentius of Troyes records that all the holders of benefices between Frisia and the Seine were ordered by the emperor in 837 to commend themselves to the young king Charles the Bald and take an oath of fealty to him, he makes no distinction between the bishops and abbots and the counts and royal vassals.[2] This state of affairs was naturally continued in the various kingdoms into which the empire broke up. In West Francia, Archbishop Hincmar of Rheims declared that where clerics were concerned the ceremony of *immixtio manuum*, which symbolized the personal *traditio*, should be

---

[1] See above, p. 48, n. 1.
[2] *Annales Bertiniani*, a. 837 (ed. Waitz, p. 15): 'episcopi, abbates, comites et vassalli dominici'.

avoided, but he fully admitted the necessity of commendation.[1]
The oath of fealty taken by bishops closely resembled that taken
by vassals. That taken by the younger Hincmar, bishop of Laon,
has been preserved: 'I Hincmar, bishop of Laon, will from this
hour forward be faithful to my lord Charles as a vassal is bound to
be to his lord and a bishop to his king, and will obey him as a
vassal is bound to obey his lord, and, as a bishop of Christ, I will
obey the will of God and aim at the safety of the king, as far as
my will and strength permit.'[2] (*Ego Hincmarus Laudunensis episcopus de hora ista inantea fidelis ero seniori meo Karolo, sicut
homo per rectum seniori suo debet esse et episcopus regi suo et
sic obediens quomodo homo per rectum seniori suo debet esse, et
episcopus Christi secundum meum sapere et posse ad Dei volun-
tatem et ad regis salutem . . .*) In East Francia, the bishops were
likewise required to become vassals of the king, and here the rite
of *immixtio manuum* was not dispensed with. This at least was
the case towards the end of the century, for when Adalgar, the
coadjutor *cum iure successionis* of St. Rimbert, archbishop of
Hamburg-Bremen, was invested with his functions shortly before
888, we hear that Rimbert 'arranged for Adalgar to become the
king's vassal by having his hands received into those of the king'
(. . . *per manus acceptionem hominem regis illum fieri . . . op-
tinuit*).[3] From the reign of Louis the Pious, and perhaps even
earlier, the king invested the bishop with his office *per baculum*,
by handing to him the staff, which symbolized his pastoral functions,[4] and this ceremony likewise went far towards attributing to
the office of bishop a 'beneficial' character.

The obligations of a bishop and of a clerk in the royal chapel
who commended himself and swore fealty to the king were fealty
and service, as in the case of other vassals.[5] In 859 we find the ex-

---

[1] *Epistola Synodi Carisiacensis* (of 858), c. 15, in Boretius-Krause, *Capitularia*, ii. 439; *Annales Bertiniani*, a. 869, 877, (pp. 101, 105, 138).

[2] Hincmar, *Libellus Expostulationis adversus Hincmarum Laudunensem
episcopum*, c. 10, in Migne, *P.L.*, cxxvi. 575.

[3] *Vita Rimberti*, c. 21 (ed. G. Waitz, Hanover, 1884, p. 97).

[4] *Actus pontificum Cenomannis in urbe degentium*, c. 23 (ed. G. Busson
and A. Ledru, Le Mans, 1902, p. 299); *Vita Rimberti*, c. 11 (ed. Waitz,
p. 90).

[5] *Libellus proclamationis adversus Wenilonem*, a. 859, cc. 6 and 13 (Boretius-Krause, *Capitularia*, ii, no. 300, pp. 451-3).

pression *consilium et auxilium* applied to the duties of a bishop arising out of his oath of fealty.[1] It was by this phrase that the obligations of a vassal to his lord were to be most typically characterized in the future.

III. *The Place of the Lord between his Vassal and the King*

The policy followed by the Carolingians failed to produce the fruits they expected from it. The great extension of vassalage, its incorporation in the framework of the institutions of government, the distribution of benefices on a large scale, all ended by diminishing the authority of the king instead of increasing it.

Even before the end of the reign of Charlemagne, it had become apparent that the bonds which united a vassal to his lord, bonds which were direct and immediately appreciable by the senses, were stronger by far than those which bound the subject to the king. When there was a conflict between the two types of allegiance, the vassal would nearly always hold to that deriving from the fealty which he owed to the lord whose 'man' he was. Already in 811, in a memorandum drafted for an assembly that had to deal with problems of military service, it is stated that some of the emperor's subjects had failed to appear with the army, on the ground that their lord had not been summoned and that their duty forbade them to leave him.[2] When the reign of the feeble Louis the Pious began the period of partitions and revolts, matters went much further. Either through sincere attachment to their duties as vassals, or because they found in them a convenient pretext, the vassals of the rebel chiefs gave in their thousands their support to their lords against their king. The consideration that service was not owed to a lord who was in arms against the king was too feeble a barrier to resist their passion or their greed.

In the case of those who may be termed higher vassals, direct agents of royal power like the counts, margraves and dukes, the appetite for benefices promised or granted by the heads of the

---

[1] *Ibid.*, c. 9 (p. 452). The expression occurs also in the *Annales Bertiniani*, a. 877 (p. 138). See also below, pp. 84 and 87. The earliest employment of the phrase seems to be in c. 6 of the second *conventus* of Meersen of 851 (*Capitularia*, ii. no. 205), but here it is applied to royal *fideles* in general and not, as in the other two texts, specifically to ecclesiastics.

[2] *Capitula de rebus exercitalibus in placito tractanda*, c. 8 (in Boretius, *Capitularia*, i, no. 73, p. 165).

warring parties was so great that in order to gratify it they were prepared to ignore not only their public duties but also those aris- ing from their position as royal vassals. The very existence of benefices had here a detrimental effect on the structure of the state. Not only was the primitive strictness of the obligations of vassalage largely ignored,[1] but the uselessness of the whole machinery of vassalage as an aid to government was thrown into sharp relief.

The development of feudal institutions did other and more serious injuries to the strength of the Frankish monarchy and the states which were its heirs.

The character of virtually hereditary benefices which public of- fices came to assume in the course of the ninth century involved, at least in West Francia, severe limitations in the power which the king could hope to exercise over his officials. Amongst the aristoc- racy, the class from which the agents of royal power were drawn, the spread of vassal engagements, created by what was in form a mutual contract, contributed to the extension of the idea that the royal power was itself only conditional. If subjects had their duties towards the king, the latter had duties towards his subjects, and by subjects, here, 'magnates' was of course to be understood. The loyalty of the king in carrying out his duties was a condition of the loyalty of the *populus*—and, here again, the 'magnates' must be understood—towards him. Charles the Bald was compelled to formulate this rule of public law in the most precise fashion at the assembly of Coulaines in 843,[2] and thenceforward it remained as the basis of the system of government of West Francia. And we may be sure that this doctrine did nothing to increase the strength of the state.

Furthermore, it is beyond dispute that the spread of vassalage involved in fact the withdrawal of many free men from the imme- diate authority of the state. It is true that in law the entry of a free man into vassalage did not release him from his duties to- wards the state. He was still bound to perform his military service and to attend the *placita generalia*; the public courts were still fully competent to bring him before them. But in each of these

---

[1] See above, pp. 32–34.

[2] *Conventus in villa Colonia*, cc. 3–5 (in Boretius-Krause, *Capitularia*, ii. 255).

public functions the lord now appeared at his vassal's side to aid
and protect him; to some extent even the lord's person was actually interposed between the state and the vassal. The vassal served
in the army under his lord's orders, and was helped or represented
by the lord in the courts. When the state now wished to touch the
vassal, and particularly the vassal who, because he was without
benefice or held only a small one, was most closely dependent on
his lord, it had more and more to address itself to the lord and
invite him to apply compulsion to his vassal.

This at least was the case in West Francia. In the Capitulary
of Servais of 853, Charles the Bald ordered the *missi* to take action
against the brigands who infested the kingdom, and commanded
that no man should offer asylum to them and that all should lend
their aid to the royal officials. If any one disobeyed this injunction,
'his lord, if he have one, shall be responsible for bringing him before the king' (*si . . . alterius homo fuerit, senior cuius homo
fuerit illum regi praesentet*). In other words, in order to secure
that a guilty person shall be handed over, the king has to apply to
the lord. Thirty years later, matters have got much worse. Carloman laid down at Compiègne in 883 that if a vassal takes to
brigandage, his lord must hand him over to the king so that he
may suffer the punishment which the law prescribes, and that if
the lord does not succeed in delivering him up he must pay the
fine on his behalf (*quod si eum adducere non potuerit pro eo secundum statuta legum emendet*).[1] The fact that the lord has now
to be made responsible for the vassal's conduct shows with peculiar clearness that the immediate authority which the state could
hope to exercise over a free man who had become a vassal had
been reduced to next to nothing. The vassals of private secular
lords had by the end of the ninth century in West Francia been
practically withdrawn from the jurisdiction of the state.

It would be wrong, however, to attribute the collapse of the
state solely to the disintegrative action of vassalage. The advance
of feudalism was not the primary cause of the usurpations which
in the late ninth and early tenth centuries led to the passing of so
many of the attributes of government from the hands of the king

---

[1] *Capitulare missorum Silvacense*, c. 4 (ed. Boretius-Krause, ii, no. 260,
p. 272); *Capitula Compendiis de rapina promulgata*, c. 3 (*ibid.*, ii, no. 286,
p. 371).

into those of territorial princes in France and Italy and, though to
a lesser degree, into those of the dukes in Germany. But we cannot doubt that the formation of these territorial principalities and
duchies was strongly favoured by the paralysing action exercised
by feudalism and vassalage over so many forms of royal activity.

IV. The Role of Royal Vassals

Side by side with these disintegrative effects, however, there were
others which operated in a contrary direction. In the first place,
there was the position of those royal vassals who were not endowed with *honores* but who none the less held benefices in the
various parts of the kingdom. These men provided the kings with
an element on which they could rely in their struggle against the
usurpations of local potentates, whether dukes, margraves or
counts. This is only true, however, of the late ninth and early
tenth centuries; in the end, at least in most places, the local magnates succeeded in 'mediatizing' these royal vassals. 'Taking advantage of the troubled situation of the state, the margraves in
their insolence succeeded in submitting the royal vassals to their
authority' as a certain contemporary authority puts it (*nam rei
publicae statu iam nimis turbato regales vassos insolentia marchio-
num sibi subiugaverat*). The same source gives a curious instance
from Auvergne of the way in which this process might operate. At
the end of the ninth or during the first years of the tenth century,
Gerald of Aurillac, a royal vassal, who had incidentally assumed
without any justification the title of count, was anxious to remain
faithful to his engagements to the king. Despite all the efforts of
Duke William the Pious of Aquitaine, he obstinately refused to
become a vassal of the latter. In the end he was compelled to give
way, but he did so in such a way that his own allegiance to the
king was maintained. He himself did not become a vassal of
William, 'but he commended to him his nephew Rainald with a
great number of his men' (*nepotem tamen suum nomine Rainal-
dum eidem cum ingenti militum numero commendavit*).[1] Rainald
was evidently his heir, and by this arrangement, while Gerald himself preserved his personal independence, the 'mediatization' of
his benefices was brought about. In Germany one must probably

[1] Odo of Cluny, *De vita S. Geraldi comitis, Auriliacensis fundatoris*, i. 32
(in Migne, *P.L.*, cxxxiii. 660, 661).

reckon the royal vassals, at least where they were able to maintain themselves, as one of those elements which allowed the monarchy to save itself from being completely eliminated at the beginning of the tenth century by the great magnates who had managed to impose themselves with the title of duke on Saxony, Franconia, Swabia and Bavaria.

V. The Feudal Bond as a Check on the Disintegration of the State

From yet another point of view, the feudal bond was a factor, a factor indeed of considerable importance, in preventing the total breakdown of the state.

The territorial princes who in the tenth century divided between them the greater part of the soil of France were all descendants or successors of some court, margrave, or duke who had been a vassal of a Carolingian sovereign and held his *honor* in benefice from him. This state of things continued so far as the law was concerned: the territorial princes remained vassals of the king and held from him in benefice—or in fief, as it would soon be said—their county, marquisate or duchy.

In the tenth and eleventh centuries, these territorial princes were in reality quite independent. They recognized the king as their superior, but his supremacy was a purely theoretical one, and the only bond which continued—not very effectively—to bind them to the crown was the fact that they were its vassals. That the consequences of this vassalage were occasionally recognized is shown when from time to time we find the princes performing certain services on behalf of the king or refraining from certain acts in his despite. Slight as was this recognition, however, it was its survival in these centuries that prevented the complete fragmentation of France.

It seems also that vassalage played a similar role in Germany. That the kings there were able to resist the usurpations of the dukes at the beginning of the tenth century was in part a consequence of the fact that a certain number of counts were still their vassals. When Otto I became king in 936 and undertook the task of creating some bond between himself and the dukes, whose power had grown up outside and at the expense of the regular institutions of government, he realized that the most satisfactory proceeding would be to make all of them his vassals. This is made clear by the chronicler Widukind, who writes of the dukes that 'they placed their hands in his, and promised him their fealty and support against all his enemies' (*manus ei dantes ac fidem pollicentes operamque suam contra omnes inimicos spondentes*).[1] In Germany, therefore, as in France, vassalage at this time did something to prevent the complete disintegration of the state.

---

[1] *Res gestae Saxonicae*, ii. 1 (ed. P. Hirsch and H. E. Lohmann, Hanover, 1935, p. 64).

PART THREE
THE CLASSICAL AGE OF FEUDALISM
(TENTH TO THIRTEENTH CENTURIES)

INTRODUCTION

What one may call the classical age of feudalism is the period between the tenth and thirteenth centuries. It is true that during this period the ties of vassalage lost much of the binding force which they had had in the preceding age, and that the formation of these ties and the granting of benefices—or fiefs as they were now more generally called—no longer played as essential a part in social life in the thirteenth century as they had in the three preceding ones. This is at least the case in France, England and Germany west of the Rhine. It is also true that it is only towards the end of the twelfth century that feudal institutions came to occupy a predominant place in the political structure of Germany. None the less, as abroad generalization, we may say that it was in this period that the system of feudal institutions arrived at its completest development.

It is during this classical age that these institutions ceased to be peculiar to those states—France, Germany, the kingdom of Burgundy-Arles, Italy—which had grown up out of the ruins of the Frankish monarchy. The conquest of England by the duke of Normandy in 1066 introduced feudalism into England; the *reconquista* brought it, at least to a limited degree, to Spain; from Germany, feudal institutions spread into the neighboring Slav countries, but developed peculiar features under the influence of the existing institutions of those countries; and the Crusades carried it overseas to the kingdom of Jerusalem, as well as to principalities created by the crusaders in Syria; as a consequence of the Fourth Crusade, feudalism was able to expand in the ephemeral Latin empire of Constantinople and the "Latin" principalities of Greece. In the eastern states, however, it was feudalism with a difference. The feudalism of the Crusader states was something that has been aptly described as 'colonial', for it was created within a political framework set up by an army of lords and vassals, which constituted a species of military 'command' particularly exposed to attack. It is therefore not surprising that it should have exhibited well-marked peculiarities of its own. The system of feudal relationships was generalized and codified to a degree never known in the west, and much stronger emphasis was laid on the rights and prerogatives of vassals. The texts which deal with the feudalism of the Latin states, and in particular the collections known as the Assizes of Jerusalem, do not therefore throw much real light on feudal institutions as they existed in western Europe.

Feudalism in Spain, save in the county of Barcelona, which was derived from the Spanish March of Carolingian times and remained in theory subject to the French king up to 1258, must also be regarded as a thing apart. The historical circumstances which attended its formation gave birth to institutions differing in many respects from those found north of the Pyrenees.

Italy, strictly speaking, was one of the constituent states of the Carolingian monarchy, but the medieval Italian kingdom and the principalities which grew up within its boundaries developed many institutions peculiar to themselves, institutions in which the Frankish contribution represented only a single element. In northern and central Italy, other factors combined in the course of centuries to give to the feudalism of these regions a character quite distinct from that which one meets elsewhere, and one cannot use, for the study of Western feudalism, various legal compilations put together in Lombardy in the twelfth century, despite the fact that they are concerned with feudal relationships and were known under such names as *Libri Feudorum* or *Consuetudines Feudorum*. Still more remote from what one may regard as the norm were those features which characterized the feudalism of the Papal States. In the Norman principalities of southern Italy, and in the Norman kingdom of Sicily into which these were finally absorbed, the feudal institutions imported from France had to be imposed on a social and political system of extreme complexity. A central government of unusual strength succeeded in formulating a remarkably coherent system of feudal relationships, in which the rights and prerogatives of the lord, and in particular those of the head of the state, were strongly emphasized. But such a development cannot be regarded as in any way characteristic of Western feudalism as a whole.

There remain France and Germany, and the kingdom of Burgundy-Arles, which was attached by a political and personal union to Germany but which was much closer to France in its social development. There also remains England.

In France, in the kingdom of Burgundy-Arles, in western and—though more feebly—in southern Germany, feudal relations became in the tenth and eleventh centuries so much a matter of general custom that a freeman of military habits, accustomed to fighting on horseback and of some status in society, was nearly always the vassal of a lord, though this did not of course prevent him holding allodial land of his own in addition to such estates as he held as fiefs. This at least was the general rule, but there were exceptions to it, and it varied somewhat from one region to another. In some places the custom of vassalage was less common, and in others it only developed at a relatively late date. These regions were often those where manorial economy and the system of great estates had not become general, as for example Frisia and Saxony. The rebellions in Saxony against Henry IV in the second half of the eleventh century were in part rebellions against the extension of the manorial system and the feudalization of the upper classes. It is possible that in certain parts of the south of France feudal relations were less developed than in other parts of the realm.

Feudalism was introduced into England in its French form, and more particularly in the form which it had assumed in Normandy, which was one of those few territorial principalities in which by the second half of the eleventh century the ruler had succeeded in creating a strong central power. It was introduced, moreover, by a conqueror at the head of an army of vassals. These two features explain the fact that feudal relationships were more universal in England than they ever were in France or Germany, for in England allodial property was completely eliminated; all land was held either directly or indirectly of the king. Moreover, the English crown succeeded in mastering the feudal structure and submitting it entirely to its own authority. English feudalism therefore shows a certain number of characteristics which are quite peculiar to itself.

Inside each of these countries, the rules in which feudal relationships were embodied were largely a matter of regional or local custom. Despite the infinite variations which these entailed, however, it is possible to determine the general principles which reg-ulated the relationship of vassal to lord and the custom of fiefs: we can disentangle the essential traits of the *ius militare*,[1] the feudal law, the *Lehnrecht*[2] of these various countries. It is even possible to go further; while recognizing the existence of these na-tional varieties of feudal law, we can isolate those elements which were common to the whole of western Europe.

In studying feudal relationships under the Carolingians, the royal capitularies were one of our main sources. We cannot de-pend to the same extent on legislation in attempting to describe and analyse feudalism in its classical age, for except in England this type of material is rare before the thirteenth century; there is almost nothing apart from the *Statute* of Count William II for the county of Forcalquier in Provence (1162), the *Assise au Comte Geoffroy* (1185) for Brittany and the *Charte féodale* (1200) for Hainault.[3] We are therefore forced to fall back on the narrative sources and the charters in which the practice of the time was embodied. In the twelfth century, however, a new type of evidence comes to hand in the form of legal treatises. They first appear in England at the beginning of the century, in France, quite at its end, in Germany, in the early thirteenth century. Although they are private compilations and relatively late in date, these *coutumiers* or *Rechtsbücher* may be used, with due caution, to complete our picture of classical feudalism.

Like Carolingian feudalism, classical feudalism can be studied from the point of view of the personal and property relationships which it involved, and in the chapters that follow each of these aspects will be considered in its turn.

---

[1] Account of the enfeoffment of the county of Hainault by the bishop of Liége to the duke of Lower Lotharingia and by the latter to the countess Richilda in 1071 (ed. L. Weiland in M.G.H., *Constitutiones*, i. 649–50).

[2] *Codex Eberhardi Fuldensis* (mid twelfth century) in E. F. J. Dronke, *Traditiones et antiquitates Fuldenses* (Fulda, 1844), no. 76, p. 154.

[3] M. Planiol, 'L'Assise au comte Geoffroy', in *Nouv. rev. hist. de droit français et étranger* (1887), pp. 120–22; N. Didier, 'Le texte et la date du statut de Guillaume II de Forcalquier sur les filles dotées', in *Annales de la Faculté de Droit d'Aix-en-Provence*, 1950, pp. 115–32; L. Devillers, *Chartes du comté de Hainaut de l'an 1200* (Mons, 1898) or C. Faider, *Coutumes du pays et comté de Hainaut*, i (Brussels, 1871), pp. 3–6.

Chapter One

VASSALAGE

I. Terminology

Vassalage, which represents the personal element in feudalism, must still in the classical age of feudalism be regarded as its most essential feature, despite the growing importance of the element of property. During the whole of the period we still meet with examples of vassals without benefices, though only a vassal could hope to obtain a fief.

At the opening of the period, the terms used to describe a vassal remain the same as under the Carolingians. The most frequent are *vassus, vassallus, homo, fidelis* and *miles*. The last was particularly used in the eleventh and early twelfth centuries. When Henry V of Germany summoned the bishop of Bamberg on an expedition against the count of Flanders in 1107, he described the latter as 'so bold an enemy, who should be one of our vassals' (*tam praesumptuosum hostem qui noster miles debet esse*).[1] In the course of the twelfth century, however, the word fell into disuse, and it gradually ceased to be employed in this sense at all, except in southwestern France, where either alone or in conjunction with *homo* it remained the normal description of a vassal up to the thirteenth century.[2] *Vassus* appears rarely after the tenth century. *Homo* and *vassallus* were everywhere employed, though one must add that *miles, fidelis,* and *homo* continued always to have a broader sense than 'vassal' and can only be given this meaning where the context justifies it. In the vernacular, *homme* and *vassal* were used in France, and *Mann* in Germany. The lord was

[1] *Mandatum de expeditione flandrica facienda* (ed. L. Weiland in M.G.H., *Constitutiones*, i, no. 81, p. 133).

[2] C. Higounet, *Le comté de Comminges de ses origines à son annexion à la Couronne*, ii (Toulouse, 1949), Pièces justificatives, no. 4 (of 1257); R. Boutruche, *Une société provinciale en lutte contre le régime féodal. L'alleu en Bordelais et en Bazadais du XIe au XIIIe siècle* (Rodez, 1947), Pièces justificatives, no. 4 (of 1274).

generally described as *senior; dominus* was rather rare. In the vernacular, *seigneur* was the term consecrated by custom; *suzerain* appeared rather late and became a synonym of seigneur only in modern times; previously it had meant the lord's lord. *Herr* was the recognized term in German.

II. The Contract of Vassalage

The vassal relationship was created by the contract of commendation, which we have already met under the Carolingian monarchy. There are numerous texts which explain how the contract creating the obligations between the two parties was concluded. Let us look at some of them.

The historian Richer describes in the following terms the process by which William Longsword, second ruler of Normandy, became vassal of Charles the Simple in 927: *regis manibus sese militaturum committit fidemque spondet ac sacramento firmat,* 'he committed himself into the king's hands in order to serve him, and promised him fealty and confirmed it with an oath'. Thietmar of Merseburg describes the arrival of the new King Henry II in eastern Germany in 1002 in the following terms: *Omnes qui priori imperatori servierant . . . regi manus complicant, fidele auxilium per sacramenta confirmant,* 'all those who had served the previous emperor placed their hands in the king's and promised him on oath their faithful aid'. The twelfth century *Gesta Galcheri,* the 'gestes' of the imperialist Bishop Galcher of Cambrai, writing of the reconciliation of Count Robert of Flanders with Henry IV, does so as follows:

> *Facto palam hominio*
> *iurat Robertus Henrico,*
> *promittit, miles domino,*
> *quia fidelis amodo*
> *regno eius extiterit,*
> *et Galcherum honorabit*
> *immo eum sustentabit*
> *contra quemcumque poterit.*

'After having done homage publicly, Robert takes an oath to
Henry and promises, as a vassal to his lord, that he will show himself henceforward loyal to his kingdom and that he will honour
Galcher and that he will further support him against all and
sundry.' [1]

These texts represent respectively northern France in the late
tenth century, Germany in the early eleventh century, and western
Lotharingia in the twelfth century. But we may add to them one
more text, since it is the most explicit and precise of all. Galbert
of Bruges, a notary of the count of Flanders, relates how the new
count, William Clito, received the vassals of his murdered predecessor in 1127. 'First they did homage in the following manner.
The count demanded of the future vassal if he wished without
reserve to become his man, and he replied "I wish it"; then, with
his hands clasped and enclosed between those of the count, their
alliance was sealed by a kiss. Secondly, he who had done homage
engaged his faith to the *prolocutor* [2] of the count in the following
words: "I promise by my faith that from this time forward I will
be faithful to Count William and will maintain towards him my
homage entirely against every man, in good faith and without
any deception." Thirdly, all this was sworn on the relics of saints.'
(*Primum hominia fecerunt ita: comes requisivit si integre vellet
homo suus fieri, et ille respondit: 'volo' et junctis manibus, amplex-
atus a manibus comitis, osculo confederati sunt. Secundo loco
fidem dedit is qui hominium fecerat prolocutori comitis in iis
verbis: 'Spondeo in fide mea me fidelem fore amodo comiti Willelmo et sibi hominium integraliter contra omnes observaturum
fide bona et sine dolo'; idemque super reliquias sanctorum tertio
loco juravit.*) [3]

The complex of formal acts, of which several examples have
been given here, is sometimes designated by the same expression
as that used under the Carolingians for the *immixtio manuum*, i.e.

[1] Richer, *Historiae*, i. 53 (ed. R. Latouche, I, Paris, 1930, p. 104); revised
text of Thietmar, *Chronicon*, v. 18 (ed. R. Holtzmann, Berlin, 1935, p. 241);
Gesta Galcheri, verse 423–4 (ed. G. Waitz in *M.G.H., SS.* xiv. 202).

[2] The *prolocutor* was necessary to speak the formal words required by the
court, for the proceedings would be conducted in Flemish and William was
presumably ignorant of this tongue.

[3] Galbert of Bruges, *Histoire du meurtre de Charles le Bon, comte de
Flandre*, c. 56 (ed. H. Pirenne, Paris, 1891, p. 89).

se commendare,[1] or the variant *se committere*.[2] These acts were of a formal character, in the sense that their validity depended on the precise accomplishment of the formalities which accompanied them. They are recognizably the same as those which we met with in texts of the eighth and ninth centuries, but the accounts of them are so much more abundant and explicit that they can be more profitably submitted to a detailed analysis.

III. Homage

The first of these acts is homage (Fr. *hommage*, sometimes *hommenage*; Lat. *hominium*, or later *hom(m)agium*, also *hominaticum*, *hominagium*; *Mannschaft* and *manschap* in German and Dutch respectively, and later *Hulde* and *hulde*, though these are used more particularly of the oath of fealty). So far as we know, the Latin terms corresponding to the French *hommage* did not appear before the first half of the eleventh century. The earliest texts in which they occur are from the county of Barcelona (*ominaticum*: 1020), that of Cerdagne in the Pyrenees (*hominaticum*: 1035), eastern Languedoc (*hominaticum*: 1035), and Anjou (*hominagium*: 1037).[3] In the second half of the century its use became general in France, and in the last quarter of the century it appears already in Germany.[4]

Two elements were comprised in the act of homage. First there was the *immixtio manuum*, the name given to the rite in which

---

[1] See above, p. 26.

[2] E. G. Flodoard, *Annales*, a. 927, 932, 943, 957 (ed. P. Lauer, Paris, 1905, pp. 39, 53, 77, 86–7, 144); Dudo of St. Quentin, *De moribus et actis primorum Normanniae ducum*, iv. 67 (ed. J. Lair, Caen, 1865, p. 221); Prou and Vidier, Chartes de l'abbaye de Saint-Benoît-sur-Loire. i., no. 51.

[3] J. Rius Serra, *Cartulario de San Cugat del Vallès* (Barcelona, 1945–7), no. 479; F. Miquel Rosell, *Liber Feudorum Maior. Cartulario real que se conserva en el Archivo de la Corona de Aragon*, ii. (Barcelona, 1947), no. 693, pp. 201–4 (D'Achery, *Spicilegium* (Paris, 1664), vi. 434); C. Devic and J. Vaissete, *Histoire générale de Languedoc* (ed. Privat, v, Toulouse, 1875), no. 206–clxxv. col. 415–7; Bertrand de Broussillon, *Cartulaire de l'abbaye de Saint-Aubin d'Angers*, i, Angers, 1903, no. 1 (though it has been questioned by L. Halphen, *Le comté d'Anjou au XIe siècle*, Paris, 1906, p. 260, there is no reason to be doubtful of this charter's authenticity). The *hominaticum* is mentioned in a charter of 978 in the county of Barcelona (F. Udina, *El Libro Blanche de Santes Creus*, Barcelona, 1947, no. 2). If it has to be considered as authentic, it would be the oldest text in which the term occurs; it seems, however, that its authenticity might be questioned.

[4] Berthold, *Annales*, a. 1077 (ed. G. H. Pertz, M.G.H., SS., v. 295).

the vassal, generally kneeling, bareheaded and weaponless, placed his clasped hands between the hands of his lord, who closed his own hands over them. Secondly, there was the declaration of intention, the *volo* which, as we have seen, was pronounced in reply to a question of the count of Flanders at Bruges in 1127. This declaration of intention was nearly everywhere made in similar terms. A treatise of customary law from western France which is traditionally but inexactly known under the title of the *Etablissements de Saint Louis* and which dates from the second half of the thirteenth century gives it in the form: 'Sire, je devien vostre hom.' The great English jurist Bracton in his *Tractatus de Legibus*, composed between 1250 and 1258, gives a rather longer formula, but one which equally begins with the words 'Devenio homo vester', of which the text given by the *Etablissements* might well pass for a translation. The lord on his side would likewise express his will in a set form of words; the *Etablissements* gives the formula 'Je vos recoif et pran a home . . .',[1] and this is no doubt a fair example of the phrases that would be employed.

Of these two elements which constituted homage, the gesture of the hand is clearly more essential than the verbal declaration of the will of the two parties. In the framework of early medieval legal ideas, as indeed in all rather primitive legal systems, a declaration of intention, even when expressed in a set form of words, or even the concurrence of declarations of intention expressed in that form by both parties, was not in itself sufficient to create rights of a character which we would describe as 'real' over things or persons. A corporeal act, generally of a symbolic character, was indispensable, and in the case of homage this act was the *immixtio manuum*. When one remembers the legal atmosphere of the time and takes into account the incapacity of early medieval man for thinking in abstract terms, and when one recollects his taste for the concrete and actual, one can understand how in his eyes the essential element in becoming a vassal was that of making some gesture of the hands. From this there arose such expressions as *manus alicui dare*, 'to give one's hands to someone', or *in manus alicuius venire*, 'to come into the hands of someone', in the sense

[1] *Etablissements de Saint Louis*, ii. 19 (ed. P. Viollet, Paris, 1881, p. 398); Bracton, *De Legibus et Consuetudinibus Angliae*, fo. 80 (ed. G. E. Woodbine, II, New Haven, 1922, p. 232).

of becoming someone's vassal, and of *aliquem per manus accipere*, 'to receive someone by the hands', in the sense of receiving some-one into vassalage. Sometimes the phrase is more explicit still; we find, for example, *alicuius manibus iunctis fore feodalem hominem*, 'to become by joined hands the vassal of someone'.[1]

The essence of the rite of homage was the self-surrender (*traditio*) of one person to another. The placing of the hands of the vassal between those of the lord symbolized the placing of the vassal's person at the lord's disposition, and the gesture by which the lord took the vassal's hands in his symbolized the acceptance of this surrender. It is true that the rite of homage might be used to create bonds other than those of vassalage, as in Hainault in the twelfth century and Flanders and Normandy in the thirteenth century, where the act of homage might be a way of bringing to an end a private feud.[2] But this use of homage to create a rela-tionship other than that of lord and vassal appears to be late in origin, and has no connection with the original objects of the legal act.

Since homage was an act which symbolized self-surrender, it is easy to understand why in Germany a *ministerialis*, who was an unfree knight, was in early times not permitted to do homage to his lord. Since the lord already had immediate and direct author-ity over the *ministerialis* in virtue of the latter's personal status, such a self-surrender would have been quite meaningless. This rule only began to break down in the second half of the twelfth cen-tury, when the rise in the social scale of the class of *ministeriales* caused the servile element in their personal status to decline in importance and eventually to be forgotten.

Homage, since it involved the surrender of one's person, should

[1] Sigebert of Gembloux, *Chronographia*, a. 1007 (ed. L. C. Bethmann in M.G.H., SS., vi. 354); account of the enfeoffment of Hainault in 1071 (see above, p.68, n. 1); *Annales Altahenses maiores*, a. 1045 (ed. E. von Oefele, Hanover, 1891, p. 39); D. C. Douglas, 'A charter of enfeoffment under William the Conqueror', E.H.R., xlii (1927), p. 427 (of 1066–1087). Of the two literary sources here cited, Sigebert was writing between 1082 and 1106, and the annals of Nieder-Altaich (Bavaria) are contemporary or almost so.

[2] C. Duvivier, *Recherches sur le Hainaut ancien*, ii (Brussels, 1866), Pièces justificatives, no. 127(6), p. 584; G. Espinas, *La vie urbaine de Douai au moyen âge*, iii (Paris, 1913), Pièces justificatives, no. 420, p. 321; *Summa de legibus Normanniae*, xxvii. 5, in J. Tardif, *Coutumiers de Normandie*, ii (Rouen, 1896). The *Summa* dates from the middle of the thirteenth century.

in law be an action freely undertaken, but in countries and periods where the authority of the lord over his vassals was strong it might occasionally happen that a lord could compel his vassal to do homage to another lord. Ordericus Vitalis tells how in 1105 Duke Robert of Normandy 'gave' his vassal the count of Evreux to his brother Henry I of England *quasi equum et bovem*, 'like a horse or an ox', and that *tunc R. dux ipsum regi per manum porrexit*, 'then Duke Robert gave him by hand to the king', i.e. caused him to pass from his vassalage into the king's by making him carry out the rite of homage.[1]

IV. Fealty

Homage, as we know already, was followed by an oath of fealty (Lat. *fides*, or sometimes *sacramentum, iuramentum*, or *iusiurandum*, with or without the addition of *fidelitatis*; Fr. *foi*; Germ. *Treue, Hulde* [2]; Dutch *hulde*,[3] or sometimes *fyauteit* [4] from the Fr. *féauté*). This oath was taken standing, the vassal placing his hand on the Scriptures or on a casket containing relics. Sometimes he began by a declaration that he undertook to be faithful and then confirmed this declaration by an oath. This separation of the sworn obligation of fealty into two sections existed quite early, for it was known to Richer in the tenth century, but it rapidly became more and more unusual and it seems to have been abandoned relatively soon. It seems to have survived in Flanders, however, until at least the twelfth century, for it is apparently to it that Count Robert II refers in 1101 when he promises his fealty to Henry I of England *fide et sacramento*, 'by his faith and oath'. It seems that it is also to it that our account of the submission of the Flemish nobles to their new count, William Clito, alludes, when we are told that the nobles, after having promised him their

[1] Ordericus Vitalis, *Historia ecclesiastica*, xi. 10 (ed. A. Leprévost, iv; Paris, 1852, p. 201). Ordericus was writing in Normandy between 1120 and 1141.

[2] E.g. *Sachsenspiegel*, Lehnrecht 47, 1 (ed. K. A. Eckhardt, 2nd ed. Göttingen, 1956, p. 66). The *Sachsenspiegel* (from Lower Saxony) dates from 1215/35.

[3] The Dutch *hulde*, like the German *Hulde* but to a greater degree, sometimes also meant homage (see above, p. 72), and frequently the whole ceremony of homage and fealty together.

[4] *Leenboek van Vlaenderen* [14th cent.], c. 2 (in L. Gilliodts van Severen, *Coutume du Bourg de Bruges*, iii (Brussels, 1885), p. 208).

fealty, confirmed their undertakings with an oath. There are like-wise grounds for supposing that the custom still existed in Hainault in the twelfth century.[1] After that it seems to disappear.

We have already noted one text of the oath of fealty in Galbert's account of the events of 1127 in Flanders, but it may be as well to give some further illustrations. As a first example we may take one of those long oaths of fealty in a Latin helped out wholesale with words from the local dialect which were much used in Languedoc between the tenth and the beginning of the twelfth century. They are very detailed in their provisions and in some sections occasion-ally recall the wording of the oaths of Carolingian times. The final formula in an oath of fealty taken about 1034 by Count Roger of Foix to Bishop Peter of Gerona ran as follows: *De ista ora inantea fidel serai ego Rotgarius, filius Garsen a te Petrone episcopo, filio Adalaiz per rectam fidem, sine ingan, sicut omo debet esse ad seniorem suum sine nulla sua deceptione me sciente*, 'from this hour henceforward I, Roger son of Gersinda, will be faithful to you, Bishop Peter son of Alix, by true faith, without mischievous intent, as a man should be to his lord and without any will to deceive'.[2] A German text of the first half of the elev-enth century describes the oath of fealty taken by Duke Brětislav I of Bohemia when he became a vassal of Henry III of Germany in 1041: *iusiurandum regi fecit ut tam fidelis illi maneret quam miles seniori esse deberet, omnibus amicis eius fore se amicum, inimicis inimicum*, 'he took an oath to the king that he would be as faithful to him as a vassal should be to his lord and that he would be a friend to all his friends and a foe to his foes'. A French oath of fealty taken in 1236 runs as follows: *Ego . . . ab ista ora inantea personam tuam non capiam, vitam et membra tua non tollam, nec homo, nec femina, meo consilio vel meo ingenio:* 'from this hour forward, I promise not to seize your person nor to

---

[1] For Richer, see above, p. 70, 71, and n. 1; F. Vercauteren, *Actes des comtes de Flandre*, 1071–1128 (Brussels, 1938), no. 30, cap. 1 (p. 89; on the date C. Johnson and H. A. Cronne, *Regesta regum Anglo-Normannorum*, ii, London, 1956, no. 515, p. 7, and F. L. Ganshof, R. Van Caenegem and A. Verhulst, 'Note sur le premier traité anglo-flamand de Douvres', *Revue du Nord*, xl, 1958); Galbert, see above, p. 71, n. 3; for Hainault, evidence quoted by N. Didier, *Le droit des fiefs dans la coutume de Hainaut au moyen âge* (Gre-noble, 1945), p. 28, n. 49.

[2] See above, p. 71, n. 3; C. Brunel, *Les plus anciennes chartes en langue provençale*, Paris, 1926, no. 2 (or Devic and Vaissete, *op. cit.*, v, no. 202).

deprive you of life or limb; I will not do this myself, nor shall any man or woman do it by my advice or at my instigation'. Finally, the text of an oath reproduced by Bracton may be quoted: *Hoc audis, domine N., quod fidem portabo de vita et membris, corpore et catallis et terreno honore, sic me Deus adiuvet et haec sancta*: 'hear this, my lord: I bear you faith in life and limb, in body and chattels and earthly honour, so help me God and these holy relics'.[1]

The probable origin and the aim of the oath of fealty have already been discussed in the section dealing with vassalage in the Carolingian period, and there is no need to discuss it again here.[2]

The fusion of these two elements which created the contract of vassalage was so complete that the act of homage was at once followed by the oath of fealty. This state of affairs is reflected in the terminology of documents in which such ceremonies are described. A charter of Count Baldwin V of Hainault relating to the homage done and the faith promised in 1187 by the mayor of Onnaing to his lords, the canons of the chapter of Notre-Dame of Cambrai, uses the following phrase: *hominii dominis a maiore facti et fidelitatis ab eodem eisdem promissae*.[3] The French expression *foi et hommage*, by which it became customary in the later middle ages to describe this series of acts, expresses perfectly the intimate character of their union. It would be said of a lord that he received someone *à foi et hommage*, meaning that he accepted him as a vassal, and of another that he held an estate (fief) *à foi et hommage*, i.e. in his capacity as vassal.

As a general rule, faith and homage seem to have been 'borne' (*portare fidem*), or in other words taken at the principal residence of the lord or at the capital of the seigneurie to which the fief held by the vassal was attached. In Normandy, for example, this had become by about 1091 a formal obligation on the part of the ducal vassals. But there were other customs, as for example that by which the holders of certain very large French fiefs which were contigu-

---

[1] *Annales Altahenses maiores*, a. 1041 (pp. 27, 28); the homage of James I of Aragon to the bishop of Maguelonne, in A. Teulet, *Layettes du Trésor des Chartes*, ii (Paris, 1866), no 2471, p. 329; Bracton, *De Legibus*, fo. 80 (ed. Woodbine, ii. 232).

[2] See above, pp. 28–30.

[3] C. Duvivier, *Actes et documents anciens intéressant la Belgique*, ii (Brussels, 1903), no. 64, p. 133.

ous to the lands of their lord did homage and took their oath of
fealty on the frontier between the two territories. This was the
normal practice for the duke of Normandy, vassal of the king of
France, from the tenth to the beginning of the thirteenth century,
and for the count of Champagne, vassal of the duke of Burgundy
and of various ecclesiastical lords, in the twelfth and thirteenth
centuries. This form of homage was described as 'frontier-homage',
homagium in marchia or *in locis in marchiam deputatis*; in French
it is known as *hommage en marche*.[1]

V. *The Kiss*

The doing of homage and the taking of an oath of fealty were
fairly frequently accompanied, especially in France, by a third act,
a ceremonial kiss (*osculum*). It is met with in Germany from the
eleventh century. The monk of St. Gallen, Ekkehard IV, who apparently died shortly after 1057, tells how Notker was elected
abbot in 971, in the presence of Otto I, and became an imperial
vassal: *meus tandem eris, ait, manibusque receptum osculatus est;
moxque ille evangelio allato, fidem iuravit,* ' "now at last you will
be mine", said the emperor, and having received him with his
hands he kissed him; then, when a Gospel book had been brought,
Notker swore fealty'. We have already seen an example of this
rite in Flanders in 1127, and in the thirteenth century we find it
provided for in the *Etablissements de Saint Louis*, according to
which the lord receiving the homage does so with the words 'Je
vos recoif et pran a home et vos en baise en nom de foi'.[2]

The kiss had not the same importance as the rite of homage
and the oath of fealty. Once these acts were accomplished, the
contract of vassalage was complete; the *osculum* was not essential
to its conclusion. It was simply a way of confirming the obligations contracted by the two parties, just as it was used to confirm
other forms of contract; a sort of analogy to it is the drink or
hand-clasp by which a bargain is still often sealed today. Like
homage, however, the kiss was a visible gesture, so that like the
immixtio manuum it was calculated to impress itself on a specta-

---

[1] *Consuetudines et Iusticiae*, c. 5, in C. H. Haskins, *Norman Institutions*
(Cambridge, Mass., 1918), p. 282; A. Longnon, *Documents relatifs au comté
de Champagne et de Brie*, i (Paris, 1901), nos. 16 (p. 473), 19 (p. 474).

[2] *Casus S. Galli*, c. 16 (ed. I, von Arx, M.G.H., SS., ii, 141). See above,
p. 71, n. 3; *Etablissements*, ii. 19 (ed. Viollet, ii. 398).

tor. In the later Middle Ages we consequently meet with such expressions, at least in France, as *hommage de bouche et de mains*, and a vassal described as *homme de bouche et de mains*.

VI. *Exceptions*

If the kiss was not essential to the contract of vassalage, homage and fealty were both indispensable, at least in France, Germany and England. The few exceptions that can be found only confirm the rule. If the king of France did not do homage, it is because he was a sovereign, and the same was true of the German king. In the eleventh century, German, French and English bishops all did homage and swore fealty to their rulers, but the obligation of homage gradually disappeared in the twelfth century as a result of the influence of those movements for reform which had triumphed within the Church, and whose main principles the Church had succeeded in imposing on civil society. In Guyenne, and in certain regions (Forez, Lyonnais, Dauphiné) in the vicinity of the Rhône which were or had been part of the kingdom of Burgundy-Arles, the relationship of vassalage was occasionally established in the thirteenth century by a simple oath of fealty, without any homage being required.[1] Here the explanation seems to lie in the influence which the property element might exercise over the personal element in the complex of feudal relationships; the rules defining these relationships were no doubt much less rigid in southern than in nothern France, and at the moment when a fief was created the vassal would be in a position to impose conditions that would have appeared quite unreasonable north of the Loire. In any case, even in the south, the phenomenon was exceptional and is only found at a late date. There was, however, one country where homage disappeared very early and over large areas: the kingdom of Italy. In Lombard Italy, homage had already gone by the twelfth century, and the oath of fealty

---

[1] *Recogniciones feodorum in Aquitania* (1273–75), no. 11, in C. Bémont, *Recueil d'actes relatifs à l'administration des rois d'Angleterre en Guyenne au XIII*ᵉ *siècle*, (Paris, 1914), p. 15; P. E. Giraud, *Essai historique sur l'abbaye de Saint-Bernard et sur la ville de Romans*, 2e partie, ii (Lyons, 1866), Preuves, no. 385, p. 94; M. C. Guigue, *Cartulaire lyonnais*, vols. i, ii (Lyons, 1885, 1893), no. 212 (1225), as well as nos. 178 (1221) and 260 (1230), compared with nos. 672 (1268), 762 (1280), and 842 (1297), which refer to grants *in feudum ad homagium*.

sufficed to create the contract of vassalage.[1] This was not the case in the Papal States or the kingdom of Sicily; in the latter, fealty and homage were practised in the same manner as in Normandy.

VII. *Written Contracts*

The various acts which we have analysed and described were of an oral character, and the same is of course true of the immense majority of legal forms of the early Middle Ages. It might happen that a charter would be drawn up recording the circumstances of the acts of fealty and homage and stating precisely the obligations incurred by the two parties. But this was rarely done except when the parties concerned were of some consequence and the contract of vassalage had political implications. A good example is the charter which determined the rights and obligations of the bishop of Liége on the one hand, and the Countess Richilda and her son Count Baldwin II of Hainault on the other, when the latter became direct vassals of the church of Liége in 1076.[2] Another is the charter drawn up when Count Robert II of Flanders became a vassal of Henry I of England in 1101.[3] There are also examples of charters by which a vassal acknowledges that he has taken an oath of fealty and done homage to a lord, and follows this up by the acceptance of penal clauses. At the end of the twelfth and during the thirteenth century, the French monarchy compelled certain of its vassals to subscribe to such charters, which it subsequently used in pursuit of its expansionist aims.[4] In the south of France, however, and in the regions of the king-

---

[1] *Consuetudines Feudorum*, Antiqua, viii. 8–11 and 12 (ed. K. Lehmann, *Das Langobardische Lehnrecht*, Göttingen, 1896, pp. 119, 120, 123).

[2] Analysed in Gislebert of Mons, *Chronique*, c. 9 (ed. Vanderkindere, Brussels, 1904, pp. 13–14). See also p. 68, n. 1.

[3] Vercauteren, *Actes*, no. 30.

[4] Charter of homage of Baldwin IX, count of Flanders, of 1196 (in F. Lot, *Fidèles ou Vassaux*, Paris, 1904, p. 255–257); charter by which Philip Augustus declares that he has received the homage and fealty of count Thibaut III of Champagne, and the charter of homage of the latter of 1198 (in Longnon, *Documents*, i, chartes 3, 4; pp. 467, 468 the first one also in *Recueil des actes de Philippe-Auguste, roi de France*, II, ed. C. Petit-Dutaillis and J. Monicat, Paris, 1943, no. 581, pp. 129–130); charter of homage of Ferrand of Portugal, count of Flanders, of 1212 (in C. Duvivier, *La querelle des d'Avesnes et des Dampierre*, ii, Brussels, 1894, Pièces justificatives, no. 7, pp. 13–14).

dom of Burgundy-Arles lying along the Rhône, where written acts
were in any case more frequent than was the case north of the
Loire, the custom of using charters to preserve the record of contracts of vassalage was in common use from the beginning of the
twelfth century onwards. These charters normally included the
oaths of fealty taken by the vassals, these being often drawn up
in the vernacular. A case in point is provided by the imposing
series of documents in which the oaths taken by the chief vassals
of the seigneurs of Montpellier were preserved from 1111 onwards.[1]

VIII. *Servile Homage*

Some cases are known in France, between the twelfth and fourteenth centuries, of homage, sometimes accompanied by oaths
of fealty, being entered into by free men and imposing on the
latter the obligation of constituting themselves serfs of some
ecclesiastical establishment. But the late date of the appearance
of servile homage and fealty justifies us in regarding them as
simply an imitation of the ordinary practice of vassal homage and
fealty.

IX. *The Effects of the Contract of Vassalage*

The consequences of the contract of vassalage, as created by the
legal acts which we have described, may be considered under
two different aspects: their effect on the power of the lord over
the person of his vassal, and the obligations they set up between
the two parties.

X. *The Power of the Lord over his Vassal*

The power of the lord over the vassal (*dominatio, dominatus,
dominium, potestas*, etc.) owed its very existence to the act of
homage, and to the *traditio personae* which it implied. In its
original conception, it must have been of such a character that
it can only be placed in the same category as a real right. It gave

---

[1] A. Germain, *Liber instrumentorum memorialium. Cartulaire des Guillems
de Montpellier* (Montpellier, 1884–86), nos. 316 ff. (seigneurs of Mont-
ferrier), 422 ff. (châtelains of Cournonsec). For Dauphiné: U. Chevalier,
Cartulaire de l'église de Die (Grenoble, 1868), no. 9, pp. 28–9 (of 1168).

the lord an immediate and direct power over the person of his vassal, and was limited only by the tacit proviso that it must not be exercised in such a way as to derogate from the vassal's status as a free man or from the allegiance which the vassal owed as a subject to the king. But in the period with which we are now concerned, this power was decidedly less than it had formerly been; it was only fully effective with regard to the lesser vassals without benefices and in those countries and periods in which the authority of the lord was exceptionally strong.

In a general way, this power of the lord over the person of his vassal can simply be conceived of as involving obedience and respect. This was clearly understood by Bracton, when in the middle of the thirteenth century he explained the rite of *immixtio manuum* as 'that which signifies, on the part of the vassal, submission and reverence' (*per quod significatur . . . ex parte tenentis, subiectio et reverentia*).[1] It was from this *reverentia* that the external marks of respect due from a vassal to his lord were derived, such services as holding the stirrup when he mounted his horse, escorting him on solemn occasions, or rendering him other 'services of honour' which varied in detail according to place and time. This authority, this power of the lord over the person of his vassal, also lay behind the many expressions which emphasized the dependence of the vassal with regard to his lord. *Mox suus effectus*, 'soon he became his', writes the author of the 'gestes' of the bishops of Cambrai in the first half of the eleventh century when he wished to describe how the count of Flanders became the vassal of King Henry II of Germany in 1007 (actually in 1012). *Ipsa vero ducis effecta* is what we read in an account of the entry of the Countess Richilda of Hainault into the vassalage of Godfrey the Hunchback, duke of Lower Lotharingia, in 1071: literally, 'she became the thing of the duke'.[2] But one cannot doubt that the dependence implied by these expressions had long ceased to correspond to the realities of feudal relationships.

---

[1] *De Legibus*, fo. 80 (ed. Woodbine, ii. 232).

[2] *Gesta episcoporum Cameracensium*, i. 115 (ed. L. C. Bethmann in M.G.H., SS., vii. 452); account of the enfeoffment of Hainault (ed. L. Weiland in M.G.H., *Constitutiones*, i. no. 441, p. 650); cf. also Thietmar, *Chronicon*, v. 14(9) (ed. Holtzmann, p. 236); 'regis efficitur'.

XI. The Obligations of the Parties

The contract of vassalage was a mutual one, and consequently imposed obligations on the two parties concerned. These obligations were created by the double action of fealty and homage, though both theorists and practising lawyers of the eleventh, twelfth and thirteenth centuries in France and England showed an inclination to derive them particularly if not exclusively from the oath of fealty.

In the first half of the eleventh century there was at least one man alive who was well acquainted with feudal relations in practice and whose intellectual development rendered him capable of expressing them in abstract terms. Bishop Fulbert of Chartres gives a remarkable definition of the obligations created by the contract of vassalage in a letter addressed to Duke William V of Aquitaine in 1020. It is so important that it is worth while reproducing the passage in its entirety. 'He who swears fealty to his lord should always have these six words present to his memory: "safe and sound", sure, honest, useful, easy, possible. Safe and sound, because he must cause no injury to the body of his lord. Sure, because he must not injure his lord by giving up his secrets or his castles, which are the guarantees of his security. Honest, because he must do nothing to injure the rights of justice of his lord or such other prerogatives as belong to his well-being. Useful, because he must do no wrong to the possessions of his lord. Easy and possible, because he must not make difficult for his lord anything which the latter may wish to do, and because he must not make impossible to his lord that which the lord might otherwise accomplish. It is only right that the vassal should abstain from injuring his lord in any of these ways. But it is not because of such abstention that he deserves to hold his fief. It is not sufficient to abstain from doing wrong; it is necessary to do right. It is therefore necessary that in the six matters aforesaid, the vassal shall faithfully give to his lord his counsel and support, if he wishes to appear worthy of his benefice and carry out faithfully the fealty which he has sworn. The lord must also in all things do similarly to the vassal who has sworn fealty to him. If he fails to do this, he will be rightly accused of bad faith, just as a vassal who will have been discovered to have been lacking in his duties, whether by positive action or simply by consent, is guilty of perfidy and perjury'.[1] (. . . *Qui domino suo fidelitatem iurat, ista sex in memoria semper habere debet: incolume, tutum, honestum, utile, facile, possibile. Incolume, videlicet ne sit domino in damnum de corpore suo. Tutum, ne sit ei in damnum de secreto suo, vel de munitionibus per quas tutus esse potest. Honestum, ne sit ei in damnum de sua iustitia, vel de aliis causis, quae ad honestatem eius pertinere videntur. Utile, ne sit ei in damnum de suis possessionibus. Facile vel possibile, ne id bonum, quod dominus suus leviter facere poterat, faciat ei difficile; neve id quod possibile erat, reddat ei impossibile. Ut autem fidelis haec nocumenta caveat, iustum est; sed non ideo casamentum meretur: non enim sufficit abstinere a malo, nisi fiat quod bonum est. Restat ergo ut in eisdem sex supradictis consilium et auxilium domino suo fideliter praestet, si beneficio dignus videri velit, et salvus esse de fidelitate quam iuravit. Dominus quoque fideli suo in his omnibus vicem reddere debet. Quo si non fecerit, merito censebitur malefidus: sicut ille, si in eorum praevaricatione vel faciendo vel consentiendo deprehensus fuerit, perfidus et periurus.*)

XII. The Fealty of the Vassal

We may now turn to consider the duties of the vassal, which involve two things, fealty (*fidelitas*) and certain concrete obligations.

The idea of fealty had in the first place a negative aspect, and this indeed seems to have been its earliest characteristic. It was the obligation of being faithful, and this fidelity was to be shown by abstaining from any act which might constitute a danger to the lord; it was therefore in the first place an obligation of *non facere*.[2] This is very apparent from the oaths of fealty which have

---

[1] Bouquet, *Recueil*, x. 463.

[2] There also exist from the south of France promises and oaths which involve no form of vassal relationship and are exclusively or almost exclusively negative in content, being essentially oaths of security; e.g. Devic and Vais-sete, *op. cit.*, ed. Privat, v, nos. 139 (c. 985), 148 (c. 989), 185 (c. 1025), 173, III (probably 1100). The phenomenon is not confined to the Midi. In Lotharingia, which was then a part of Germany but quite close to France, Bishop Gerald I of Cambrai required the friends of the châtelain Walter to take such an oath in 1023 (*Gesta episcoporum Cameracensium*, iii. 41; ed. L. C. Bethmann, *M.G.H., SS.*, vii. 481).

been preserved from the south of France. They all begin with the principal obligation, which is purely negative in character. The count of Besalu expresses himself as follows in an oath of fealty to the archbishop of Narbonne which dates from c. 1053: *De ista hora inantea non tolra ne dezebra Guilielmus comes filius Adalaiz Guifredum archiepiscopum, filium Guisle comitissae, de sua vita neque de sua membra que in corpus suum portat et in suum corpus se tenent, neque de ipsa sede Sancti Justi que est sita intra muros urbis Narbone, neque de ipsa forteza que est constructa insupra de dicta sede, neque de ea omnia que in suprascripta civitate ad suprascriptam sedem pertinere debentur,* 'from this hour henceforward. I, Count William son of Alix, will neither deceive Archbishop Wifred, son of the countess Gisela, nor injure him in his life nor in the limbs which he bears and which are attached to his body, nor of the cathedral of Saint-Juste which is situated within the walls of Narbonne nor of the fortress which is built up against the said cathedral nor of the other things which are in the said city and ought to belong to the said cathedral.[1]

That the same concept was widely held in northern France is apparent from the famous letter of Fulbert of Chartres to the duke of Aquitaine.[2] Nor was this purely a matter of theory. In 1007 or shortly afterwards this same Fulbert had to write a letter to Renaud of Vendôme, bishop of Paris, who was a vassal of the church of Chartres, reminding him of his duties. He stresses above all *securitatem de mea vita et membris et terra quam habeo vel per vestrum consilium acquiram,* 'security about my life and limbs and about the land which I possess or may acquire by your counsel'.[3] It is well expressed in the treaty of alliance concluded at Dover in 1101 between Count Robert II of Flanders and Henry I of England, in which the count, on becoming a vassal of the king, 'on his faith and oath assured King Henry of his life and limb and freedom, so that the king through him should come to no hurt' (*fide et sacramento assecuravit regi Henrico vitam suam et membra que corpori suo pertinent et capcionem corporis,*

---

[1] Brunel, *op. cit.,* no. 3 (or Devic and Vaissete, *op. cit.,* ed. Privat, v, no. 237).

[2] Above, pp. 83–84.

[3] Bouquet, *Recueil,* x. 447.

ne rex eam habeat hanc ad dampnum suum).[1] Traces of the
same idea are also found in the forms of oath which French and
English texts of the thirteenth century have preserved for us.[2]
It is probably this quality that twelfth-century texts of Flanders
and Hainault mean by *securitas*, used in contrast to *fides* or *fidelitas*, which in this context would refer to the more positive side of
the concept of fealty.[3] For fealty was likewise a mental attitude
which was supposed to dominate and colour all the actions of
the vassal, and which in particular should determine his attitude
to the various obligations whose fulfilment formed the other
aspect of his duty.

XIII. *The Services of the Vassal*

These services formed, par excellence, the positive aspect of the
duty of the vassal. Fulbert of Chartres provides us with both doc-
trinal and practical evidence on this point. In his letter to the
duke of Aquitaine, after enumerating the acts from which the
vassal must abstain if he wants to respect his oath, he adds that
all this is not sufficient if he wishes to be faithful and that he
owes positive services as well to his lord. Similarly, in his letter to
Renaud of Vendôme, Fulbert deals first with the negative aspect
of *securitas* and then turns to deal with positive duties in respect
of services.[4] Similarly the treaty of 1101 between the count of
Flanders and the king of England, after setting out what the
count promises by his faith and oath not to do against his new
lord, goes on to state what he promises to do on his behalf: he
'will help him to keep and defend the realm of England against
anyone who may live or die' (*et quod juvabit eum ad tenendum
et ad defendendum regnum Angliae contra omnes homines qui
vivere et mori possint*).[5] These services were not so much, indeed,
a matter of giving (*dare*) but of acting (*facere*). Fulbert sum-

---

[1] Vercauteren, *Actes des comtes de Flandre*, no. 30, c. 1.
[2] See above, p. 76.
[3] Galbert, *Histoire*, cc. 52, 55, 56, 102, 104 (pp. 83, 87, 89, 147, 150);
Gislebert of Mons, *Chronique*, cc. 43, 82 (ed. L. Vanderkindere, Brussels,
1904, pp. 75, 121).
[4] See above, pp. 84–85.
[5] See above, p. 85- 86; Vercauteren, *Actes des comtes de Flandre*, no. 30,
cap. 1 (p. 89).

marizes them in the words *auxilium* and *consilium*, aid and counsel, which we have already seen in use in the Carolingian period.[1]

XIV. *Auxilium*

Auxilium consisted in the first place of the service due to the
lord, and, in the period of 'classical' feudalism, this normally
meant military service as a mounted knight. Over and above this
'service' in the narrow sense, it included other types of material
aid. A summary of the obligations due from the count of Hainault
to the bishop of Liége at the end of the eleventh century implies
this duality when it declares that 'the count of Hainault owes to
his lord, the bishop of Liége, his service and aid in all matters
and against all men' (*comes Hanoniensis domino suo episcopo
Leodiensi servitium et auxilium ad omnia et contra universos
homines . . . debet*).[2] The word *servitium* is here, as very frequently, reserved for military service proper, while *auxilium*
appears to cover the other aspects of aid; this is a more restricted
sense than that in which it is used by Fulbert of Chartres and
many other writers. In England, the military service of the
vassal was generally described more precisely by the terms *militare
servitium* or *servitium militis*.

The military service due from the vassal was, from the lord's
point of view, at least during the greater part of the period with
which we are at the moment concerned, the essential object of
the contract of vassalage. The lord possessed vassals in order that
he might have soldiers at his disposition, and the institution still
had primarily a military character. With regard to the actual
form of military service, however, a good deal of variation was possible. The vassal might be bound to service with complete
equipment, or only with the most essential elements of it. In
parts of western France, for example, the latter was the case for
the *vavassores*, the subvassals of territorial princes and great lords,
and the numerous vassals who held only very small fiefs. Some
vassals were bound to render personal service only, while others
were bound to serve with a fixed number of knights, who would
generally be their own vassals. Here once again many variations

[1] See above, p. 56.
[2] See above, p. 80, n. 2.

were possible. Some vassals were bound to appear on their lord's summons with all their forces, *cum omnibus viribus hominum suorum tam equitum quam peditum*, as the count of Hainault was obliged to do according to regulations taken in 1076, as a vassal of the bishop of Liége.[1] In other cases the numbers required might be quite small. At the beginning of the twelfth century, the count of Flanders was quit of his obligations towards his lord, the king of France, when he joined the 'ost' of the latter with only twenty knights (*R. comes ad Philippum regem ibit cum XX militibus tantum*). On the other hand, the contract of vassalage into which he entered in 1101 with regard to the king of England obliged him to serve the latter with a thousand knights in England of Normandy, and with 500 knights in Maine.[2] From the eleventh century onwards, these quotas generally bore some relation to the importance of the fief held by the vassal. An exception to this was England, where they seem to have been fixed by the monarchy and were determined by the structure of the royal army. In France and Germany, the service quotas were frequently the subject of a detailed agreement between the parties, particularly when newly established contracts of vassalage were in question. In England, · where the monarchy succeeded in retaining control of the whole feudal organization, it was a rule, though not one that was always observed, that the lord had the right of summoning his vassals to arms only for the king's service. The earliest charter of enfeoff-ment that has been preserved illustrates this rule. At some date between 1066 and 1087, William the Conqueror laid down that a knight named Peter, to whom the abbot of Bury St. Edmund's had at his command granted a fief, should be required to furnish his service only if the abbot himself had been called upon to render service first of all to the king (*priusquam ex parte regis*).[3]

The nature of the service might also vary. In France and Eng-land, it was customary to distinguish the *expeditio* or *hostis* from the *equitatio* or *cavalcata*, the 'ost' from the 'chevauchée'. The first implied a military enterprise of some importance, while the second meant only a short expedition or even simply the

[1] *Ibid.*

[2] Treaty of Dover of 1101 between Robert II of Flanders and Henry I of England, c. 12 (cf. also c. 1 and caps. 2, 11 and 14), in Vercauteren, *Actes des comtes de Flandre*, no. 30, pp. 89, 90, 92.

[3] Douglas, 'A Charter of Enfeoffment . . . , *E.H.R.*, xlii (1927), 247.

duty of escort. In Germany, from the second half of the 12th century onwards, the expedition of the king to Rome (*Römerzug*) to be crowned emperor was a particular type of military service imposed on vassals and subvassals of the crown; this at least was the case from the time when Frederick Barbarossa substituted feudal obligations for those arising out of the status of a man as his subject as the basis of this service. Bishop Otto of Freising in his account of the 'gestes' of the emperor speaks of the *universorum equitum agmen feoda habentium*, 'the army of all the knights holding fiefs', and of the princes who had called to arms *singulos beneficiatos suos*, 'each of those who held some benefice from them'.[1] Another form of military service was that of castle-guard (Lat. *stagium, custodia*; Fr. *estage*; Germ. *Burghut*), which involved guard duties in one of the lord's castles.[2] One also frequently meets with the duty of the vassal to hold his own castle open to his lord and at his disposition. Gislebert of Mons, for example, declares that this was the case for all vassals of the count of Hainault who held a castle or some other fortified dwelling-house: *ita quod comiti Hanoniensi . . . ad omnes monitiones suas . . . castrum suum vel munitionem suam debeat reddere*.[3]

Service was due from the vassal without any particular remuneration. But vassals necessarily directed their efforts towards limiting the extent of their obligations, and in France, by the end of the second half of the eleventh century, it was generally agreed that the vassal could only be held to a certain number—often forty—days of service, beyond which the lord could only retain him by paying him wages. Sometimes it was also understood that service was due only in certain regions. In any case, this whole question was frequently the object of private agreements

---

[1] *Gesta Friderici I Imperatoris*, ii. 12 (ed. G. Waitz and B. von Simson, Hanover, 1912, p. 113).

[2] E.g., for Hainault in the twelfth century, the many passages in Gislebert's *Chronique* referring to the 'estage' owed by the count's vassals at his castles of Mons, Valenciennes and Beaumont (see the glossary in Vanderkindere's edition, s.v. *stagium*); for France, the list of royal liege vassals who owed castle-guard at Monthléry in the early thirteenth century in the *Scripta de feodis* (ed. L. Delisle in Bouquet, *Recueil*, xxiii. 671–5) and the long list of vassals of the count of Champagne, c. a. 1172 owing the same service to their lord (*feoda Campaniae*) (ed. Longnon, *Documents relatifs au comté de Champagne*, I, p. 1–74).

[3] *Chronique*, c. 43 (ed. Vanderkindere, p. 75).

between the parties concerned, which fixed such limitations as there might be, agreed on the wages due if a case for them arose, established what excuses would be acceptable if the vassal failed to appear, and so on. Limitations on the military service due from the vassal came at a later date in Germany, apart from Lotharingia, and there they were also much less usual and precise. In England it is not certain that they existed at all before the middle of the twelfth century.

Forms of *servitium* other than military obligations are known to us from the texts. Sometimes they might be related to knight service and complementary to it, but they were often of a quite different character, involving duties in the administration of the manor or in the lord's household, the carrying of messages, the providing of escorts, and so on. As examples of unusual types of service we may note that one of the obligations of several of the chief vassals of the bishop of Paris was that of carrying on their shoulders the newly consecrated bishop on his formal entry into his cathedral, and that an English tenant-in-chief held his Kentish estates in return for the service of 'holding the king's head in the boat' when he crossed the Channel from Dover to Wissant.[1] But these are probably late extensions of vassalage into spheres which it had not entered for many centuries; in Germany, at least, such instances may be explained by the fact that they were due from *ministeriales*, and that these were only effectively admitted to the status of vassal in the course of the twelfth century.

Military service was sometimes replaced by a money payment known as scutage (Lat. *scutagium*; Fr. *écuage*). In England, at a quite early date, the monarchy permitted money payments in lieu of *servitium militare*, at least in the lower ranks in the feudal hierarchy,[2] and the Plantagenets, in the second half of the twelfth century, systematically favoured the substitution of scutage for service, even in the case of tenants-in-chief of the crown. Their object in doing so was a financial one. The revenue provided by this levying of scutage made possible the hiring of paid troops, who were more trustworthy and more flexible than

[1] B. Guérard, *Cartulaire de l'église Notre-Dame de Paris*, i (Paris, 1850), no. 5 (of 1197/1208) pp. 5–11; T. Madox, *Baronia Anglica* (London, 1741), p. 245. A still odder form of service is cited by A. L. Poole, *Obligations of Society in the Twelfth and Thirteenth Centuries* (Oxford, 1946), p. 66, n. 2.

[2] See below, pp. 120–121.

an army of feudal knights could be at this time. In France, where scutage likewise existed, there were other forms of non-military service, such as the provision annually of a horse (*servicium de equo*) which would be at the lord's disposal for a certain specified time, or even more commonly the delivery of a pack-horse or an equivalent in money ('roncin de service') each time the fief changed hands. These methods of 'redeeming' military service are found in the twelfth and thirteenth centuries throughout a great part of north-western France: in Beauvaisis, the Ile de France, Orléanais, Anjou, Maine, Touraine and Poitou. In Maine and Anjou, and to a lesser degree in the other regions just enumerated, there also existed annual money payments (*servicium* or *servitium militare*) which in the case of certain vassals were accepted instead of personal knight service or *servicium de equo*; they are found in the twelfth and still more frequently in the thirteenth century. There were also other less effective substitutes for service, such as the presentation of a pair of gloves, a sword, a set of horseshoes, and so on. These were regarded as being a kind of honorary service—*ad honorem*,[1] as it is put in a charter of 1199 of the abbot of Murbach and Zürich in favour of the abbey of Engelberg in Switzerland—and in consequence they received the name of *Ehrschatz* in German feudal law. In Germany, from the second half of the twelfth century onwards, a money payment was allowed in lieu of personal participation in the *Römerzug*. Cases where similar payments instead of service were due from very small or newly created fiefs are not unknown in Germany and France; there were, for example, some instances in Flanders in the second half of the twelfth century.[2] In south-western France one even finds fiefs of some importance, with a castle which formed the centre of a seigneurie, from which only a money rent, generally known as *obliae* ('oblies'), was due.[3] But the general rule in France and Germany was that of personal military service.

There is good reason to suppose that the growth of household

[1] *Quellenwerk zur Entstehung der schweizerischen Eidgenossenschaft. I. Urkunden* (ed. T. Schiesz, Aarau, 1933), no. 205.

[2] E.g. F. Van de Putte and C. Carton, *Chronicon et cartularium Sancti Nicolai Furnensis* (Bruges, 1849), a° 1179 (pp. 231–2).

[3] E.g. Higounet, *Le comté de Comminges*, ii, Pièces justificatives, nos. 3 (1199), 7 (1276/7).

services, as well as services of an honorary character and those involving trivial obligations, all to the detriment of military service proper, was accentuated in the thirteenth century. It was certainly a very widespread phenomenon. In Flanders, for example, we know that in 1325 only 87 out of more than 500 vassals of the count in the châtellenie of Bruges actually had to perform services of a military nature; the remainder performed other types of service of the kinds indicated above.[1]

In addition to its military aspect, the obligation of *auxilium* covered also that of rendering financial aid to a lord in case of need. In the twelfth and thirteenth centuries, such 'aids' were raised only on rare occasions, and since these were nearly always the same, the rule gradually crystalized out that they should be limited to them. The number of recognized occasions was not always identical. In Normandy, for example, three such occasions were admitted, while in the royal domain and in the greater part of France four were allowed. The *aide aux quatre cas* was held to include the payment of the lord's ransom if he were captured, the knighting of his eldest son, the marriage of his eldest daughter, and his departure on a crusade. Such *auxilia* were also generally recognized in England, but in Germany they were less usual.

XV. *Consilium*

Consilium is cited side by side with *auxilium* by Fulbert of Chartres as one of the services due from a vassal to his lord. The vassal was bound to assist his lord by his advice, and since this advice was a form of service it implied an obligation on the vassal to attend his lord when the latter summoned him. In Germany the service of *Hoffahrt*, which when the king was concerned had been an obligation falling on all subjects, assumed under the Hohenstaufen in the twelfth century the character of a general feudal duty, but in France and western Germany it was, at least since the end of the eleventh century, often limited to a certain number of journeys a year. It was in virtue of this same service that a vassal sat with his lord and his co-

[1] J. De Smet, *Le plus ancien Livre des fiefs du Bourg de Bruges vers 1325*, Tablettes des Flandres, 1953.

vassals in his lord's court (*curtis, curia*), and it was in consequence of this fact that the word *consilium* came to be applied
to the assembly at which he deliberated with his lord. The object
of such deliberation might be any subject on which the lord
desired to know the opinion of his vassals. One of the most important aspects of this duty of 'counsel' consisted of judging,
under the presidency of the lord, cases which came before the
latter's court, and it was in virtue of the fealty sworn to him that
the lord required his vassals to declare the law. As Count Charles
the Good of Flanders expressed it in 1122 to his vassals, when they
were sitting in his court to give judgment in a dispute between
the abbot of St. Vaast's of Arras and a knight named Englebert:
'My lords, I adjure you by the faith which you owe me that
you should go aside and decide in unimpeachable fashion what
it is necessary to reply to Englebert and what to the monks'
(*Domini, obtestor vos per fidem quam michi debetis, ite in par-
tem et iudicio irrefragabili decernite quid Ingelberto, quid mona-
chis conveniat responderi*).[1]

XVI. Vassals owing no Services

In the lands situated on the banks of the Rhône in the kingdoms
of France and Burgundy-Arles, and in the greater part of Languedoc and on the northern slopes of the Pyrenees, cases can be
found where the obligations of the vassal were either non-existent
or negligible, amounting perhaps to no more than the duty of
placing his castle at the lord's disposal or offering him 'albergue',
entertainment for himself and a limited number of his suite during a prescribed period. The vassals who enjoyed this particularly
favourable arrangement were said to hold by 'franc fief' (*feudum
francum, feudum honoratum*),[2] and their very existence is yet
another illustration of the influence which the property element
could exercise over the personal one in the complex of feudal
relationships. In this case the results directly contradicted the very
essence of the bond which ought in feudal theory to have existed
between the vassal and his lord.

[1] Vercauteren, *Actes des comtes de Flandre*, no. 108 (p. 249).
[2] See below, pp. 119–120.

XVII. The Obligations of the Lord

The obligations of the lord show a marked parallelism with the obligations of the vassal. Fulbert of Chartres tells us that the lord must *in omnibus vicem reddere*, and Philippe de Remi, sire de Beaumanoir, the greatest French jurist of the thirteenth century and a man thoroughly familiar with the practice of his time, echoes the phrase in his *Coutume du comté de Clermont en Beauvaisis* when he says 'Nous discns et voirs est selonc nostre coustume, que pour autant comme li hons doit a son seigneur de foi et de loiauté par la reson de son homage, tout autant li sires en doit a son homme'.[1] For the lord, as for the vassal, these obligations included a general duty of keeping faith, as well as certain specific obligations. We need not pause to discuss the duty that the lord should keep faith, for it did not differ in any respect from the fealty due from the vassal. It involved the duty of not acting in any way that would injure the life, honour, or property of the vassal, and at the same time it expressed the sentiment which should dominate and pervade the whole of the lord's conduct towards his vassal.

The material obligations may be classified under two headings, whose existence we have already seen in the Carolingian period. The lord owed to his vassal protection and maintenance.

It was the duty of protection that Bracton had in mind when he declared that homage signified 'on the part of the lord, protection, defence and warranty' (*ex parte domini protectio, defensio et warantia*).[2] It implied, and all our sources agree on this point, that the lord was bound to come to his vassal's aid when the latter was unjustly attacked, and that he was bound to defend him against his enemies. This defence might take various forms, which were sometimes provided for by specific agreements between the two parties. The most essential aspect was the military one, which might compel a lord to go to war in defence of his vassal. It was this, for example, that led Philip I of France to come to the aid of his vassals, Countess Richilda of Flanders and her son Arnulf III, against the attempted usurpation of

---

[1] See above, pp. 83–84; Philippe de Beaumanoir, *Coutumes de Beauvaisis*, no. 1735 (ed. A. Salmon, ii, Paris, 1900, p. 383).
[2] *De Legibus*, fo. 80 (ed. Woodbine, ii. 232).

Robert the Frisian, though in this case the protection was inadequate and Robert made good his usurpation at the battle of
Cassel in 1071. Another important aspect of protection lay in
the field of justice. The lord was bound to defend his vassal in
a court of law, even in the king's court. These two aspects of the
duty of protection are clearly alluded to in the conditions for the
enfeoffment of the county of Hainault granted to Richilda and
her son Baldwin II by the church of Liége in 1076: 'if the lord
emperor of the Romans summon the count of Hainault to his
court for any matter, the bishop of Liége is bound to make himself the defendant, and answer instead of the count. Moreover
if any person shall attack the land of Hainault with intent to
do it an injury, the bishop of Liége shall bring his army to assist
the count of Hainault at his own expense' (*Si dominus imperator
Romanorum comitem Hanoniensem ad curiam suam invitaverit
ob aliquam causam, episcopus Leodiensis . . . debet . . . pro
eo in curia juri stare et respondere. Preterea si quis terram Hanoniensem ad malefaciendum aggressus fuerit, episcopus Leodiensis comiti Hanoniensi debet exercitum contra exercitum in pro-
priis expensis episcopi.*)[1]

The lord was equally bound to assist his vassal by his advice
and to act fairly and justly by him. Moreover, if he had granted
him a fief, he was bound to guarantee him its possession by
defending it against any attempts which might be made to deprive him of it. The complex of these obligations was sometimes
summarized in the same formula, *consilium et auxilium*,[2] which
was used for the obligations due from the vassal.

As far as maintenance was concerned, its primary object, from
the lord's point of view, was the necessity of making it possible
for the vassal to provide the service, and in particular the military
service, which he owed him.

This maintenance might, as in times past, be provided by the
lord in one of two different ways, either by maintaining the vassal
in his court and household or by granting him a fief. He might
also, though this occurred more rarely, grant him an allod, a
precarial tenure, or a tenure 'en mainferme'. The distinction be-

[1] See above, p. 80, n. 2.
[2] See above, p. 80; William Clito required it from his lord, the king of
France, in 1128 (Galbert of Bruges, *Histoire*, c. 107, p. 154).

tween these two methods of providing for the vassal is made very clearly by Dudo of Saint-Quentin, writing at the beginning of the eleventh century. He tells how William Longsword, ruler of Normandy, refused in the following words to grant a request for fiefs by certain of his subjects: 'The land which you ask of me I cannot give you, though all that I possess in movable goods I will grant you willingly: armlets and baldricks, breastplates and helms and greaves, horses, axes and wonderful swords marvellously adorned with gold. If you show yourselves willingly devoted to my service, you will enjoy my benevolence and rejoice in the military distinction of my household'.[1] (*Terram quam a me requiritis non possum largiri vobis; omnem tantum suppellectilem quam possideo concedam libenter vobis: videlicet armillas et balteos, loricas et galeas, atque cambitores, equos, secures, ensesque praecipuos auro mirabiliter ornatos. Gratia mea continua, militiaeque palma in domo mea fruemini, si incumbentes meo servitio voluntarie fueritis.*)

Beside this French example, which distinguishes so clearly the lot of the beneficed vassal from that of what one may call the domestic vassal, one may place a contemporary German instance. A letter written at the beginning of the eleventh century by a monk of the abbey of Tegernsee in Bavaria to a count who is related to him, pleads in favour of a vassal of this count who has complained that he 'has not yet received a benefice', *se adhuc carere beneficio.*[2]

In France there were still vassals who were *non casati*—they were often called 'bachelors', Fr. *bacheliers, baccalarii*—during the whole of the period under consideration. There was a similar class of household knights in England till at least the twelfth century, and the same class existed in Germany. It was even numerically fairly important. But the general desire for fiefs and the efforts made by vassals to acquire them hastened a development whose beginnings we have already seen in the reign of Charlemagne. The proportion of *vassi non casati* to *vassi casati* declined without a pause. Already by the eleventh century it was normal for a

[1] *De moribus et actis primorum Normanniae ducum*, iii. 44 (ed. J. Lair, Caen, 1865, p. 187).

[2] *Die Tegernseer Briefsammlung*, ed. K. Strecker in M.G.H., *Epistolae* (octavo series), iii (Berlin, 1925), no. 72, p. 80.

vassal to hold a fief, and one who did not was quite the exception. In many cases this unbeneficed situation would be of a temporary character; the vassal in question would count on obtaining a fief at the end of some years of faithful service, and it would be rare for him to be disappointed.

In early times, the grant of a benefice did not necessarily exclude other forms of maintenance at the lord's expense. A survival of this state of affairs occurs in the obligation sometimes found by which lords were required to give annually a suit of clothing (*vestes*) to their vassals, even to those who were beneficed. The bishop of Liége, for example, was bound every year at Christmas to give three suits of clothing to the count of Hainault and his three principal châtelains.[1]

XVIII. Lords and Sub-vassals

The mutual obligations created by homage and fealty were of a personal character, and so could affect nobody outside the two contracting parties. No legal relationship was established between the lord and the sub-vassal. This rule was formulated in France in the fourteenth century—'the vassal of my vassal is not my vassal' (. . . *queritur utrum homo hominis mei sit meus homo. Et dicendum est quod non* . . .)[2]—but was certainly then no novelty; it takes its place naturally in the general framework of feudal ideas and institutions as revealed to us in the texts. A vassal might be bound to bring to his lord's service some or all of his own vassals, but the latter had no direct obligation towards their 'suzerain', as the lord of a lord came to be termed in France towards the close of the Middle Ages.[3]

To this general rule there was one important exception. The influence of the property element in feudal relationships gave rise to the custom that when a lord died without a certain heir, his vassals were regarded as the vassals of his lord until an heir to

---

[1] See above, p. 80, n. 2 (1076).

[2] Jean de Blanot, *De homagiis*, c. 12 (ed. J. Acher, 'Notes sur le droit savant au moyen âge', in *Nouvelle revue historique de droit français et étranger*, 1906, p. 60); it is repeated by Durandus in his *Speculum iuris* (*Speculi Gulielmi Durandi . . . pars tertia et quarta*, [Lyons], 1532, fo. 120v.: Liber iv, Particula iii, *De feudis*, 28).

[3] Bloch, *Société féodale*, i. 225, n. 1. It was only later that 'suzerain' in French came to be a simple equivalent of 'seigneur'.

the deceased was legally established. To put it another way, the rights of a lord in the fiefs of his vassals necessarily reverted on his death without heirs to the lord of whom he ultimately held those fiefs. It was in virtue of this practice that after the murder of Charles the Good (1127), who left no certain heir, King Louis VI treated the count's vassals in Flanders as if they were now his own vassals and caused them to sit in his court.[1]

XIX. Breach of Engagements

Originally, as we have seen, the vassal had not the right to denounce the contract that bound him to his lord, unless the latter had wilfully abused his power over him. At the beginning of the eleventh century, at least in certain parts of Germany, this custom remained in force. The monk of Tegernsee, in the letter which we have just mentioned, asked the count if he would not grant his vassal 'some aid in the form of a benefice' (*aliquid auxilii . . . in beneficio*), to allow him 'freely to seek out another lord with your consent' (*cum gratiosa licentia vestra alium sibi dominum conquirere*).[2] We see here that before a vassal could acquire another lord, he must have secured the dissolution of his first contract, and this could not be brought about by its unilateral denunciation by either party. But from the end of the eleventh century and certainly by the first half of the twelfth century, it was admitted, in France and western Germany (Lotharingia), that a vassal might break his engagement on condition that he made a solemn statement to that effect and renounced his fief. Here once again we see the effect which the existence of the fief could have upon the relationship of vassalage, for the terms used to describe the act are hopelessly confused; to renounce one's faith—and one's fief—was called *renunciare* or *diffiduciare* (Fr. *défier, désavouer*; Eng. *defy*, in a now obsolete use of the word), and the renunciation was called *diffidentia, diffiduciatio, diffidatio* (Fr. *défiance, défi, désaveu, démission de foi, démission de fief*). In actual fact, of course, a vassal renouncing his 'foi' was normally rebelling against his lord and hoping at the same time to retain his fief; it was in this way that 'to defy' came to bear its modern ·

---

[1] Galbert, c. 52 (p. 82).
[2] See above, p. 96, n. 2.

meaning of 'to challenge' in both the English and French languages.

XX. Sanctions

This topic of *diffidatio* leads on naturally to the question of the sanctions envisaged in the case of one party or the other failing in his obligations. Such sanctions existed, but it must be admitted that up to the twelfth and even the thirteenth century they were often quite ineffective and that in practice the conflicts which followed such breaches of engagement were most often settled by recourse to arms.

The failure of one or other party to fulfil his obligations was technically known as 'felony'. The first sanction would itself be the breach of 'faith', the breaking off of friendly relations; it would be the same as the *diffidentia, diffiduciatio, diffidatio* which we have already met with as the process of terminating a contract of vassalage without any implication of a wrong having been committed by either party. As a sanction, however, a denunciation of his 'foi' might be solemnly made by a vassal, as when in 1173 Jacques d'Avesnes, having protested in vain against what he regarded as infringements of his rights by his lord, Count Baldwin V of Hainault, broke off relations with the countess, who was governing the country in her husband's absence, and dared to break his faith to her' (*ab ea recedens, ipsam diffiduciare presumpsit*). Similarly a rupture of faith might be a sanction resorted to by a lord. A scribe, a *dictator* of the school of Orléans at the end of the twelfth century, drawing up an imaginary letter to be addressed by Philip Augustus to Philip of Alsace, count of Flanders, summoning the latter to appear before his court, finished it with these words: *alioquin a nobis et a nostris baronibus vos esse noveritis diffidatum*, 'otherwise you must know that we and our barons will break our faith with you'.[1]

But a more effective sanction could be taken with regard to the fief, affording yet another indication of the influence exercised by feudal conceptions on the personal relationship between lord

---

[1] Gislebert of Mons, *Chronique*, c. 74 (ed. Vanderkindere, p. 114); A. Cartellieri, *Philipp II August, König von Frankreich*, i (Leipzig, 1900), Beilage 13, B. no. 3, p. 91.

and vassal. A serious fault on the part of a vassal would entail the confiscation of the fief, a necessary consequence of the breach of fealty, since the grant of the fief was conditioned by the contract and obligations of vassalage. In charters of Anjou of the first half of the eleventh century we already meet with what was to become the classical terminology by which such confiscation was to be described: *forsfacere fevum, fevum forsfactum*. A charter of 1039 tells us how a court adjudged that a certain Walter, vassal of Count Geoffrey Martel, 'had entirely forfeited the fief that he held of Count Geoffrey' (*totum ex integro fevum secum forsfecerat, quod de Goffridi comitis beneficio tenebat*) since he had killed a relative of the count and the latter had summoned him before the court. In 1101 Count Robert II of Flanders agreed with Henry I of England that if the French king, his lord, called out the *ost* against England he would obey the summons, but would do so with the smallest body of troops compatible with his not being called upon 'to forfeit the fief which he held of the king of France' (*ita tamen ne inde feodum suum erga regem Francie forisfaciat*).[1] Other terms were also used to indicate forfeiture of a fief as a sanction for misconduct. Jacques d'Avesnes, who has just been mentioned, having subsequently come to terms with his lord the count of Hainault, was required by the latter in 1176 to give up to him the castle of Condé. When he refused, it was adjudged by the count's court *quod Jacobus in castro suo nihil juris ulterius habere videretur*, 'that Jacques had lost all rights over his castle'.[2] Confiscation of a fief was termed *commissio* or *commissum* (French "commise"). In practice, however, the progressive development of the rights of the vassal over his fief, a topic which we shall deal with later, made confiscation difficult, except in England, where the monarchy was strong enough to carry it out when need arose. In twelfth-century France a less drastic sanction of a provisional character was developed: the temporary 'seizure' or occupation of the fief (*saisia, saisimentum*; Fr. *saisie*). In England, where confiscation always remained a possibility, there was less need to have recourse to such a 'seizure' of the fief, but the 'distress' of movable property was constantly practised

---

[1] C. Métais, *Cartulaire de la Trinité de Vendôme*, I (Paris, 1893), no. 16; cf. also nos. 62, 66, 67; Vercauteren, *Actes des comtes de Flandre*, no. 30, c. 1.
[2] Gislebert of Mons, *Chronique*, c. 80 (ed. Vanderkindere, p. 119).

as a temporary measure. The 'désaveu' of the lord by his vassal for a serious failure of his obligations also entailed consequences for the fief; the vassal might claim to hold the fief directly of the lord who was superior to him whom he had disavowed, or, if there was no superior lord, he might claim to hold it in full ownership.

Whether or not provoked by the fault of either party, the action of 'désaveu' had to be carried out by a formal rite known as *exfestucatio*, the solemn rejection of the *festuca* (corn-stalk) or other object that served as a symbol of the fief. When William Clito, count of Flanders, took offence at the attitude of his vassals Ivain of Alost and Daniel of Termonde in 1128 and wished to break the faith that bound them to him, Galbert of Bruges tells us that he 'leapt forward and would have thrown back the *festuca* to Ivain had he dared to do so, declaring "this is my will, that, by casting aside the homage which you have done me, I make myself your equal" ' (*prosiliens exfestucasset Iwannum si ausus esset . . . et ait: Volo . . . reiecto hominio quod mihi fecisti, parem me tibi facere . . .*). A little later, Ivain and Daniel, considering that the count had failed in his obligations, sent a message to him to say that 'the homages which up till now they have inviolably maintained towards you, they now renounce through us [i.e. their messengers] by throwing away the 'festuca' (*. . . hominia, quae inviolabiliter hactenus vobis servaverunt exfestucare per nos non differunt*). And Galbert adds, 'these messengers then proceeded to throw away the *festuca* in their masters' names' (*Et exfestucaverunt ex parte dominorum suorum internuntii illi*).[1]

XXI. Heritability

The relationship of vassal to lord was not in itself hereditary, but the wish of a vassal to secure that the benefice which he held should pass to one of his children was bound sooner or later to confer on this relationship an hereditary character. The question of inheritance can therefore be more appropriately studied when we come to deal with fiefs. When there were no fiefs, the relationship of lord and vassal was not hereditary; it did not exist, for example, in the case of *vassi non casati*.

[1] Galbert of Bruges, *Histoire*, c. 95 (ed. Pirenne, pp. 139, 140).

XXII. *Plurality of Allegiance*

We have already seen that before the end of the ninth century the practice had come to be tolerated, at any rate in France, of a vassal doing homage to several lords, and we noted that it was the desire for benefices that caused this breach in the primitive strictness of the relationship of lord and vassal. This breach was indeed a serious one, for a vassal of several lords might be compelled to choose between them, if they were at odds, and might profit by this conflict of loyalty to behave as if he were the vassal of none. We sometimes hear of persons who feared this consequence, and refused to become the vassal of more than one lord. We have already met with one such man, Gerald of Aurillac, who lived at the beginning of the tenth century. Another was Count William of Evreux, who lived in the first quarter of the twelfth century and who, according to Ordericus Vitalis, made the following declaration: 'I love both king (Henry I of England) and duke (Robert of Normandy), but I will only make myself the vassal of one and I will serve him lawfully as lord' (*Regem et ducem diligo . . . sed uni hominium faciam, eique ut domino, legaliter serviam*).[1] But these were heroic and quite exceptional cases. If the letter of the monk of Tegernsee shows that the custom of multiple vassalage was not yet generally admitted in Germany at the beginning of the eleventh century,[2] it became so during the next hundred years; a count Siboto of Falkenstein in Bavaria was vassal, in the twelfth century, of no less than twenty different lords. The custom was probably allowed in France in the tenth century, and was later widespread in England.

Naturally attempts were made to prevent this state of affairs from too seriously weakening the binding force of the tie of vassalage. Already before the end of the ninth century it had come to be realized that some action was necessary. The text of 895 which provides us with our earliest example of double vassalage shows that some contemporaries at least held the view that the lord whom one was most strictly bound to serve was the one from whom one held one's largest benefice: Patericus was more the

---

[1] Odo of Cluny, De Vita S. Geraldi, I, c. 32 (Migne, Patr. lat. cxxxiii, col. 660, 661); Ordericus Vitalis, *Historia ecclesiastica*, xi. 10 (ed. Leprévost, iv. 201).

[2] See above, p. 96, n. 2 and p. 98.

vassal of Robert than of Berengar 'because he held the larger benefice from him' (*quia plus ab ipso beneficium tenebat*).[1] In some places it was held that the closest bond was that which was the earliest in date; this was the principle which was generally received in northern Italy. Elsewhere subsequent acts of homage might carry an explicit reservation in favour of earlier ones.

XXIII. Liegeancy

It was the system of liegeancy (Fr. *ligesse*) which eventually became dominant in France, where it appeared in the middle of the eleventh century. By the end of the century it was known in Lotharingia,[2] and from Normandy, where possibly it was born, it was carried in the second half of the century to southern Italy and England. In this system, it was recognized that there was one among the lords of a vassal who must be served with the full strictness that was characteristic of primitive vassalage: *integre*, entirely, without reserve; *contra omnes*, against all men.[3]

This lord was the *dominus ligius*, the liege lord. The word is related to the German *ledig*, which means 'empty' or 'free', the implication in this case being that of 'freedom' from all other ties. The notion of 'liege' passed also to the vassal, and to the homage which he did and to the fief which he held, so that one made use of such expressions as *homo ligius, ligius miles, hominium ligium*,

[1] See above, p. 49, n. 1.
[2] *Cartulaire de la Trinité de Vendôme*, i (ed. Métais, Paris, 1893), no. 62, p. 117; Gislebert of Mons, *Chronique*, cc. 8, 9 (ed. Vanderkindere, pp. 12, 13); *Gesta episcoporum Cameracensium. Continuatio: Gesta Lietberti episcopi*, c. 9 (ed. L. C. Bethmann in *M.G.H., SS.*, vii. 493). These examples come respectively from 1046 Vendômois, 1076 (Liége-Hainault) and shortly after 1076 (Cambrai).
[3] 'Si integre vellet homo suus fieri' (Galbert of Bruges, *Histoire*, c. 56; ed. Pirenne, p. 89; cf. above, p. 71), cited by N. Didier, *Le droit des fiefs dans la coutume de Hainaut au moyen âge* (Paris, 1945), p. 31. 'Contra omnes': engagement of vassalage offered in 996 by count Fulk Nerra of Anjou to the son of count Eudes I of Blois (Richer, iv. 91; ed. Latouche, ii, 294-6); letter of Fulbert of Chartres to Renaud of Vendôme c. 1007 (Bouquet, *Recueil*, x. 447; cf. above, p. 85); as a consequence of his *hominium ligium*, the Count of Hainault had, since 1076, to serve his lord, the bishop of Liége, *ad omnia et contra universos homines* (see above, p. 80, n. 2); by the treaty of Dover (1101), the count of Flanders, Robert II, after he became a vassal of the king of England, Henry I, pledged him his service *contra omnes homines qui vivere et mori possint* (c. 1; see above p. 88, n. 2); for a case of 1205, see below, p. 142 and n. 1.

ligia fidelitas, feodum ligium. In the same sense and with the same meaning such words and conceptions as *dominus ligius, homo ligius, ligantia* passed on to England and southern Italy, where they were maintained and developed in the course of the twelfth century. In the county of Barcelona the liege vassal was described as *solidus.* Primitively, of course, there could only be one liege lord, and this rule was particularly emphasized in England,[1] where it was observed until late in the twelfth century. But in France and Lotharingia use was made of the institution of 'liege homage' to create new bonds whose binding force was identical with that of the homage done to the first liege lord, and with the evident intention of obtaining further fiefs. So in the twelfth century an individual in France or Lotharingia might be the liege man of several lords. Attempts were made to range these engagements of liege homage in an order of preference by formally reserving, in the later acts of homage, the obligations arising out of earlier acts. The French monarchy tried to enforce on its vassals a reservation of allegiance to the king. As early as 1101 we see the count of Flanders, when becoming a vassal of Henry I of England, reserving his fealty to the king of France (*salva fidelitate Philippi regis Francorum*)[2], but it was only in the thirteenth century that such a reservation became fairly general. Other forms of homage were described as 'simple' homage (Lat. *homagium planum*; Fr. *hommage plain, plane* or *ample*); its obligations were less strict than those of liege homage, and it was often created by a less elaborate rite.

In England, where from the time of Henry I every contract of vassalage carried with it a reservation of allegiance to the king,[3] liege homage ended by being monopolized by the Crown. In Germany, the need for liegeancy was not felt till about the middle of the twelfth century, for the king, the ecclesiastical and lay princes, and the greater magnates had their 'serf-knights', their *ministeriales*, knights who were narrowly and exclusively subordinated to their authority. Consequently the existence of the *homo ligius, ledichmann,* did not penetrate further eastwards than

---

[1] *Leges Henrici I,* 43.6, 55.2, 82.5 (ed. F. Liebermann, *Die Gesetze der Angelsachsen,* i, Halle, 1903, pp. 569, 575, 599); the date is 1114/18.
[2] Vercauteren, *Actes des comtes de Flandre,* no. 30, cap. 1 (p. 89).
[3] *Leges Henrici I,* 82.5 (p. 599).

Lotharingia and some regions adjacent to it. But when *minis-teriales* began to receive fiefs from other lords and when the mass entry of free knights into their ranks made the subordination of their class much less effective, the situation changed. In the second half of the twelfth century, the Hohenstaufen, in imitation of the French practice, tried to introduce into Germany, for the benefit of the monarchy, the concept of liegeancy. Frederick Barbarossa in particular attempted to secure that liege homage should be done to the king by the princes of the empire, and that it should be done to him alone, as was generally the case in France with the peers (*pairs*), as the chief territorial princes were called. He also tried to secure that a reservation in favour of the Crown should be made when homage was done to the princes by their vassals. But in this effort he was unsuccessful, and in Germany multiple vassalage was able to pursue unchecked its destructive course.

Chapter Two

FIEFS

I. Terminology

The property element in feudal relationships was still in the 'classical' period the same as it had been under the Carolingians, at any rate if one reduces it to its essential element—a tenement granted freely by a lord to his vassal in order to procure the latter the maintenance which was his due and to provide him with the means of furnishing his lord with the services required by his contract of vassalage.

At the start of the period now under discussion the term used for a feudal tenure was *beneficium*, as it had been in Carolingian times. This word, however, was also applied to precarial tenures, to tenures involving some menial kinds of service, and to ecclesiastical benefices. It is consequently essential to take into consideration the context when we are trying to arrive at its meaning in any particular case. The meaning that interests us is that which the word most frequently possesses, the 'benefice' in the sense of the property granted to the vassal.

In Germany *beneficium* was at this period and for long afterwards the technical term for this that was most in use. Examples abound in writers of the eleventh and twelfth centuries—Thietmar, Wipo in his biography of Conrad II, and so on.[1] Wipo tells us how King Conrad II, wishing to attach to his service Duke Ernest of Swabia after the latter had served him for some time in the course of an Italian expedition, granted him an important 'benefice': 'the duke received from the king the abbey of Kempten in benefice' (*Campidonensem abbatiam . . . in beneficium accepit a rege*).[2] Royal and imperial charters from Conrad II to

---

[1] Thietmar, i. 7, iv. 52, 69, vi. 29 (pp. 10, 190, 210, 222, 308); Wipo, *Gesta Chuonradi imperatoris*, c. 11, 28, 31 (ed. H. Bresslau, Hanover, 1915, pp. 33, 46, 50).
[2] Wipo, c. 11 (p. 33).

Henry IV include many references to benefices granted to vassals.[1]

In France likewise *beneficium* was the accepted term in the tenth and the first half of the eleventh centuries. In 1022 Count Eudes II of Blois and Chartres complained to his immediate overlord King Robert II, perhaps by the pen of Fulbert, that the king had judged him unworthy 'to hold of yourself any benefice' (*ullum beneficium tenere de te*).[2] A charter of 1058 declares that Fulk Nerra, count of Anjou, has divided up the estates of Montrevault 'and distributed it in benefices to his vassals' (*et militibus universa per beneficium donaverat*).[3] In a charter of 1023 the count of Mâcon refers to the fact that he had bestowed on the abbey of Cluny the estate of Jully-lez-Buxy *una cum consensu suorum fidelium qui predictam potestatem vice beneficii acceperant*, 'with the consent of his vassals who had received this seigneurie in benefice'.[4] *Beneficium* is employed in the royal charters of the last Carolingians and the first Capetians,[5] and in a great number of private charters; we have found it in Anjou, including the region of Vendôme, in Burgundy, in Champagne, in the region of Chartres, in Flanders, in Languedoc, in the Limousin, in Maine, in Normandy, in the Orléanais and Gâtinais, in the region of Paris, in Poitou, and in Touraine.[6]

Another term, however, appears in this period: *feodum*, which is met with frequently in the form *fevum* and sometimes *feudum*. In French it is *fief* or *fieffe*, in German *Lehen*, in Dutch *leen*.

It is at the end of the ninth century that the word first appears, in the form *feos* or *feus*, in southern Burgundy. It is applied to movable objects of value and is used in an oblique case and in the

---

[1] See the indices to the various volumes in the quarto series of *M.G.H.*, *Diplomata*, s.v. *beneficium*.

[2] Bouquet, *Recueil*, x. 501–2.

[3] L. Halphen, *Le comté d'Anjou au XIᵉ siècle*, Paris, 1906, p. 160, n. 1.

[4] A. Bernard and A. Bruel, *Recueil des chartes de l'abbaye de Cluny*, iii (1884), no. 2782.

[5] See the indices to the volumes which have appeared in the collection of *Chartes et diplômes pour servir à l'histoire de France*. For reigns where no edition of charters exists we have assembled an extensive collection of texts, largely with the help of the catalogues drawn up by W. M. Newman (*Catalogue des actes de Robert II, roi de France*. Paris, 1937) and F. Soehné (*Catalogue des actes d'Henri Iᵉʳ, roi de France*. Paris, 1907).

[6] This assertion is based on an extensive though of course not exhaustive study of collections of charters.

plural. The charters in which it occurs are concerned with sales in which the price is paid partially or entirely in kind, in *feos* or *feus* to which a pecuniary value can be attached. An example is a sale of landed property in the *pagus* of Mâcon in 889. The vendor declares that 'we have received from you the price cash down, as it was agreed between us, to wit in movable objects of value worth 21s.' (*accepimus de vobis precium in presente, sicut inter nos convenit, in feus compreciatus valentes solidus XXI*).[1] We have a whole series of charters from the same region of the last quarter of the ninth and the first of the tenth century in which the same clause and the same terminology is found.[2] The meaning assigned to the *feos* and *feus* is confirmed by the fact that the phrase *in feus compreciatus* is in one charter replaced by the words *in re preciata*.[3]

Several scholars have given interpretations of the evolution of the word *feodum*, which began by meaning a "movable object" of some kind and was in due course transferred to "benefice," i.e. landed property held in return for service. I still believe that Marc Bloch's hypothesis may be considered to be the most satisfying explanation of this rather surprising evolution.[4] The evolution began with the Frankish * *fehu-ôd*. The first element of this, parallel to the Gothic *faihu*, 'herd', meant 'cattle' (cf. Germ. *Vieh*, Lat. *pecus*), the movable wealth par excellence of early peoples. The second element *ôd* appears to have meant 'goods', so that the combination would imply 'a movable object of value'. This is one sense in which *feod* and *feus* are certainly used, and it appears that the derivation of these from * *fehu-ôd* presents no serious philological difficulties. Lords gave *feos* or *feus* to their vassals to allow them to maintain themselves; we have seen a good

---

[1] *Cluny*, i. (1876), no. 39.

[2] *Cluny*, i, nos. 24 (881), 36 (889), 50 (893), 54 (895), 68 (900), 100 (908), 236 (923), 243 (924). The term appears in the kingdom of Italy in the second half of the ninth century (P. S. Leicht, *Storia del diritto pubblico italiano. Lezioni*, Milan, 1938, p. 164).

[3] *Cluny*, i, no. 38 (889). A parallel text from the Auvergne in A. M. and M. Baudot, *Grand Cartulaire de Saint-Julien de Brioude. Essai de restitution*, Clermont-Ferrand, 1935, no. xviii (893; or also H. Doniol, *Cartulaire de Brioude*, Paris, 1863, no. 18). There are analogous texts of the 10th century for Rouergue in G. Desjardins, *Cartulaire de l'abbaye de Conques en Rouergue*, Paris, 1874, nos. 128 (908), 208 (932), 113 (943), 162 (965), 223 (974).

[4] *Société feodale*, i. 254-56.

example of this described by Dudo of St. Quentin.[1] This resulted in the second meaning of the word, 'that which provides for the maintenance of a vassal', and in regions of romance speech where the origin of the word was forgotten it was this last sense which became the chief one. So the word could be used with regard to real property as well as in connection with movable wealth.

We consequently find that in the same period as the charters we have been studying were being drawn up, others in more southern lands were already using *fevum* in the sense of *beneficium*. The earliest text of this sort is a charter of 899 which describes a legacy left by Countess Guillemette of Melgueil to the cathedral of Maguelonne.[2] This legacy included an allod situated at Saint-André-de-Novigent in eastern Languedoc. The countess forbade the granting of this allod 'to any man as a fief' (*ipsum alodem supranominatum donare per fevum ad ullum hominem*), a prohibition quite analogous to those of other charters in which the alienation of benefices is forbidden in the same manner.

The term occurs in many charters of Languedoc of the tenth century either in form *fevum* or in forms closer to the spoken language—*feum, feo,* or even the frankly 'vulgar' form *feuz*. It is found either in prohibitory clauses resembling that just cited or in the main dispositive clauses, where it refers to a previous or current grant of a *fevum* to a man of high social rank. The will of Countess Garsinda of Toulouse (c. 972), for example, contains several such references: *Illum fevum quem tenuit Rostagnus de Veharea, pratos et boscos et condaminas . . . dono Aymardo et Bernardo filiis Bernardi . . . et illum fevum quem tenet Isarnus vicecomes, teneat ipse Isarnus dum vivit,* 'the fief containing pasture and woodland and demesne lands, which is held by Rostagnus of Veharea . . . I give to Aymard and Bernard, the sons of Bernard . . . and as for the fief which the Viscount Isarn holds,

---

[1] Above, p. 96.

[2] J. Rouquette and A. Villemagne, *Cartulaire de Maguelone*, i, Montpellier, 1912, no. 3. The text given has been checked against the cartulary (Reg. C., f. 127v.), in the Archives Départementales de l'Hérault. Devic and Vaissete, and the scholars responsible for the revision of their work, published the charter in vol. v, no. 48, but with the faulty manuscript reading of *per fidem* for *per fevum,* which is impossible. Sainte-André-du-Novigent is within the present territory of Montpellier.

he—the said Isarn—shall continue to hold it till his death'.[1] The
texts become more numerous still in the first half of the eleventh
century, and it is probably true to say that by this time *fevum*
was more generally used in Languedoc than *beneficium*.

The word was also employed in other parts of France, but less
generally. In Burgundy it appears in the sources as a synonym
for *beneficium*, though it did not displace the latter. *Fevum* is
found in the Limousin and perhaps in Berry, *fedum* in Poitou.
Anjou—including the Vendômois—is probably the only part of
France north of the Loire where *fevum* appears in private charters
of the first half of the eleventh century in the meaning of benefice.
Sometime between 1006 and 1040 Viscount Hubert of Vendôme
ceded to his overlord Fulk Nerra, count of Anjou, the 'manor' and
the church of Mazé (Maine-et-Loire) which he held of him in
chief and which the count wished to add to his *dominicatum*:
*Curtem et ecclesiam Maziaci Hubertus Vindocinensium vicecomes
Fulconi comiti, de cuius tenuerat fevo . . . guerpivit.*[2] But neither
fevum or *feodum* seems to be found in this period in Normandy,[3]
Brittany, Champagne, Flanders, or the Paris region,[4] and the
words do not occur in royal charters before the last years of the
reign of Philip I.[5]

Feodum only puts in a timid appearence in western Germany
at the beginning of the eleventh century, but it was not applied exclusively to vassal tenures and it was never used by those respon-

[1] Devic and Vaissete, *op. cit*, ed. Privat (henceforward in this footnote
HGL), v, no. 126. Other tenth century texts: G. Desjardins, *Cartulaire de
l'abbaye de Conques*, no. 262 (916); Migne, *Patrol. lat.*, cxxxii. 469–70
(923–35); E. Germer-Durand, *Cartulaire du chapitre cathédral de Notre-
Dame de Nîmes*, 1874, no. 44 (943); HGL, v, nos. 100 (956), 106 (c. 959),
111 (961); *Conques*, no. 340 (961); HGL, v, no. 122 (972); P. Alaus, L.
Cassan, E. Meynial, *Cartulaire de Gellone*, Montpellier, 1898, no. 174 (c.
984); *Gallia Christiana*, xiii, Instr. eccl. Tolos., col. 6 (985); HGL, v, no.
143 (987), 150 (990); *Conques*, no. 294 (c. 990/6); HGL, V, no. 155
(997); *Conques*, no. 480 (tenth cent.).

[2] C. Métais, *Cartulaire de la Trinité de Vendôme*, i, Paris, 1893, no. 44.

[3] Save perhaps in a text of 1035–87 cited by R. Carabie, *La propriété foncière dans l'ancien droit normand*, Caen, 1943, p. 248, n. 2.

[4] No. 247 (1006) of J. Tardif, *Monuments historiques. Cartons des Rois*,
Paris, 1866, is a forgery of the end of the eleventh century (J. Favier, 'La
fabrication d'un faux à Saint-Maur-des-Fossés vers la fin du XIe siècle',
Bibliothèque de l'Ecole des Chartes, CXIX, 1961).

[5] The charter of Robert II of 1008 for Saint-Denis (Tardif, no. 249 or also in
Bouquet, *Recueil*, x. 592–4; no. 120 in Newman's list) is a forgery of c. 1101
(L. Levillain, *Études sur l'abbaye de Saint-Denis à l'époque mérovingienne.
III, Bibliothèque de l'Ecole des Chartes*, lxxxvii, 1926, pp. 90–94).

sible for drawing up royal and imperial charters before the end of
the reign of Henry IV.[1] Its use became general in Lotharingia in
the second half of the eleventh century, though it was not yet accepted as a technical term; a charter of Hainault of 1087 refers to
'a benefice that in vulgar parlance is called a fief' (*beneficium
quod vulgo dicitur feodum*).[2]

There were some regions in which these terms were used with
a general significance in addition to a purely technical one. In
Normandy, Brittany, Guyenne, Gascony, and the region of Toulouse, the words *feudum* and *fief* or *fieffe* were used to describe
any form of tenement, and in order to avoid confusion, the tenement of a vassal was often described as *feodum militis*, 'knight's
fee'. The expression *feodum militare* was also used in Lotharingia
and other parts of Germany to differentiate between a true fief
and the tenements granted to certain types of servant. The chronicle of the abbey of Saint-Trond, for example, tells us that sometime between 1108 and 1136 the servant who had the duty of
bleeding the monks, providing the abbot's saddle and spurs, re-
pairing the abbey windows and performing other minor services
claimed, though unsuccessfully, that the tenement which he held
in return for these services (*terram . . . quae debet servire fratri-
bus ad omnem minutionem sanguinis*) was a free knight's fee
(*pro libero militari feodo*).[3] In England the word *feudum*, which
was employed in its technical sense on the morrow of the Conquest, was extended very early to cover any form of free heritable
tenement; it became in consequence necessary to specify further
when a vassal held his land by knight service (*per militare servitium*), and it became increasingly the practice in the twelfth and
thirteenth centuries to describe his tenement as a knight's fee

[1] Waitz, *op. cit.*, vi, 2nd ed. revised by Seeliger, p. 132. We have not
carried out a systematic study of the royal and imperial charters beyond the
reign of Henry IV.

[2] C. Duvivier, *Actes et documents anciers intéressant la Belgique*, ii, Brussels, 1903, no. 6, p. 18. Cf. the *loco beneficii sub nomine fedii* in a charter
of Count Eudes of Vermandois of 1036/43 (F. Vercauteren, 'Note sur un
texte du cartulaire d'Hombl:ères', in *Recueil . . . offert à M. C. Brunel*,
Paris, 1955, p. 655, n. 1). The sentence to which the words quoted in this
note belong might be considered as perhaps having been interpolated at a
more recent date.

[3] *Gesta abbatum Trudonensium*, ix. 12 (ed. R. Koepke in M.G.H., SS., x.
p. 124 or ed, C. de Borman, *Chronique de l'abbaye de Saint-Trond*, i, Liége,
1877, pp. 151-2).

(*feudum militis*). Occasionally, both in England and on the Continent, some paraphrase might be employed instead of the technical term; one could speak, for example, of an estate being held *iure militari* or *iure feodario*, or describe the estate itself as *terra feodalis*.[1]

In addition to *beneficium* and *feudum* in its various forms, there were other words which might be used to describe a fief, though they were often rather general terms implying any form of tenement. Examples of these are *casamentum*,[2] which was already known in the Carolingian period, *tenementum*, *tenura*, and above all *liberum tenementum*. The last of these was commonly employed in England in the twelfth and thirteenth centuries. But in such cases the terms of the contract would have to make it clear that these words are being used to describe the tenement of a vassal, as where, for example, in the English documents, when the free tenement (*liberum tenementum*) was specifically related to knight service (*servitium militis*).

A vivid light is thrown upon the archaism of German legal terminology by the famous incident which occurred in 1157 at the diet of Besançon. At this diet the Emperor Frederick Barbarossa received papal legates bearing a letter from Adrian IV in which the pope, after making various complaints against the emperor, reminded him that it was he who had crowned him emperor and declared that he would have been pleased to confer further *maiora beneficia* upon him. It is highly probable that at Rome, where the German use of the word *beneficium* was perfectly well known, some ambiguity may have been intended, but the official sense of the expression was not open to dispute. The papal chancery used the word *beneficium* only in the same sense as the modern 'benefit', and never with any other meaning. But the imperial chancellor Rainald of Dassel, the future archbishop of Cologne, when translating the text into German, apparently, and probably deliberately, used the German 'Lehen', which at that time was in Germany the equivalent of *beneficium*, instead of 'Wohlthat',

---

[1] Some examples of these from Hainault are in Duvivier, *Hainaut ancien*, ii, no. 105 (of 1114/15), p. 512, and unpublished texts of the same region of 1216 and 1251 are cited by Didier, *Droit des fiefs*, p. 7, n. 41 and p. 2, n. 5.

[2] E.g. the letter of Fulbert of Chartres to William of Aquitaine (above p. 83–84).

which meant 'benefit'. In this way the pope's words were made to imply that the imperial dignity was held as a fief from the pope, and some expressions used by the legates appeared to bear out this impression. There was an immediate uproar amongst the German princes, and the Count Palatine Otto of Wittelsbach would have killed the legate, Cardinal Roland Bandinelli, if the emperor had not intervened.[1]

II. Content of a Fief

A fief normally consisted of a landed estate, which might vary enormously in size, from thousands of acres down to only a few acres or even a few perches. Sometimes it might be a castle, but carry no land with it, as for example in Hainault, where every castle in the second half of the twelfth century was held as a fief of the count. This was the case even if it was built on a fief held of some other lord or on allodial land.[2] A fief might be some form of public authority, or a duty or right. The French territorial princes, who were successors by usurpation of the royal officials of Carolingian times, held their offices in fief from the king, fiefs of this kind being what were subsequently known as 'fiefs de dignité'. The same was true in Germany of the dukes, of many of the margraves and counts, and of the imperial bishops (Reichsbischöfe). In the second half of the twelfth century, when Frederick Barbarossa attempted to reorganize the state on a feudal basis, the princes of the empire (Reichsfürsten), a class which included the majority of the bishops, some of the abbots, the dukes, the majority of the margraves, and a few counts, held their offices directly in fief of the king; margraves and counts who were not admitted to the rank of princes of the empire held their offices indirectly of him as arrière-fiefs. But by the side of these offices which by their nature were of a superior character and always public in origin, there was an infinite number of other duties and rights which might be held as fiefs, such as the right to tolls and market dues, the rights of minting and justice, the functions of châtelain, advocate, mayor, provost, receiver, and so on.

In all these cases, even if the fief was not itself a landed estate,

[1] Rahewin, continuation of Otto of Freising, Gesta Friderici, III, c. 9, 10 and 17 (ed. Waitz and von Simson, pp. 174–7, 187–9).
[2] Gislebert of Mons, Chronique, c. 43 (ed. Vanderkindere, p. 75).

it was normally not without a territorial or at least a local basis. The king of France granted the county of Flanders as a fief, and the king of Germany the duchy of Brabant; the count of Flanders granted as a fief the châtellenie of Bruges; an abbey granted as a fief the 'avowry' of a particular group of estates; an individual held in fief a particular seigneurie, or the tolls at a particular place or on a particular bridge, the office of mayor in a particular village, the right of aubaine in such and such a locality. A fief might have no territorial or local basis, but consist in the right to certain payments made at regular intervals; this from the thirteenth century onwards would be called an annuity (*rente*). These fiefs are called 'money fiefs' (Lat. *feodum de bursa*; Fr. *fief de bourse*; Germ. *Kammerlehen*); writers on French feudal law ('feudalistes') sometimes used the expression 'fiefs de revenue'; [1] some modern scholars have preferred that of 'fief-rente'. They existed in France and Germany, and in the Low Countries, from the eleventh century onwards. An early Flemish example dates from 1087, when the abbot of St. Bertin's declares that two brothers, Arnulf and Gerbodo, 'have become our vassals and receive, as a fief, a payment each year of two marks of silver apiece on an appointed day, to wit at Michaelmas' (*homines nostri manibus effecti quatuor marchas argenti, unusquisque videlicet duas, et hoc constituto tempore, id est in festivitate Sancti Micaelis, in benefitium singulis annis recipiunt*).[2] But it was the English monarchy under the Normans and Angevins which made the most extensive and systematic use of such money fiefs. One of the earliest examples of which the details are known is that by which King Henry I of England granted to Count Robert II of Flanders a money fief amounting to 500 pounds sterling a year: *propter praedictis conventiones et praedictum servitium dabit rex Henricus comiti R. unoquoque anno CCCCC libras anglorum denariorum in feodo.* In the twelfth and thirteenth centuries the English monarchy used grants of this character to make many of the greater and lesser nobles of France and Germany, and particularly those of

[1] F. Ragueau and E. de Laurière, *Glossaire du droit françois* (Paris 1704), s.v.

[2] B. Guérard, *Cartulaire de Saint-Bertin* (Paris, 1841), pp. 202–3; cf. D. Haigneré, *Les Chartes de Saint-Bertin*, i (Saint-Omer, 1886), no. 85, p. 33. Gerbodo was advocate of St. Bertin's; he was also earl of Chester for some years, having followed William the Conqueror to England.

the Low Countries, its vassals. The first king of France to grant a money fief was, as far as we know, Louis VII in 1155/56,[1] and his successors methodically followed the same policy from the moment when their financial resources permitted it, i.e. from the reign of Philip Augustus onwards.

The money fief might assume a number of different aspects. It might be constituted by the delivery to the vassal of a sum of money with which to acquire an estate or office which would bring him a regular income. We hear, for example, of Richard d'Orcq, a vassal of Count Baldwin V of Hainault, being given £200 to be spent in acquiring some 'liege fief' (200 *libras . . . ut in feodum ligium eas converteret*). Or the fief might consist of a fixed revenue to be paid from a definite source, as for example when the same count created in favour of Baldwin of Neuville a fief consisting of an annual payment of £30 from the 'winage' of Maubeuge (*unde ei winagio Melbodiensi 30 libras annuatim assignavit*). But in most cases the source of the money was not specified, and the payment was simply made from the lord's treasury. This was so for the majority of money fiefs granted by sovereigns or princes to foreign lords, as in the case of the 100 marks sterling of annual revenue with which an English king in the twelfth century enfeoffed Counts Baldwin IV and V of Hainault (*ei super 100 marchis sterlingorum magno pondo annuatim habendis hominium fecit . . . sicut pater ab ipso rege et ab ejus avunculo Henrico rege Anglie infeodatus fuerat*).[2]

French feudal lawyers sometimes gave the name of 'fiefs en l'air' to all fiefs whose objects were incorporeal, but the expression led to confusion and was never generally adopted.[3]

In the tenth and eleventh centuries, lay vassals of any importance usually held churches—abbeys, *altaria* or parish churches, chapels—amongst their fiefs. This gave them the profits of the tithe and the endowments of the church, and even in some cases the income arising from the spiritual offices themselves (offerings of the faithful, church dues, etc.). It was indeed the case that

---

[1] Treaty of 1101, Vercauteren, *Actes*, no. 30, c. 18; A. Luchaire, *Etude sur les actes de Louis VII* (Paris, 1885), Pièces justificatives, no. 353.

[2] Gislebert of Mons, *Chronique*, cc. 115 and 69 (ed. Vanderkindere, pp. 175, 109).

[3] Brussel, *Nouvel examen de l'usage général des fiefs en France*, i (Paris, 1727), p. 397.

revenues of an ecclesiastical character, and particularly tithes, were amongst the most sought after types of fief. Almost all sovereigns and princes, and lesser lords when they were in a position to do so, enfeoffed their vassals with churches or ecclesiastical revenues. In private charters one frequently meets such clauses as that which accompanies the restitution of the church of Chouzy in the Blois region to the abbey of Marmoutiers by Count Eudes II of Blois and Chartres: *Alanus, Britannorum comes clarissimus et Eudo, frater eius qui de me praedictam ecclesiam in beneficio tenebant, pro lucro aeternae hereditatis consenserunt,* 'Alan, the most illustrious count of Brittany, together with his brother Eudes, who held of me the aforesaid church in benefice, have consented to it in order to obtain in return the inheritance of everlasting life.' [1]

The reform movement of the late eleventh century had as one object the abolition of this type of fief, and it did succeed, to a degree that varied from country to country, in checking and limiting it, but it was unable to suppress it entirely. In the early twelfth century we often hear of such fiefs being terminated, either after open conflict, or by some arrangement between the parties. In 1114 the abbey of Montiérender recovered the church of Ceffonds (Haute-Marne) through the intervention of the bishop of Troyes, one of whose predecessors had usurped it (*violentia cujusdam mei predecessoris injuste sibi ablatum,* as the charter of restitution puts it) and enfeoffed it to the count of Brienne, who in turn had granted it in fief (*in casamento*) to his vassal Englebert. The same charter records that the count of Brienne had restored the half of the church of Sommevoire (Haute-Marne) which he also held in fief of the bishop, and which had been usurped in the same way to the detriment of the same abbey. A few years later, in 1128, we find William Clito, Count of Flanders, restoring to the church of Noyon-Tournai twelve parish churches in Flanders which a bishop of Tournai had granted in fief to Count Baldwin IV (*ob.* 1035). According to a trustworthy account of this earlier transaction, 'the magnates of Flanders (i.e. the principal vassals of the count) had petitioned the count to grant them to them in benefice, and when they had received them, the

---

[1] *Gallia Christiana,* xiv, Instrument. eccl. Turon., no. 48, col. 68. The restitution was made probably in 1033.

magnates had granted them in fief to their own vassals' (*optimates Flandrenses a comite petierunt ea sibi concedi in beneficium. Que accepta, optimates militibus sibi servientibus rursus in feodum distribuerunt*). These churches had therefore been made the objects of three successive enfeoffments. The death of Count William deprived the restitution of any effect, and by the middle of the century the church of Noyon-Tournai had not yet recovered its *altaria*, though some of them came back to it in the end.[1] Amongst the ecclesiastical revenues which were longest retained by princes and lay lords must be counted the *decimae novalium*, the tithes on land newly brought under cultivation. As late as the thirteenth century, in the diocese of Utrecht, these tithes were still held in fief of the church by the counts of Guelders and Holland within the limits of each of their respective counties.[2]

III. Different Types of Fief

Many fiefs existed which could be described by special titles, as for example the 'liege fiefs' and 'fiefs plains' or 'amples' which corresponded to the homages of these types noticed above.[3] There were also those which were termed honours (*honores*). As we have seen, this word was used in the Carolingian period to describe public offices and lay abbacies with the benefices which constituted their endowment. This tradition was maintained in Germany, where the word *honor* was applied in the tenth, eleventh and twelfth centuries only to public offices held in benefice, and not to other types of fief. It is constantly employed by Widukind and Thietmar in this meaning. When Wipo records that the Emperor Conrad II pardoned his cousin Conrad in 1027 and *honorem suum sibi restituit*, he meant by this his counties in Franconia. When at the end of the same century Lampert of Hersfeld refers to the *honores publicos* of the duke of Carinthia, he meant by this phrase his ducal office and his counties. The monk of Cambrai who in the

---

[1] C. Lalore, *Cartulaire de l'abbaye de la Chapelle-aux-Planches. Chartes de Montiérender . . .* (Paris, 1878), no. 60, pp. 189–90; Galbert of Bruges, *Histoire*, c. 107 (p. 154); *Historiae Tornacenses*, iii. 9 (ed. G. Waitz in M.G.H., SS., xiv. 338).

[2] L. A. J. W. Sloet, *Oorkondenboek der graafschappen Gelre en Zutfen* (The Hague, I, 1872–76), no. 435, p. 443 (1213–1216); L. P. C. van den Bergh, *Oorkondenboek van Holland en Zeeland*, ii (Amsterdam and The Hague, 1873), no. 431, p. 192 (1281).

[3] See above, pp. 103–105.

second quarter of the twelfth century compiled the chronicle of the abbey of St. André of Câteau-Cambrésis remained, like a good Lotharingian, faithful to this practice, and used the term in reference to the county of Flanders, although this was not in Germany; he makes Robert the Frisian, before the coup d'état, complain *se . . . omni honore Flandriae exclusum esse*, meaning that he had been excluded completely from the government of the county of Flanders. Even more interesting is the fact that at the end of the twelfth century we find Gislebert of Mons, a former chancellor of the county of Hainault, when describing the sale of her allods in Hainault by the Countess Richilda to Bishop Theoduin of Liége in 1071, writing of *tanta allodia tanto honore insignita*, 'allods which such an honour made illustrious'.[1]

In France a distinction must be made. In charters of Languedoc of the tenth and eleventh centuries the idea that *honor* meant the endowment of some office, whether public or not, and generally held as a fief, seems to have existed, but in the twelfth and thirteenth centuries the word is applied to a seigneurie of any description, even an allodial one. In western France in the eleventh century it sometimes means a county held in benefice.[2] As a general rule, however, the word is in French texts no more than a synonym for *feudum*. It was usually applied to fiefs of some consequence, though not necessarily only to 'fiefs de dignité', i.e. those whose holders enjoyed the title of viscount, count, duke, and so on.

The word was never in post-conquest England a simple synonym for fief. Especially in the twelfth and thirteenth centuries did the word 'honour' have a particular meaning, for it was

---

[1] Widukind, II, 13, 25, pp. 78, 88, III, 21, 32, 50, pp. 115, 118, 729; Thietmar, I, 1, p. 5, II, 14, 26, pp. 54, 70, IV, 39, p. 176, V, 21, p. 245; Wipo, *Gesta Chuonradi imperatoris*, c. 21, p. 41 (ed. H. Bresslau, Hanover, 1915); Lampert of Hersfeld, *Annales*, a° 1073 (ed. O. Holder-Egger, Hanover, 1894, p. 153); *Chronicon S. Andreae Castri Cameracensis*, ii. 33 (ed. L. C. Bethmann in M.G.H., SS., vii. 537); Gislebert, *Chronique*, c. 8 (p. 11).

[2] For Languedoc: endowment, e.g., Brunel, *op. cit.*, no. 1 (or Devic and Vaissete, *op. cit.*, ed. Privat, v, no. 201), of c. 1034; seigneurie, e.g., Higounet, *op. cit.*, P. J., nos. 3 and 5, of 1199 and 1261; C. Douais, *Cartulaire de l'abbaye de Saint-Sernin de Toulouse*, Paris, 1887, no. 260, of 1128; Germain, *op. cit.*, nos. 231 and 556, of 1139 and 1187. For western France, Métais, *Cartulaire de la Trinité de Vendôme*, i, no. 6, shortly after 1050.

there applied to great complexes of fiefs, united in a permanent fashion as single lordships and held by the chief barons of the kingdom, tenants-in-chief of the crown. The 'honour' carried with it military obligations of particular importance. It is worth noting how Wace, in his *Roman de Rou*, written *c.* 1160, describing the inducements offered by William the Conqueror to those who were to accompany him on his expedition, contrasts the money fiefs promised to the vavasours with the 'honours' reserved for the 'barons':

> *Rentes promist a vavasors*
> *E as barons promist enors.*[1]

In the lands lying east and west of the Rhône, in Languedoc and in the region comprised between the Pyrenees and the Garonne, we find in the twelfth century a well-defined type of unusually privileged feudal tenement know as the 'free fief' (Lat. *feudum liberum, feudum francum, feudum honoratum*; Fr. *franc fief*). When a vassal declared in 1181 that he would do the service due from a particular fief 'according to the rules and customs of a free fief' (*serviemus iamdictum feudum secundum consuetudinem et recionem feudi honorati*),[2] he knew that this meant something quite clear and generally recognized by contemporaries. A vassal in possession of a 'free fief' had in general no obligations other than those of fealty and of holding his castle—if the fief had one— at his lord's disposal. The conditions which William VII, seigneur of Montpellier, imposed on Pierre de Sauteyrargues in 1168 for a free 'fief de reprise' (*ad feudum honoratum*), would certainly apply to many, and perhaps to most, 'free fiefs'; 'you are not bound to any other service save that of fealty towards me' (*et aliud servicium . . . non teneris facere sed fidelis semper esse michi debes*).[3] When actual military service did happen to be owed, it was only on terms that were strictly limited, as for example

---

[1] *Roman de Rou*, iii. 6371–2 (ed. H. Andresen, Heilbronn, 1879, ii. 282).
[2] L. Cassan and E. Meynial, *Cartulaire de l'abbaye d'Aniane* (Montpellier, 1900), no. 23 (of 1181).
[3] Germain, *op. cit.*, no. 313 (of 1168), and oath of fealty in no. 312 (of 1168); see above, p. 93.

through the vassal placing his castle at his lord's disposal or supporting him against a specifically named enemy.[1] The explanation of this relaxation or total disappearance of the obligations to which vassals elsewhere were accustomed seems to be that when the fief was constituted—and especially when it was a 'fief de reprise'—or altered its character, the vassal had been in a position to impose his own terms on an impoverished lord. The phenomenon of 'free fiefs' is in any case, with but rare exceptions, found only in the south of France and the kingdom of Burgundy-Arles.

Yet another type of fief was the 'fief de haubert', *feodum loricae*, so called from the long coat of mail (hauberk) which was an essential part of the defensive equipment of a knight between the late eleventh and thirteenth centuries. In those parts of France where the expression is found, and particularly in Normandy, it was used in reference to a fief held by a vassal whose duty it was to serve with full equipment, including such a coat of mail. In England, on the other hand, it seems to have been synonymous with a knight's fee, *feodum militis,* and this wider use is also found in some parts of France. In Germany we hear of fiefs described as *beneficium castrense* or *beneficium castellanum* (Germ. *Burglehen*), which were held by vassals who owed the service of castle-guard in their lord's castles.

Such terms as *vavassoria, feodum* or *terra vavassoris,* the fief or the land of a vavasour, are as imprecise in their meaning as the form vavasour itself. We have seen already that this word had in early times meant a sub-vassal, and usually a sub-vassal of low social rank: in northern Italy a sub-vassal of the crown, in the greater part of France a vassal who was only required to serve with a limited amount of equipment, in Normandy and in post-conquest England a free man, perhaps not necessarily a vassal at all, from whom military service was due. Even in twelfth-century England the word *vavassoria* often meant no more than the small fee of a knight of only middle rank.

The word *vavassoria,* at any rate in Normandy and often in England, cannot therefore be necessarily regarded as signifying a

---

[1] Eastern Languedoc: Germain, *op. cit.,* no. 556 (of 1187); Dauphiné (where the name 'franc fief' is not always found): U. Chevalier, *op. cit.,* nos. 9 and 29 (of 1168 and 1220); Forez: G. Guichard, Comte de Neufbourg, E. Perroy and J. E. Dufour, *Chartes de Forez,* iii (Mâcon, 1934), nos. 303–4 (of c. 1180).

fief in the sense in which we understand the word, i.e. a tenement which formed the endowment of a vassal. The same is true of the serjeanty (Lat. *serjanteria*; Fr. *sergenterie*; Germ. *Dienstlehen*) Although these often are described as *feodum* in the texts, no doubt as the result of a process in which the habit of imitation and the hope of assimilating them to tenures of greater social consequence played a part, they were in fact tenements which had originally been intended to provide the maintenance of manorial and domestic servants, of serf-knights (*servientes, ministeriales*) and so on. But there can be no doubt that by the twelfth century many French serjeanties must be regarded as, and had in fact become, true fiefs. The same is true in England, though here lands held in serjeanty (*per serjenteriam*) were regarded as inferior to true knight's fees. In Germany the same was probably the case in practice for the fiefs (*Dienstlehen*) of *ministeriales*, though the *Sachsenspiegel*, in the early thirteenth century, still refuses to regard them as true fiefs (*echte Lehen*).[1] For most men of the time, however, these may have been indeed inferior categories of fiefs, but fiefs they certainly were. The essential criterion in the eyes of men of the twelfth and thirteenth centuries, with the exception perhaps of the feudal lawyers, must have been whether or not the tenement was held by a person living as a knight and did not, at least normally, involve the payment of a rent in money.

Some types of fief owed their character to the circumstances of their creation. One of the most important was the 'fief de reprise' (Lat. *feudum oblatum*; Germ. *aufgetragenes Lehen*), which was undoubtedly very common between the ninth and twelfth centuries. Such a fief was as a rule created in the following fashion: the owner of an allod abandoned this by the process known as *werpitio*, the transfer of his rights over it to another person by a solemn formal act; then having become vassal to the latter—if indeed he was not one already—by swearing an oath of fealty and doing homage to him, he received back as a fief the property which he had just given up. The reasons for such a proceeding might be very various; one might be compelled to give up one's allod under pressure, or one might surrender it willingly to another person in order to obtain his protection, or one might have agreed to sell it on condition that one received it back as a fief.

[1] *Lehnrecht*, 63. 1 (ed. K. A. Eckhardt, 2d edit., pp. 81–82).

An excellent example of this last type of transaction is given by the proceedings which determined the status of the county of Hainault after Robert the Frisian had usurped the county of Flanders in 1071. We are told that Richilda, the countess of Flanders and Hainault, widow of the last count Baldwin VI and mother of Arnulf III (who had been killed during the struggle) and of the young Baldwin II of Hainault, who was claimant to the throne of Flanders, 'sold all her allods in Hainault to the bishop of Liége in order that with the purchase money she might hire mercenaries to use against Robert. Bishop Theoduin gladly received these great allods, which such an honour made illustrious, and granted them back to Richilda and her son Baldwin to be held as a liege fief from him, and he paid a very great sum for them' (*allodia sua omnia in Hanonia sita episcopo Leodiensi . . . danda obtulit, ut . . . accepta ab eo pecunia, stipendiarios . . . contra . . . Robertum conduceret. Theoduinus autem episcopus . . . tanta allodia tanto honore insignita gratanter suscepit, que quidem ipsi Richeldi et ejus filio Balduino in feodo ligio tenenda concessit, maximamque pecuniam proinde eis tribuit*). It was even stipulated a little later that 'if the count should acquire some allod in the county of Hainault he should hold it also of the bishop of Liége with the rest of his fief' (*si aliquod allodium intra terminos sui comitatus . . . sibi in proprietatem acquisierit ipse statim ea ab episcopo Leodiensi cum alio feodo suo tenet*). All the count's allodial possessions were thus, with his own consent, converted into a 'fief de reprise'.[1] Another interesting case is that of the allods of the count of Looz, which in 1203 were converted by him into 'fiefs de reprise' held of the bishop of Liége, from whom he already held his comital authority, his *comitatus*, in fief since before 1190. Hugh of Pierrepont, bishop of Liége, describes the proceeding as follows: 'Be it known to all that Louis count of Looz, who was our liege vassal, knowing us to be well disposed towards him, has given to our church the castle of Montenaken with the land attached to it, and likewise the castle of Brustem with the land attached to it, and also the allod of Hasselt with the fortress which stands there and all the land attached to it, and the whole allod of Tessenderloo and the allod and castle of Lummen; the count has placed all these in our hands and

[1] Gislebert, *Chronique*, cc. 8, 9 (pp. 11, 14).

received them back as fiefs from us.' (*Notum sit . . . quod Lodo-wicus, comes de Los . . . quia et nos cuius erat ipse homo legius . . . propitios . . . senserat, ecclesie nostre contradidit castrum de Montegni cum omni territorio . . . similiter et castrum de Brusteime cum omni . . . territorio suo . . . et allodium etiam de Halud cum munitione eius cum omni etiam territorio suo . . . et totum allodium de Tessendrelos . . . et allodium et castrum de Luman . . . ipse comes in manus nostras reportavit; et hec omnia supradicta in feodum recepit a nobis.*)[1] Finally, here is an example from a famous literary text of the eleventh century, the *Chanson de Roland*: Marsile's offer made to Charlemagne and interpreted by Ganilo:

> *Quant ço vos mandet li reis Marsiliun*
> *Qu'il devendrat jointes ses mains tis hom*
> *Et tute Espaigne tendrat par vostre dun.*[2]

If the offer had been accepted, Spain would have become what a feudal lawyer would term a 'fief de reprise'.

Closely related to the process by which a 'fief de reprise' was created (Germ. *Lehensauftragung*) was the practice by which a vassal resigned his fief to his lord, who thereupon invested another person with it, the original holder then becoming the vassal of the latter to hold the fief of him. Such an arrangement might be convenient in contracts in which three parties were involved: political agreements, arrangements involving monetary transactions, and so on. We have already seen something of the dispositions made by the Countess Richilda of Hainault with regard to her allodial property in 1071. So far as her late husband's fiefs—mainly the county of Hainault and the offices of lay abbot and advocate of St. Waudru's of Mons (*abbatiam et advocatiam Montensis ecclesie et justiciam comitatus Hanoniensis*)—were concerned, she surrendered them (*omnia feoda que comes Hanoniensis ab eo tenebat*) to the king. Henry IV gave them to the church of Liége, and Duke Godfrey the Hunchback of Lower Lotharingia 'received them from the bishop as a benefice and became his vassal' (*miles*

[1] E. Poncelet, *Actes des princes-évêques de Liége, Hugues de Pierrepont* (Brussels, 1946), no. 11, pp. 10–11.
[2] Verses 222–4. *La chanson de Roland publiée d'après le manuscrit d'Oxford et traduite par J. Bédier* (Paris, 1922), p. 18.

effectus est domni episcopi . . . accepto ab eo hoc beneficio).
Finally Richilda, 'having become a vassal of the duke, received
this benefice in her turn from him' (*ducis effecta, hoc idem accepit a duce beneficium*). These various proceedings clearly pre-
suppose payments made by the bishop of Liége to the king as well
as to Richilda.[1] From being a direct vassal of the king, the count
of Hainault had become his sub-sub-vassal; even after the death
of Godfrey without an heir he was still left only a sub-vassal again.
When Godfrey died leaving no male heir, the count became the
vassal of the Church of Liége.

Another example, French this time but dating likewise from the
eleventh century, may perhaps be given. The county of Vendôme
was held of the crown, and the young Count Burchard and his
mother, Countess Adela, resigned it to King Henry I. Thereupon
'Count Geoffrey (i.e. the count of Anjou, Geoffrey Martel) received it in fief of the king, on condition that the mother and her
son (i.e. Adela and Burchard) should hold it of him; and so it
was done' (*Eo quidem pacto Gaufredus comes a rege percepit
honorem quatenus et mater et puer ejus ab eo tenerent quod et
factum est).*[2]

Another type of fief characterized by the circumstances of its
creation was a fief which served as a pledge. It was frequently
created, especially during the later centuries of the Middle Ages,
when a debtor, in order to give his creditor an estate producing
an income as a pledge, enfeoffed him with a piece of property. A
fief created in this fashion was known in France as an *engagère*,
in Germany as a *Pfandlehen*. It might be created either by the
enfeoffment of an allod or by sub-enfeoffment of a fief which the
debtor himself held, though in the latter case the consent of the
lord from whom the fief was held in the first place would as a
rule be necessary. Gislebert of Mons provides us with an excellent example of the way such a fief was created in his account of
the conflict in 1188 between Henry the Blind, count of Namur,
and Count Baldwin V of Hainault. Henry the Blind approached
the young duke of Brabant, Henry I, who had been associated

---

[1] Gislebert, *Chronique*, c. 8 (p. 12); notice of the enfeoffment, ed. Weiland in M.G.H., *Constitutiones*, i, no. 441 (p. 650).

[2] Métais, *Cartulaire de la Trinité de Vendôme*, no. 6.

with his father Godfrey III, in order to borrow some money. We are told that 'the count of Namur gave to the young duke all the country situated on this side (i.e. on the west bank) of the Meuse and the Sambre, both fiefs and allods, to be held as a pledge, in return for a sum of 5000 marks' (*Ibique duci juniori comes Namurcensis . . . totam terram suam ex hac parte Mose et Sambre vadio tenendam concessit, tam in feodis quam in allodiis pro 5 milibus marcis*).[1] If the lord, as debtor, paid his debts to his creditor who had become his vassal, the latter had to surrender his fief to him.

IV. Investiture

The legal conceptions of the early Middle Ages required, as we have seen, the performance of some corporeal act in order to bring about the creation or the transfer of what we would call a property right. This corporeal act was nearly always of a symbolic character. In the case of enfeoffment, the symbolic act was known as investiture (Lat. *vestitura* or *investitura*; Fr. *investiture*; Germ. *Lehnung*). It followed the oath of fealty and the act of homage, generally at once. Only in northern Italy, where homage, as we have seen, was quite exceptional, did investiture precede the taking of the oath of fealty.[2]

We have already seen how Galbert of Bruges describes the manner in which the vassals of the murdered count of Flanders, Charles the Good, constituted themselves vassals of William Clito in 1127. The account continues as follows: 'Then, with the wand which he held in his hand, the count gave investiture to all those who had done homage to him and promised him their fealty and taken an oath on it' (*Deinde virgula, quam manu consul tenebat, investituras donavit eis omnibus, qui hoc pacto securitatem et hominium simulque juramentum fecerunt*).[3] Another vivid picture of the ceremony of investiture is given in the twelfth-century *Chanson des Saisnes*, by Jean Bodel of Arras, which describes how Charlemagne, after receiving fealty and homage from Bérard of Montdidier and giving him the *osculum*, invests him with his fiefs by handing him a standard:

[1] *Chronique*, c. 148 (p. 228).
[2] *Constitutiones Feudorum*, Antiqua, viii. 9 (ed. Lehmann, p. 120).
[3] Galbert of Bruges, *Histoire*, c. 56 (p. 89); see above, p. 71.

Berɜrs de Monsdidier devant Karle est venuz;
A ses piez s'agenoille, s' est ses hom devenuz;
L'amperes le baise, si l'a' relevé suz;
Par une blanche ansaigne, li est ses fiez renduz.[1]

The rite of investiture consisted in the handing over by the lord of some symbolic object, representing either the action of vesting or the object vested (Germ. *Handlungssymbol* or *Gegenstands-symbol*). In the first case, the object was intended to symbolize the act of concession which was taking place, and the lord retained the object employed, which might be a sceptre, wand, ring, knife, glove, etc.; when the object was one of little value, as for example a knife, it might be formally broken after the ceremony. The count of Flanders in 1127 used his wand in the case of all the investitures and, since we must assume that he retained it, it can be regarded as a symbol of the act of concession. In the second case, the object remained in the vassal's hand and symbolized the fief itself. It might be a corn-stalk, a piece of earth or turf, a lance, a banner or banners, a pastoral staff in the case of the investiture of imperial bishops in Germany and Italy before the Concordat of Worms, and so on. When Henry II of Germany enfeoffed his brother-in-law Henry of Luxemburg with the duchy of Bavaria at Regensburg in 1004, the chronicler Thietmar of Merseburg relates that 'he conferred the duchy of Bavaria on his vassal and brother-in-law Henry with a banner' (*militi suimet generoque Heinrico . . . cum . . . hasta signifera ducatum dedit*).[2]

By the ceremony of investiture the vassal was 'vested' with the fief; it conferred on the vassal the seisin (Lat. *saisina*, sometimes *tenura*; Fr. *saisine* or *tenure*; Germ. *Gewere*; Dutch *weer*) of the fief, or at least the seisin of it in his capacity of vassal. In other words, from the moment at which he was invested with the fief and by reason of the fact of this investiture, the vassal had acquired a right in the fief, and this right was legally protected against invasion from any quarter. The protection accorded by seisin suggested a comparison with the 'possession' of Roman law; in fact, one of the consequences of the revival of Roman law in western Europe in

---

[1] *Jean Bodels Saxenlied* (ed. F. Menzel and E. Stengel, Marburg, 1906), iii. 1151 ff.
[2] *Chronicon*, vi. 3 (ed. R. Holtzmann, p. 276).

the twelfth century was to bring about, first in Italy[1] and later in France and elsewhere, a contamination of the idea of seisin by that of possession, particularly in so far as fiefs were concerned. A treatise of feudal law from fourteenth-century Flanders speaks regularly of *possessien* when referring to fiefs.[2]

V. Written Records

Sometimes the parties drew up a written record not only of the oath of fealty and the act of homage but also of the enfeoffment. Such records are met with early and in all countries in the form of *noticiae* and charters. A *noticia* of this type, of an unusually detailed character, is that which describes how in 1143 Count Thibaud II of Blois and Troyes (Champagne) did homage *in marchia* to Duke Eudes II of Burgundy at Augustines, and recognized that he held in fief of the later the abbey of Saint-Germain of Auxerre and a number of estates and castles, as well as the county and town of Troyes (*Notum sit . . . quod comes Theobaldus Blesiensium Odoni duci Burgundie apud Augustinam fecit hominium et cognovit quatinus abbatia Sancti Germani Autissiodorensis de feodo ducis erat et tenebat, et . . .*).

Written documents are not very frequent before the thirteenth century, save in southern France and the kingdom of Burgundy-Arles, but from the thirteenth century onwards they become more numerous in the whole of France, as well as in England and the Low Countries. Sometimes the lord would give his vassal a charter attesting the completion of the acts of fealty and homage and the investiture of the fief. On other occasions the vassal might draw up a charter declaring that these ceremonies had been accomplished and that he had received seisin of the fief[3]; this would be handed to the lord and would serve him as a kind of title deed, which was known in French as *aveu*. In such cases the vassal often

[1] *Consuetudines Feudorum*, viii. 3, 12 and *passim* (ed. Lehmann, pp. 115–16, 123 and *passim*).

[2] *Leenboek van Vlaenderen*, c. 9, ed. L. Gilliodts van Severen in *Coutumes du Bourg de Bruges*, iii (Brussels, 1885), p. 210.

[3] Longnon, *Documents*, i, Chartes, no. 1 (p. 466); charter of Baldwin IX (VI) of Flanders (and Hainault) delivered to Philip Augustus in 1196, in F. Lot, *Fidèles ou Vassaux?* (Paris, 1904), pp. 255–7; charter of Ferrand of Portugal, count of Flanders and Hainault, delivered to the same king in 1212, in C. Duvivier, *La querelle des d'Avesnes et des Dampierre*, ii (Brussels, 1894), Pièces justificatives, no. 7 (pp. 13–14). See above, p. 80 and n. 3.

undertook to make what was known as an *ostensio feodi*, an indication on the spot of what he regarded as forming part of his fief. This *monstrée de fief* or *montrée de la terre* might be replaced by a written description known as a 'dénombrement'. Here, by way of example, is the analysis of an *aveu* of 1228 with the undertaking to provide a 'dénombrement': 'Messire J. d'Estenville has done homage to William, bishop of Paris, for what he holds of him near Sainte-Croix, at Saint-Denis, and he undertakes to provide within forty days to the said bishop a list in writing of what these things are' (*Dominus J. de Estenville fecit homagium Willelmo, Parisiensi episcopo, de hiis que tenet de eo prope Sanctam Crucem, apud Sanctum Dionisium et infra XL dies debet tradere in scriptis dicto episcopo que sunt illa*).[1] In England, however, similar records are rare, and the same is true of Germany, at least up to the end of the Middle Ages.

VI. *Renunciation of Fiefs*

The renunciation of a fief, which where necessary would be preceded by a renunciation of fealty (*démission de foi*), was a ceremony modelled on the act of investiture itself. The man renouncing the fief formally 'divested' himself of it between the hands of the lord. This was done by an act corresponding to that which had been used to 'vest' him with the fief, and was known as *werpitio* (Fr. *déguerpissement*). The vassal would hand the lord an object symbolizing the act of enfeoffment or the fief itself; in the latter case at least, it would generally be the same as that which had been used for the original investiture. In the last quarter of the eleventh century, we find a reference in the 'gestes' of Bishop Lietbert of Cambrai to the legal formalities accompanying the renunciation of a fief. The bishop refused to lift the excommunication which he had pronounced against the rebel châtelain Hugh of Oisy, 'unless he first consents to renounce with his own hands—*werpire*, to use the common expression—every fief which he holds within the city of Cambrai' (*nisi prius dimissionem manu propria, quod et vulgo werpire dicitur, faceret ex omni beneficio quod infra ambitum Cameracae civitatis habebat*).[2]

[1] B. Guérard, *Cartulaire de l'église Notre-Dame de Paris*, i (Paris, 1850) no. 174, p. 148.
[2] *Gesta Lietberti episcopi Cameracensis*, c. 20 (ed. L. C. Bethmann in *M.G.H., SS.*, vii. 495).

VII. Mouvance

It was considered from early times that some sort of connection continued to exist between a land or a right granted in fief and the allod or fief from which it had been detached. This was usually expressed by saying that the land or right 'descended' (*descendere*), or more frequently that it 'moved' (*movere*), from this allod or fief. Hainault charters of 1200 and 1229, for example, can write *de cuius feodo ista descendunt*, 'of whose fief these properties descend', and of a *decima que de meo movebat feodo*, 'a tithe which "moved" from my fief'.[1] The relationship was described in French as 'mouvance', and the word was used also to describe the relationship existing between the fief which had been granted and the lord granting it. French feudal lawyers described, not very happily perhaps, the fief which was granted as the 'fief servant' and the allod or fief from which it was detached as the 'fief dominant'.

'Mouvance' might be used, however, to describe connections of a purely artificial character. Sometimes fiefs were attached to lands, to castles, to seigneuries or later to administrative units for reasons which were simply military or administrative. This was the case, for example, with the fiefs attached in twelfth century Hainault to the count's castles of Mons and Valenciennes for no other reason than that it was at these castles that the vassals holding the fiefs owed their duty of castle-guard. In the early thirteenth century many fiefs held of the king of France were attached in' similar fashion to his *châtellenies*, *prévôtés* or *bailliages*.[2]

VIII. The Rights of Lord and Vassal over the Fief

One of the most fundamental problems involved in the study of the fief is that of the nature of the rights which the lord and the vassal possessed over it. It can most easily be approached by regarding fiefs as falling into two categories, the differences between which can be best described from the point of view of the lord from whom they were held.

[1] Unpublished documents cited by Didier, *Droit des fiefs*, p. 107, n. 1 and 2.

[2] Gislebert of Mons, *Chronique*, cc. 41, 130 (ed. Vanderkindere, pp. 74, 196); charter of Philip Augustus of 1205 for Dreu, son of the constable Dreu de Mello, in *Recueil des actes de Philippe-Auguste*, II, ed. Petit-Dutaillis and Monicat, no. 885, pp. 473–474 (also in Bouquet, *Recueil*, xvii. 59). *Scripta de feodis*, nos. 510 (of 1204/12), 178 ff., 184 ff., 283 (of 1220), in *ibid.*, 714–15, 646 ff., 647 ff., 668.

The first category was that of fiefs which were held directly of lords whose allodial property they were. This category existed in every country. In England, however, as a result of the Conquest, the king had become in law the only allodist, so that this type of holding was confined to the tenants-in-chief (*tenentes in capite*) who were direct vassals of the Crown. In many parts of France, lay allodial property became rare at an early date. In Normandy it had actually disappeared by the late eleventh century, and the same seems to have been the case in Brittany in the twelfth century; elsewhere this result had not yet come about by the end of the period with which we are concerned, but already in the thirteenth century the rule of 'nulle terre sans seigneur', which excluded the presumption and sometimes even the possibility of allodial property, was recognized in many regions.[1] This tendency was in part the consequence of a state of society which strongly favoured the relationship of vassalage, but it was in part also the result of a policy followed systematically by the monarchy, by some of the territorial princes, and by many important secular and ecclesiastical lords. In Germany, the steady movement towards feudalization in the twelfth century, largely promoted by the Hohenstaufen, who hoped to base their authority on a framework of feudal relationships, led to a similar but not identical result. Lay allodial property became steadily less and less common, so that there was even a tendency to assimilate the status of the allod to that of the fief by describing it as a *Sonnenlehen* (Lat. *feodum solis*), a 'fief held of the sun', but neither the rule of 'nulle terre sans seigneur' nor anything approaching it was ever generally recognized. Allodial property remained in existence in all parts of Germany, and in some regions—Frisia, Saxony, Thuringia—was even of considerable importance. It also survived in Upper and Lower Lotharingia and in some parts of the kingdom of Burgundy-Arles: in Franche-Comté, in Lyonnais, Dauphiné and Provence, and in what is today Switzerland. Parts of France—Flanders, some regions of eastern France, and a great part of the south (Bordelais and Bazadais, Comminges, Languedoc, Auvergne, Forez, Nivernais) must also be reckoned among the areas where allodial property managed to

[1] For the region of Beauvais, see Beaumanoir, *Coutumes*, ed. Salmon, i, no. 688, p. 349.

maintain itself, though in some of them it showed a marked tendency to decline from the thirteenth century onwards.

A vassal, then, might hold his fief of an allodial proprietor, whether king, layman or church; in the last case it was often called frankalmoign (Lat. *franca* or *libera elemosyna*; Fr. *franche aumône*), which in France and in neighbouring regions was a privileged form of ecclesiastical allod. It was this type of property which was in question, for example, in a charter of 1060 drawn up with regard to the gift of an allod to the abbey of Gellone by Peter, son of Almeras d'Anduse; William of Montpellier and Peter, son of Gaucelin de Lunel, held this allod as a fief (*et hoc alodem tenent ad fevum Willelmus de Montepistillario et Petrus, filius Gaucelini de Lunello*). Next to this evidence from Languedoc, we may quote an instance from Flanders: an entry of 1164 in the *Liber Traditionum* of the abbey of St. Peter of Ghent, which declares that Simon, son of Baldwin of Landskouter, got 3-½ bonniers of his own allodial land at Musehole back from Dirk of Alvana, who had up till then held them of him as a fief, and that he then gave them in alms to the church for the upkeep of the altar of St. Peter (*quidam Symon, filius Balduini de Landeskoutre, 3½ bunaria terre allodii in Musehole, a Theodorico de Alvana, qui eandem terram de se actenus tenebat in feodo, recepit et ad altare Sancti Petri in elemosina optulit ecclesie*).[1]

At the beginning of the period which we are studying, there could be no doubt of the nature of the rights enjoyed by the two parties over the fief. The lord was invested with rights which were of the same nature as the bare ownership envisaged in Roman law, while the vassal had rights corresponding to the Roman idea of usufruct and which were still, as in earlier centuries, often described as *ususfructus* in the texts. There was consequently a division of ownership between the parties. But the fact that it was the vassal who was the effective occupier of the fief permitted him to strengthen and extend his real right, while that of the lord tended correspondingly to decline. This development had already begun in the ninth century, but it gathered force in the course of the centuries following, since the vassals were in a position to

[1] Devic and Vaissete, *op. cit.*, ed. Privat,V., no. 258, III; *Liber traditionum Sancti Petri Blandiniensis*, ed. A. Fayen (Ghent, 1906), no. 173, p. 175.

exercise constant pressure on their lords owing to the fact that their services were required for the political or military enterprises in which their lords were engaged. Already in the eleventh century the rights of a vassal over his fief had extended far beyond those allowed by the Roman conception of usufruct. The uncertain terminology employed in acts of the twelfth and thirteenth centuries to describe the rights respectively enjoyed by lord and vassal is characteristic of a period of transition. We hear of the lord's *dominium*, his *dominium feodale*, his *supremum dominium*, his *possessio*, and of the vassal's *jus hereditarium*, his *proprietas*, his *dominatio*. When in the twelfth century the study of Roman law revived in the West, and attempts were made to arrive at a clear definition of the rights of the two parties, the romanists attempted to fit them into the framework of Roman legal ideas. After a good deal of groping and uncertainty, they finally, in the thirteenth century, reached a doctrine based on a somewhat incorrect interpretation of the laws of Roman landed property. Since it was impossible for them to admit that a vassal could hold only a real right over a thing belonging to another, a *ius in re aliena*, they preferred to allow a deeper division of the right of property and invented the doctrine of divided *dominium*. The lord who had allodial rights over the property retained over it the *dominium directum*, which modern scholars sometimes call 'eminent domain,' while the vassal acquired the *dominium utile*, the useful ownership. This conception appears already in the *Glossa Ordinaria* of the illustrious glossator Accursius of Bologna towards the middle of the thirteenth century. It began to be applied in France in the same century. It is possible that this distinction was used in practice in France during the 13th century, before the theory had been elaborated. It later passed to Germany by way of Lotharingia.[1]

The second category was that of fiefs held by a vassal of a lord who himself held them in fief of the allodial proprietor; they were consequently subfiefs. The real right of the vassal was consequently only a fraction of his immediate lord's right, which was in turn derived from the division of a real right which itself had been separated from the initial property right of the allodial proprietor. When the doctrine of divided *dominium* was formu-

[1] Charter of the abbot of Kornelimünster, a° 1280, State Archives, Namur, "Chartes des comtes de Namur," nr. 126 (unpublished).

lated, the lawyers evinced a good deal of uncertainty regarding the attribution of the *dominium* as between the mesne lord and his sub-vassal. There were some who argued in favour of the multiplicity and the relativity of both 'direct' and 'useful' *dominia*, but the view generally accepted in France was that the *dominium directum* belonged exclusively to the lord whose allodial property the fief had originally been, while the vassals and sub-vassals shared only in the *dominium utile*.

IX. *Dealings with Fiefs*

The vassal had originally only the *ius utendi et fruendi*, the right of using and enjoying the fief and appropriating its produce. He was not entitled to alter its substance, to divide it up, to 'abridge' it by diminishing its value, or to alienate it; in short, he did not possess the *ius abutendi*, the right of disposing of it. But in the course of the period with which we are now dealing, the vassal succeeded in acquiring most of these rights over his fief, apart from that of 'abridging' it, a privilege which generally was denied him.

X. *The Heritability of Fiefs*

We have already seen how the benefice, originally a form of life tenure, had begun to assume an hereditary character, at least in the direct male line, by the end of the ninth century. This was particularly the case in France and Italy. In France, heritability became increasingly common during the tenth and eleventh centuries, until it was in the end the normal practice, especially in the case of the more important fiefs. Two examples may be given to indicate the spread of the practice. The first is one of collateral succession, a circumstance in which the lord still retained a certain freedom of action at the beginning of the eleventh century. A knight named Hamelin asked (*c.* 1028) Count Fulk Nerra of Anjou to be permitted to succeed to a fief held in turn from the count by his father Goscelin of Rennes and his brother Giroire of Beaupreau. The count, to whom he had given offence, refused (. . . *postulans in honore paterno succedere, vix hoc assequi potuit a Fulcone inclito comite*), but ended by giving way through the intervention of his wife, whom Hamelin had won over to his side by presenting her with a church.[1] The second case is that of

[1] P. Marchegay, *Cartulaire de l'abbaye du Ronceray d'Angers* (Angers. 1854), no. 125.

a fief which had been explicitly granted for life. In the tenth century, Duke Hugh the Great had deprived the abbey of Saint-Germain-des-Prés of the estate of Combs-la-Ville (Seine-et-Oise), and had given it as a fief to his vassal Count Hilduin, while limiting the enfeoffment *expressis verbis* to the life of the tenant. On Hilduin's death, Hugh the Great gave it to his own son Hugh Capet, and it passed in turn to the latter's son Robert the Pious, who restored it to Saint-Germain. Later, at the request of Hilduin's nephew Manasses, Henry I again deprived the abbey of the estate and gave it as a fief to Manasses for his life. When Manasses died, the king gave it back again to Saint-Germain, but Manasses' son Eudes considered that he had an hereditary claim to it, and induced Philip I to deprive the abbey of it again and enfeoff him with it, though on condition that the abbey should recover it on his death. This last stipulation, however, was never executed.[1] Enfeoffments of this sort for life became progressively rarer in France after the end of the eleventh century, though they never entirely disappeared; money fiefs in particular were often granted for life. These observations hold good also for Lotharingia.

The evolution in Germany was a much slower one. There are relatively numerous examples, in the ninth and tenth centuries, of the son of a vassal succeeding to his father, but by the early eleventh century the custom had not become as general as it was in France, particularly in the lower ranks of the social hierarchy. Inheritance could not yet be considered something to which one was entitled, even in the case of direct succession from father to son. In a letter of a monk of Tegernsee there is a reference to the *beneficium* of a vassal *paterno quidem iure . . . si dici fas est, sibi in hereditatem collatum*, 'a fief which this vassal has inherited from his father, if one may put it thus'.[2] The development of heritability was greatly accelerated in the first half of the century by the policy pursued by Conrad II. In northern Italy, he issued a constitution which established the rule that for the fiefs of both tenants-in-chief and vavasours, i.e. the sub-vassals of the crown, a son or a brother might inherit. In Germany a similar rule was applied. As his biographer Wipo puts it, 'he assured himself the loyal support of the vassals by refusing to allow them

[1] M. Prou, *Actes de Philippe I* (Paris, 1908), no. 13 (of 1061), pp. 38–41.

[2] *Die Tegernseer Briefsammlung*, ed. K. Strecker, no. 116, pp. 124–5.

to be deprived of fiefs which their parents had formerly held' (*Militum vero animos in hoc multum attraxit quod antiqua beneficia parentum nemini posterorum auferri sustinuit*).[1] But in the twelfth and even in the thirteenth century there was still a certain number of fiefs for life in Germany, and even in the second half of the twelfth century the succession of collaterals was regarded as a favour and not a right.

In England, the heritability of fiefs was far from being generally established in the period immediately following the Norman Conquest. The two earliest charters of enfeoffment which we possess, dating from 1066/87 and 1085, seem to have contemplated nothing more than grants for life, though it is worth noting that in both cases the fiefs did in fact become hereditary.[2] In the twelfth century, however, heritability must be regarded as a characteristic feature of the English fief.

The heritability of the fief was, however, an heritability of a quite particular character. Since the fief was intended to provide the vassal with the means of furnishing the services due from him, its grant should naturally have come to an end when the vassal died. The heir could not expect to inherit it with the same fullness of title as he could his allodial property, for he had to carry out the ceremonies of fealty and homage and investiture before he could claim seisin. He had a claim to investiture, however, on condition that he took an oath of fealty and did homage, and the opportunity of performing these acts could not be denied him. What occurred in practice was that an heir immediately occupied a fief left vacant by the predecessor from whom he hoped to inherit, and then addressed his request to the lord for investiture. This action had to be taken within a certain time-limit determined by local custom, and an heir who failed to comply with it was held to have committed a serious fault, which in France was known as 'défaute d'homme' (*defectus hominis*).[3] Since the death of a vassal brought the enfeoffment

[1] *Constitutiones*, i, no. 45 (pp. 90–1) of 1037, and Wipo, *Gesta Chuonradi*, c. 6 (p. 28).

[2] D. C. Douglas, 'A charter of enfeoffment . . .', *E.H.R.*, xlii (1927), p. 247; V. H. Galbraith, 'An episcopal land-grant of 1085', *ibid.*, xliv (1929), pp. 371–2.

[3] *Établissements de Saint Louis*, ii. 19 (ed. Viollet, ii. 396); Beaumanoir, *Coutumes*, i, no. 78 (ed. Salmon, p. 51).

to an end, the legal rights of the lord over the fief revived in their entirety, and if he was the allodist the tenant's *dominium utile*, at least in theory, reverted to the lord, and merged with the *dominium directum*. Originally, therefore, it was argued that in the lapse of time between the death of the *de cujus* and the investiture of the new vassal the latter did not have seisin of the fief. But with the passing of time this view was weakened by the constant endeavours of vassals to improve their position and 'patrimonialize' their fiefs, and more than one custom came into existence to nullify the claims of the lord desiring vacancies.

A good example of a demand for admission to homage, fealty and investiture as put forward to his lord by the heir of a fief is provided by the following extract from a *noticia* of 1237 from the Tyrol. It describes how Cunz Fafe von Griffenstein demanded the investiture of a fief which his late father had held of the count of Eppan. 'He requested the investiture of a fief of the Lord Egeno, count of Eppan, for himself and from the latter, which fief the late Lord Morhard had formerly held of him and previously of the late Count Ulrich, and he gave his hands to him and declared himself ready to do homage' (*peciit . . . investitura feudi unius a domino Egenoni, comiti de Epiano pro se et ab eo . . . de quoddam feudo, quod quondam dominus Morhardus . . . habebat ab eo . . . et a condam domino Ulrico comite, et porrexit ei manus suas et volebat sibi facere minuitatem*).[1]

XI. Reliefs

At the beginning of the period with which we are dealing, and consequently at a time when the heritability of fiefs had not yet become an established custom, the lord could impose his conditions before admitting the heir of a vassal to fealty and homage and investing him with the fief. He could, in other words, demand some recompense in return for his consent. The payment which the lord exacted on this account is called in the texts *relevium*, 'relief' (Fr. *relief*, from which came the medieval Flemish *verlief*[2]; Germ. *Lehnware*); it was the sum paid by the heir, the

[1] H. Loersch, R. Schroeder, L. Perels, *Urkunden zur Geschichte des deutschen Rechtes* (3rd ed., Bonn, 1912), no. 122.

[2] *Leenboek van Vlaenderen*, c. 4 (p. 209). The usual term is *verheffings-recht*.

candidate for vassalage, for authorization to take up seisin of the fief which had, symbolically speaking, fallen to the ground in consequence of the death of the former holder. One meets also the word 'redemption' (Lat. *rachetum*[1]; Fr. *rachat*), and in south-western France and the region of Toulouse a number of expressions which have essentially the same signification (Lat. *adcaptatio, reacaptatio, reiracapta, retroacaptis*; Fr. *acapte, arrière-acapte*.)[2] A Flemish charter of the twelfth century gives both the Latin and an equivalent vernacular term when it speaks of *emptionem que vulgo dicitur cop*; the last word, which is possibly misspelt, corresponds to the modern Dutch 'koop', meaning a purchase.[3] In the fourteenth century Jacques d'Ableiges, the compiler of the Parisian custumal which is most inappropriately known as the *Grand Coutumier de France*, gives an explanation of reliefs which fully justifies this second series of terms: 'And yet it seems, according to common belief, that we may say that on the death of a vassal the fief falls and lies in such manner that it can be possessed by neither overlord nor heir; it can only be taken up by the immediate lord. And it is from the taking up of the fief by the lord and its transference to the heir when the lord accepts him and holds him in his fea¹ that the lord derives the right known as "relief", or "rachat" as it is sometimes called, which amounts to a year's revenue of the fief . . . and until the relief is paid the lord enjoys the revenue of the fief as a consequence of "défaute d'homme".' (*Et semble encores selon la commune oppinion, que a plus proprement parler, l'on peult dire que par la mort du vassal le fief chiet et gist par telle manière qu'il ne peult estre possédé ne par le seigneur, ne par l'heritier, fors quant il est relevé par le seigneur direct, et de ce relief que le seigneur faict a*

---

[1] E.g. in the Treaty of Péronne of 1200 between Philip Augustus and count Baldwin IX (VI) of Flanders and Hainault, in *Recueil des Actes de Philippe-Auguste*, II, ed. Petit-Dutaillis and Monicat, no. 621, pp. 167–168, and also in Duvivier, *La querelle des d'Avesnes et des Dampierre*, ii, Pièces justificatives, no. 1, p. 2.

[2] E.g. Douais, *op. cit.*, nos. 98 (of 1133), 260 (of 1128), 335 (n.d.) and 698 (of 1176); Higounet, *op. cit.*, ii, Pièces justificatives, no. 3 (of 1199).

[3] Charter of Thierry of Alsace, count of Flanders, of 1160, in A. Pruvost, *Chronique et cartulaire de l'abbaye de Bergues-Saint-Winnoc*, i (Bruges, 1875), pp. 118–19. Other examples of the use of the Dutch 'koop' in the sense of 'relief' are to be found in K. Stallaert, *Glossarium van verouderde rechtstermen*, i (Leyden, 1890), s.v., pp. 96–7.

*l'heritier en le prenant et laissant en sa foy, il a le droit qui est
appelé relief, que l'on dit aucunes fois rachat, qui vault le revenu
d'ung an . . . En tant longuement que le relief demourera a
faire, le seigneur fera les fruicts siens par défaulte de homme.)*[1]

Originally the figure of the relief was arbitrarily fixed by the
lord or was arranged by negotiation between the two parties. This
is what Louis VI was in a position to do with regard to the new
count of Flanders, William Clito, in 1127, when the men of
Bruges reproached him with having openly demanded and received the sum of a thousand marks for the price and redemption
of the fief (*mille marcas pro pretio et coemptione aperte · sus-
ceperit*).[2] Enormous reliefs were sometimes exacted in the twelfth
and thirteenth centuries for the investiture of the larger fiefs, as
for example the great French territorial principalities, when the
heirs were not in a direct line of succession. Ferrand of Portugal,
for example, had to pay 50,000 pounds in 1212 before he was
admitted to fealty and homage for Flanders and authorized to
marry the heiress Joan.[3] In similar cases high and arbitrarily fixed
reliefs seem to have remained the rule in Germany for important
fiefs held from the Crown. In France, however, certain rules for
calculating reasonable reliefs came to be generally accepted. In the
French 'domain of the Crown,' it was customary at the beginning of
the twelfth century to fix the relief at one year's revenue of the fief,
and this practice spread generally through France. Gislebert of
Mons tells us that at the agreement reached at Péronne in 1192
between Baldwin VII (V) of Flanders (and Hainault) and Philip
Augustus, 'the count contracted to pay to the lord king five thousand marks of pure silver as the relief for Flanders, since it is the
law in France that every vassal shall give to his lord for the relief
of his liege fief as much as the fief is worth to him in a single year'
(*comes 5 milia marchas puri argenti . . . pro relevio terre Flandrie
domino regi pepigit, cum iuris sit . . . in Francia, ut quilibet
homo pro relevio feodi sui ligii tantum det domino suo, quantum*

---

[1] *Le Grand Coutumier de France*, ed. E. Laboulaye and R. Dareste (Paris,
1868), pp. 234–5.
[2] Galbert, *Histoire*, c. 106 (p. 151).
[3] 'Anonymous of Béthune', *Chronique française des rois de France*, ed. L.
Delisle in Bouquet, *Recueil*, xxiv. 564.
[4] Gislebert, *Chronique*, c. 186 (p. 275). See also the text of Jacques
d'Ableiges reproduced on pp. 137–138.

ipsum feodum intra annum valeat).[4] The same reckoning is met with outside France, as in certain Lotharingian principalities, and more particularly in the county of Namur. In England a figure of 100 shillings was generally accepted as that proper for the relief of a knight's fee, at least in the thirteenth century.

In certain cases, though generally only in those of less important fiefs, the relief consisted not of a sum of money but of a horse and the equipment, more or less complete, of a knight. This type of relief (Germ. *Heergewäte* or *Heergeräte*) is to be explained by the fact that often the mount and military equipment of the vassal had in early times been provided by the lord, and that the latter required their restoration, or the restoration of the equivalent, before granting the fief to the vassal's heir. In the county of Hainault and in the Cambrésis, a relief of that type was called *liget*.

The system of reliefs existed everywhere. In France and England, it became an important source of income for lords, and even more so for the crown. It was also important for some principalities in the Low Countries, as for example the counties of Hainault and Namur and in the episcopal principality of Cambrai. As a rule, it was more generally admitted in cases of collateral than in those of direct succession to a fief.

The contract of vassalage had originally been ended by the death of the vassal (Germ. *Mannfall*) or that of the lord (Germ. *Herrenfall*; *Thronfall* when the lord was the king), and in either case the lord would in theory have the right to levy some form of relief. But the levying of a relief on the occasion of a change of lord was less generally maintained. In France, the fiefs where the custom was retained were known as 'fiefs relevant de toutes mains'. One must be careful not to confuse with reliefs another payment which was often made to the chamberlain of the lord on the occasion of the ceremonies of fealty, homage and investiture (Fr. *chambellage*; Dutch *camerlinggeld* or *hoveschede*).

XII. *The Succession to Fiefs*

The object for which a fief was granted provides the explanation for a number of peculiarities in the laws of feudal succession. It is evident that simple division between heirs, which was an invariable custom where allodial property was concerned, would seriously compromise the services due to the lord. In early times, therefore, the fief was regarded as indivisible. This rule was maintained, or in some cases was re-established after temporary departures from it, for a considerable period; it was customary in the case of the duchies and margravates and many of the counties of Germany up to some time in the twelfth century, and for a number of the territorial principalities of France. This meant that it was necessary to assign the inheritance to one of a number of possible heirs, as for example the sons of the deceased vassal, each of whom might feel that he had a claim. Sometimes the choice remained at the arbitrary disposition of the lord, but generally a definite custom sooner or later came into existence. That of male primogeniture was very common; in England it was the invariable practice in the case of fiefs. The justiciar Glanvill, or the author of the treatise on English law generally attributed to him, formulated it as follows in the second half of the twelfth century: 'in the case of a knight or a man holding by military tenure, then according to the law of England the eldest son shall succeed his father in everything' (*si miles fuerit vel per militiam tenens, tunc secundum jus regni Angliae primogenitus filius patri succedit in totum*).[1] The indivisibility of the fief has here been extended, no doubt to the great profit of the crown, to the indivisibility of feudal succession. Other customs preferred the succession of the youngest son, the 'droit de juveigneur', which existed also in England, but only for some non-feudal tenures, under the name of 'Borough-English'.

What one may call the growing 'patrimonialization' of the fief prevented the general triumph of the rule of indivisibility. The more that a vassal came to regard a fief as one of the elements in his personal fortune, the more he regarded it as natural that all his children should benefit from it, as they did from his other family possessions. It was as a consequence of this that the practice of partition eventually established itself over the greater part of France and Germany.

In some regions, customs were evolved which attempted to conciliate the interest of the lord in maintaining the indivisibility of the fief or of the feudal succession with the desire of the vassal to see it divided between his heirs. One of these was the system

[1] Ranulf Glanvill, *Tractatus de legibus et consuetudinibus regni Angliae*, vii. 3 (ed. G. E. Woodbine, New York, 1932, pp. 101–2).

known as 'parage' (*paragium*) sometimes called 'f.érage', which
was very generally practised in northern and western France and
in some of the principalities of the Low Countries. So far as the
lord was concerned, the fief or the feudal succession was not
divided at all; its partition was carried out by a private agreement
between the brothers, the younger ones holding portions of it
from the eldest, with the obligation of assisting him to carry out
his duties as vassal but without necessarily doing homage to him.
It was in Normandy that the system of 'parage' was most fully
developed, for the authority of the dukes was strong enough to
make it work in their interest. In some regions, as that of Paris,
the younger brothers did homage to the eldest. But this system
provided in the long run no satisfactory solution to the problem,
for after two or three generations so many complications always
arose that the services due for the fief were seriously compromised
and the lord in addition saw himself deprived of the reliefs which
· a series of simple partitions would have provided him with. The
result was the general disappearance of 'parage' in fact, if not
in law, in the thirteenth or fourteenth century.

In Germany another system was evolved to attain a similar
end. In order to ensure that partition would not compromise
the services due from the vassal, the practice was invented of collective enfeoffment, enfeoffment *una manu*, which was emplqyed
in various ways with different objects in view. Recourse was had
to it, for example, when in 1076 the Countess Richilda of
Hainault and her son Count Baldwin II became jointly vassals
of the church of Liége, receiving 'all their allods and serfs and
fiefs under a single hand and a single liege homage' (*sub una
manu et uno hominio ligio universa allodia sua et familias et
feoda*).[1] In the case of a feudal succession that could not be
divided, fealty and homage were done by the heirs acting in
unison,· and placing their hands simultaneously between the hands
of their lord. Investiture would likewise be conferred on them
all at the same time. This collective enfeoffment is referred to in
the early thirteenth century by the *Sachsenspiegel*, where it is
called *Belehnung zu gesammter Hand*.[2] But by the end of the

[1] Gislebert, *Chronique*, c. 8 (p. 12).
[2] *Lehnrecht*, 32. 1–3 (ed. K. A. Eckhardt, 2nd ed., pp. 55–6).

century the institution had clearly broken down, for feudal suc-
cessions and even separate fiefs were being partitioned even after
an enfeoffment of this kind.

XIII. The Succession of Minors

It was naturally possible for a fief to descend by hereditary succession to a minor, and various methods were evolved to safe-
guard both the essential interests of the lord in securing the
services due to him and the legitimate interest of the child who
would be unable to carry out these services. Common to all
these methods, which were known as *procuratio, ballia, ballium,
custodia* (Fr. *bail, garde*), was the principle that a person known
as *procurator, bajulus*, or *custos* (Fr. *ballistre* or *gardien*; Germ.
Muntwalt, Momber or *Vormund*) should be appointed to act
on behalf of the heir. Who this person should be was a matter
of local custom. The 'garde seigneuriale' of Normandy and the
practice of wardship in England—there were analogous proced-
ures in Germany—permitted the lord to take over the fief for the
time being and enjoy the usufruct of it, on condition of providing
for the maintenance and education of the heir during his
minority. Another system was represented by that of the 'bail' or
'garde noble' of the Paris region—once again similar systems are
found in Germany—whereby the nearest relative of the heir became a vassal of the lord and was invested with the fief, and saw
to the upkeep and education of the heir during his minority. In
1206, for example, the Marquess Philip of Namur, uncle of the
Countess Joan of Flanders, who was still a minor, and acting on
her behalf, took an oath of fealty and did liege homage to the
king of France, and then entered upon the office of 'baillistre' for
the county of Flanders. Philip Augustus declares in a charter that
Philip of Namur 'has promised us under oath as his liege lord
that he will serve us in good faith and without evil intent and
will help us against all men' (*nobis juravit, tanquam domino suo
ligio, quod nobis serviet bona fide et sine malo ingenio et nos
juvabit contra omnes homines*).[1] Whatever the solution adopted,
the child who was 'en garde' had the right, on attaining his

---

[1] *Recueil des actes de Philippe-Auguste, roi de France*, II no. 952 ed. C. Petit-
Dutaillis and J. Monicat (Paris, 1943), no. 952, pp. 544–5 (also in Duvivier,
Querelle, II, P.J., no. 2, p. 4).

majority, of demanding to be allowed to do homage and take the oath of fealty and so obtain for himself the investiture of the fief.

XIV. Female Succession to Fiefs

If a woman was the heir to a fief, the services due from it might equally be imperilled. There can be no doubt that originally women were entirely excluded from any right of feudal succession, but here again the gradual 'patrimonialization' of fiefs came to affect the issue. Exceptions are already being made to the rule at an early date, for women were inheriting fiefs in France, particularly in the south, at the end of the tenth century. What had first been only an exceptional favour gradually became a general practice and finally a right; it had become universal in France by the twelfth century. The custom came to be tolerated only much later in Germany, and even in the twelfth and thirteenth centuries, when instances of female succession were reasonably numerous, they could not yet be regarded as of right; they were privileged cases, or the result of some particular act of grace. An exception, however, must be made for several principalities in the Low Countries, where the custom was generally admitted at an early date, and it was by way of Lotharingia that the practice of female succession to fiefs entered Germany. When Henry IV ratified the enfeoffment of the county of Hainault by the duke of Lower Lotharingia to the Countess Richilda in 1071, and approved the arrangements which had been agreed upon for the future, he included amongst these articles one which envisaged the possibility of the succession again passing to a woman.[1] It would be rash to affirm that this was the first case in Germany of a fief being granted to a woman, but it seems likely that it was the first case where a fief so important as a county was concerned.

Since the service of the vassal had to be fulfilled and a woman *ob imbecillitatem sexus*, owing to the weakness of her sex, could not furnish it, someone had to assume the duty on her behalf. This representative would be approved by the lord and if necessary would swear fealty and do homage to him. If the woman was married, the representative would be her husband, and it was on this ground that lords claimed to intervene in the marriage

[1] *Constitutiones*, i, no. 441 (p. 650).

of their female vassals or women who could lay claim to the status of vassal. When on the death of Count Hermann of Hainault in 1051, his widow Richilda married Baldwin, the son and heir of the count of Flanders, without first securing the approval of the Emperor Henry III, the latter made of it a *casus belli*. When the statute regulating the status of the county of Hainault was drawn up in 1071, on the occasion of the mediatization of the county to the profit of the church of Liége and the duke of Lower Lotharingia, Henry IV laid it down that a daughter might succeed *si consilio episcopi voluerit uxorari*, 'if she consented to marry in accordance with the wishes of the bishop' whose sub-vassal—or vassal in the event of the duke dying, having no son—she was.[1] This right of intervention on the lord's part might involve compulsion, but more often it was a matter of consent. It existed in France and Germany, but it was in England that it was carried to its fullest development, and was even extended to the marriage of male heirs, to the very great advantage of the Crown.

XV. *Subinfeudation*

Having now dealt with the chief aspects of the transfer of fiefs as a result of the death of one or other party, it is necessary to say a few words on how the transfer of fiefs could be effected between persons still living. So far as subinfeudation is concerned, the question need not detain us long. Originally, no doubt, the subinfeudation of all or part of his fief was certainly not permitted to the vassal without the lord's authorization; it would have been regarded as an 'abridgment of the fief'. But from the eleventh century onwards it seems to have been generally and freely practised in France and Germany without any intervention on the lord's part. The requirement that the consent of the latter was necessary was retained in the case only of some fiefs and in certain particular regions in the two countries.

XVI. *The Right of Alienation*

The question of how far the vassal had the right of alienating his fief· is one that requires more prolonged discussion. There

[1] *Ibid.*

can be no doubt that originally the vassal had no right to sell
or give away his fief. The fief was connected with the service
which the lord expected from a particular vassal, and its alienation would have rendered this service difficult or impossible.
Furthermore, the right enjoyed by the vassal over his fief was
regarded as a simple *ius in re aliena*, and thus could not include
the right of disposing of it. None the less, we know of cases of
the gift or sale of fiefs by vassals from the tenth century onwards
in France and from the eleventh in Germany, and atfer the Norman Conquest in England. But in all these alienations the lord
played some role. It might be part of the agreement, concluded
between the parties and approved by the lord, that the estate
which was sold or given away should remain a fief of the same
lord, but in the hands of the new owner. In this case, the vassal
would have to resign his fief into the hands of his lord, who
would then invest the purchaser with it after having received his
fealty and homage. Or the estate might be given away or sold on
condition that it was to become an allod or even be held by the
new owner in return for a money rent; this would be the normal
practice when the new owner was the Church. It would be necessary in such a case for the vassal to surrender the fief into the
hands of the lord; the latter would then give it as an allod to the
new owner, or sell it to him, or exchange it for some other estate,
or transfer it to him in return for the payment of a rent. The
one thing essential was that it must be the lord who gave the
new owner seisin of it. If the immediate lord was not the allodist,
it would be necessary to go back by a series of surrenders to
the ultimate allodial proprietor, since he would be the only person capable of alienating the fief in this way.

A few examples may make these operations somewhat clearer;
they were indeed common enough. An excellent example is provided by a charter of 1032–34 relating to land which a certain
Archambaud proposed to sell to the count of Anjou, Geoffrey
Martel, and his wife, who wished to use it for the construction of
the abbey of La Trinité at Vendôme. Archambaud held this land
in benefice of a certain Leudon, whose allodial property it was:
*Quapropter ego Leudonius deprecante fidele meo Archembaldo
alodos quos in beneficium de me hactenus tenere videbatur, illi*

vendere iure concessi comiti Gausfrido, 'on which account I
Leudon, at the request of my vassal Archambaud, have granted
him permission to sell lawfully to Count Geoffrey the allods
which up to now he has held in benefice from me'.[1] A little later
Leudon declares that he transfers the land to the new owners as
allodial property (*nunc trado in hereditatem*), using the time-
honoured formula for the transfer of allods (*ut a die presenti
quiquid memorati possessores loci facere voluerint, liberam et
firmissimam in omnibus habeant potestatem, nemine contra-
dicente*). Here also is an example from Champagne. In the
year 1157, Oliver of Drosnay gave to the abbey of La Chapelle
aux Planches (Marne) an estate held in fief of Count Henry
of Troyes. The latter's intervention in the operation is described in his declaration that 'since this estate was held of me
in fief, Oliver and his son Gaucher, as they were bound to do,
divested themselves of it and invested me with it, and I invested
the abbot with it' (*hoc autem, ut ratum est, Oliverus et filius ejus
Gaucherus, cum de feodo meo erant, manum suam devestiverunt
meamque investiverunt et ego manum abbatis investivi*).[2] Or
again, from Flanders, Count Thierry of Alsace declared in a
charter of 1159: 'it is my wish that the following facts be known,
that 45½ measures of land held of me in fief by Leonius and of
the latter by his brother Guy were resigned by Guy to Leonius
and by the latter to me, and that I have now given them to the
church of St. Nicholas of Furnes to possess freely and for ever.
And in exchange for them I have received from the church 91
measures of land which I have given to the said Leonius to be
held in fief of me and he has handed them over to his brother
to hold them in fief of him' (*notum esse volo . . . quia 45 mensuras terre et dimidiam quas Leonius a me et frater eius Wido ab
ipso feodi jure tenuit, ab eodem fratre suo sibi et ab ipso michi
. . . redditas, ecclesie Sancti Nicolai de Furnes, perpetuo iure
libere possidendas, donavi. In quarum concambium ab eadem
ecclesia nonaginta unam mensuras de terra . . . recipiens easdem
predicto Leonio a me feodi iure possidendas tradidi et ipse nichi-*

---

[1] Métais, *Cartulaire de la Trinité de Vendôme*, i, no. 8.
[2] C. Lalore, *Cartulaire de la Chapelle aux Planches . . .*, no. 17 (pp. 17–
18).

lominus predicto fratri suo, easdem feodali iure, ab ipso possidendas, tradidit).[1]

In all these cases we find the juxtaposition of at least two separate types of act, without including the resignation of the fief carried out by the vassal who is alienating it. One of these acts takes place between the vassal alienating the fief and the person acquiring it, whether it be sale, exchange or gift; this is the only act which carries with it economic consequences, but it is not in itself sufficient to bring about the legal changes desired by the two parties. The other takes place between the lord and the person acquiring the estate, and it generally takes the form of a gift, an enfeoffment, or a grant in return for rent, but it may sometimes be a sale or exchange. There is no necessary correspondence between the first and the second of the two acts. The vassal, for example, may sell the fief to the acquirer and the lord may give it to him; indeed, in most charters there is normally only a reference to gift. A clearer case perhaps than those which we have just analysed is provided by the sale to St. Nicholas of Furnes in 1174 of a fief held of the count of Flanders at Alveringem for 550 marks by Everard Radoul, châtelain of Tournai and vassal of the count. The sale was carried out *me concedente*, with my consent, according to Count Philip of Alsace; the fief was resigned into the hands of the latter, and he, for the salvation of his soul and those of his parents, gave the property in frankalmoign to the church (*hereditario iure possidendam prefate ecclesie in elemosinam dedi*).[2]

But from the twelfth century onwards we begin to find that in France, and even in Germany, at least in certain regions and in the case of certain fiefs, the actual resignation of the fief into the hands of the lord and the investiture of the new holder with it by the latter no longer takes place. The procedure of what in France was called 'vest et devest' or 'dessaisine-saisine' is often replaced, sometimes only implicitly, by the express or tacit consent of the lord. In England, during the thirteenth century, lords

[1] A. Vandeputte and C. Carton, *Chronicon et Cartularium abbatiae S. Nicolai Furnensis* (Bruges, 1846), pp. 87–8. See also the text of 1164 cited above, p. 131, n. 1.

[2] Vandeputte and Carton, *Chronicon et Cartularium abbatiae S. Nicolai Furnensis*, pp. 217–18.

steadily lost, in practice, the power of preventing alienations by their tenants, until in 1290 the statute *Quia Emptores* forbade all subinfeudation, but gave to tenants complete liberty of substituting new tenants in their place.[1]

It must be admitted that from the twelfth century at latest in France and in Germany the lord could not effectively oppose the alienation of a fief, save in certain exceptional cases or for certain types of fief. In an agreement with the bishop of Thérouanne in 1150, Count Thierry of Alsace laid down that donations of fiefs to the church must be carried out with a strict observance of the procedure of 'dessaisine-saisine', but added that lords 'can in no fashion forbid them, unless for just cause or reasonable motive' (*domini eas nullo modo poterunt impedire, nisi justam causam et rationabilem conditionem opponant*).[2] In early times, a lord could exact a payment for his consent and approval, as in the case of succession by inheritance. This is the origin of the payments levied by a lord on the occasion of a change of holder, and often these assumed the character of a tax which bore some proportion to the price paid for the fief. Taxes of this kind appear under very varied names in the texts: *relevium, laudationes et ventae, investitura*, 'lods et ventes', 'quint', 'requint', etc.

In cases of gifts or sales to the Church, measures were developed by the lords in the twelfth and thirteenth centuries to make their explicit consent essential and the procedure of 'dessaisine-saisine' became strictly obligatory on pain of very severe sanctions. The custom grew up, particularly in France, of imposing on the church acquiring the property a tax 'of mortmain' (*de mainmorte*), which would indemnify the lord for the loss of the payments which would normally be made to him whenever the property changed hands. In other cases it was customary to designate an individual under the title of 'homme vivant et mourant', and the church would pay the relief when he came to die.

The lord could also exercise yet another right when a fief changed hands, that of pre-emption (Fr. *retrait*; Germ. *Vorkaufsrecht*; Dutch *naastingsrecht*). The feudal pre-emption was the

---

[1] W. Stubbs, *Select charters and other illustrations of English constitutional history*, 9th ed. by H. W. C. Davis (Oxford, 1948), 473–474.

[2] T. Duchet and A. Giry, *Cartulaire de l'église de Térouanne* (Saint-Omer; 1881), no. 27.

lord's right to substitute himself if he wished for the purchaser by paying him back the price which he had paid for the fief. In the customary law of some parts of France from the twelfth century onwards, precedence was given to what was called the 'retrait lignager', that is to say a right of pre-emption vested in the relatives of the seller. This may be regarded as yet another manifestation of the 'patrimonialization' of the fief. Neither of these institutions was known in England as far as military fiefs were concerned.

The real rights of the lord over the fief, which in the ninth century had amounted to full *proprietas*, at least in the case of the lord who was also the allodist, had thus been reduced to very small limits: the levying of certain dues, the right of intervening in, or consenting to, alienations between persons still alive, the right of pre-emption. The lord could alienate the fief, but only within the framework of his rights and provided he did not injure those of the vassal. With but few exceptions, as for example a fief in northern Germany held of an allodist other than the king or the Church,[1] the lord had not the power of compelling a vassal to give up his fief, even if he undertook to provide him with another in exchange for it. When Count Robert II of Flanders, on the eve of leaving for the First Crusade in 1096, gave to St. Peter's of Lille two-thirds of the tithes (*bodium*) of Lesquin (Nord), which Englebert of Cisoing and the châtelain Roger of Lille held of him in fief, he stated explicitly that both of these, after having received other goods in exchange, had surrendered it to him free of all charge (*accepto a me concambio, ab omni exactione liberum michi reddiderunt*).[2] In this way he emphasized the voluntary character of the restitution. The right of disposal had thus become much more restricted in the case of the lord than it had in that of the vassal.

---

[1] *Sachsenspiegel, Lehnrecht*, 71. 6 (ed. Eckhardt, 2nd ed., p. 105).
[2] Vercauteren, *Actes des comtes de Flandre*, no. 20 (p. 62).

Chapter Three

THE RELATIONSHIP BETWEEN VASSALAGE AND FIEF

I. The 'Realization' of Feudal Relationships

We have already seen that in the ninth century the process had begun by which the 'real' element of benefice or fief had begun to play the essential role in the complex of feudal and vassal relationships. This development had only become more accentuated during the centuries that followed. The growing custom of granting fiefs to vassals, and the importunity with which vassals demanded more and more of them, made the grant of a fief the most effective inducement to one man to become the vassal of another. It was, for example, in the hope of retaining the benefice which he had held from the late emperor and of receiving new benefices from Duke Henry of Bavaria, the pretender to the German crown, that Liuthar, margrave of the Nordmark of Saxony, was prepared in 1002 to recognize himself a vassal of the latter (*spem retinendi et augendi beneficii*.) It was by the bait of a great benefice of more than a thousand *mansi* that Archbishop Adalbert of Hamburg-Bremen induced his enemy Duke Magnus of Saxony to become his vassal in 1066 (*ut qui hostis erat, miles efficeretur, offerens ei de bonis ecclesiae mille mansos in beneficium et amplius*).[1] These examples make it clear that even in Germany, where the Carolingian tradition had in this respect lasted much more effectively than it had in France, a causal link was being created in the eleventh century between the grant of the fief and the establishment of a vassal relationship.

II. The Fief as Justification of Fealty and Service

From the existence of this causal relationship it was easy to draw the conclusion that the fealty itself of the vassal was bound up

---

[1] Thietmar of Merseburg, *Chronicon*, v. 3 (ed. R. Holtzmann, p. 222); Adam of Bremen, *Gesta Hammaburgensis ecclesiae pontificum*, iii. 49 (ed. B. Schmeidler, Hanover, 1917 p. 192).

with the fact that he held a fief of his lord, and that the service due from him was due in return for the grant of this fief. When in 1039 or a little later the châtelain Walter II of Cambrai became the vassal of Bishop Gerard I, he promised him his fealty 'as I promised it to you, as long as I shall be your vassal and shall hold your land' (*fidelitatem, sicut tibi promisi, adteneam quamdiu tuus fuero et tua bona tenuero*). It will be remembered that Fulbert of Chartres, in the first half of the eleventh century, had declared that the vassal should furnish his aid and counsel to his lord *si beneficio dignus esse vult*, 'if he wished to show himself worthy of his benefice'. In a charter of 1092 the services due from the Archbishop of Rouen to King Philip I of France are explicitly justified by the fact that he holds of the king a fief in the Vexin. In the treaty of 1101 by which Robert II of Flanders became vassal of Henry I of England and received of him a money fief, the services due from the count are linked to the fact that he has received a fief: *regem Henricum per fidem juvabit, sicut suum amicum et dominum de quo feodum tenet*, 'he will faithfully aid King Henry as his friend and his lord whose fief he holds'.[1] None the less, the duty of fealty and the services owed were in origin and in law created by a contract into which the element of property did not in theory enter.

III. *The Connection between Homage and the Grant of a Fief*

This situation allows us to understand the relationship which existed in the twelfth century between the act of homage, which created the relationship of vassalage, and the grant of a fief. In the charters and narrative sources of the period, we constantly meet with some such expression as that 'a person did homage' or 'is a vassal for such and such a fief.' Such phrases were even used by men who had a profound knowledge of the actual working of feudal institutions. For example, Gislebert of Mons, who was confidential adviser and chancellor of Count Baldwin V of Hainault (1168–95), and who was familiar with conditions in both Germany and France, tells us that in 1172 the count went to

---

[1] *Gesta episcoporum Cameracensium*, iii. 40 (M.G.H., SS., vii. 481); cf. above, pp. 83–84; Prou, *Actes de Philippe I*, no. 127; Vercauteren, *Actes*, no. 30, c. 10 (p. 91).

Liége and did homage to Bishop Raoul of Zähringen for Hainault (*debitum pro Hanonia fecit hominium*). Or again, he tells us that in 1173, Gilles of Saint-Aubert and his son 'did liege homage to the lord count [of Hainault] for this castle [of Busigny]' (*de ipso castro domino comiti . . . fecerunt hominium ligium*).[1] The phenomenon is in fact a general one. Here are two examples, one from southern Burgundy and the other from the region of Toulouse. A charter of 1096/1124 is concerned with the grant of a fief by the chapter of Saint-Vincent of Mâcon, and it is said of the vassal obtaining the fief that 'he did homage and swore fealty for this benefice' (*pro hoc beneficio . . . hominium et fidelitatem iuravit*). Pons Berenger of Brugières recognized himself in 1128 as being vassal of the abbot of St. Sernin of Toulouse and owing him homage in virtue of a seigneurie which he held of him: *et pro omni cetero honore qui est de isto fevo, Poncius Berengarii est homo ipsius abbatis manibus junctis*.[2] The assumption of such a relationship even penetrated the actual rite of homage, as we can see in legal texts of the thirteenth century. Bracton gives the rite in the following words: 'I become your man in respect of the tenement which I hold of you' (*devenio homo vester de tenemento quod de vobis teneo*), and a little further on the same author speaks of 'the tenement for which homage has to be done' (*tenementum per quod obligatur ad hominium*).[3]

IV. The Connection between Fealty and the Grant of a Fief

There are some cases from Languedoc and the kingdom of Burgundy-Arles where the texts seem to imply a relationship between the grant of a fief, or the fact of holding a fief, and the oath of fealty taken by the vassal; this is evident from many of the charters in which such oaths are embodied.[4] But whether fealty or homage is in question, it is in each case a matter of being or becoming vassal for a particular fief.

---

[1] Gislebert of Mons, *Chronique*, cc. 68, 75 (pp. 108, 115).
[2] C. Ragut, *Cartulaire de Saint-Vincent de Mâcon* (Mâcon, 1864), no. 567; Douais, *op. cit.*, no. 261, p. 181.
[3] *De legibus*, fo. 80b (ed. Woodbine, ii. 232, 233).
[4] See above, p. 81, n. 1.

V. *The Attachment of the Vassal Services to the Fief*

The preponderance acquired by the property element in the complex of feudal relationships is also made apparent by the fact that the services due from the vassal to the lord came more and more to be regarded as the services due by the fief or at least in return for the fief. An unpublished text from Hainault of 1224 puts this clearly when it speaks of 'all the service for which the said fief was bound to me' (*omne servicium in quo dictum feodum mihi tenebatur*). Even in the twelfth century, Gislebert of Mons had already used such an expression as 'the lord of the castle, who owed the service of castle-guard regularly at Mons for certain fiefs which he held' (*dominus castri, qui pro quibusdam feodis continuum in Montibus debebat stagium*).[1]

This linking of services and fief explains the abnormal customs which we have noticed in the working of feudal relationships in the south of France and the kingdom of Burgundy-Arles, and in particular the absence of virtually any service, and sometimes even the waiving of homage, for vassals holding 'free fiefs'.[2]

VI. *The Fief as the 'Cause' of the Vassal's Obligations*

When the canonists, glossators and post-glossators fully isolated the idea of the 'cause'—what an English lawyer would call the consideration—of contractual obligations, they defined it as the *id quod inducit ad contrahendum*, as the immediate end in view of which the obligation was incurred, and they regarded it as a necessary element in the contract. A new stage in the 'realization' of feudal relationships was reached when this doctrine was applied to them. Already in the thirteenth century, in the case of mutual contracts, the 'object' of the obligation of one of the parties was held to be the 'cause' of the obligation of the other. Similarly, when an advantage was lacking to one of the parties, the obligation on the other party lacked a 'cause', and therefore could be regarded as null and void. When this doctrine was applied to feudal relationships, it was widely held that the 'cause' of the vassal's obligations was not the maintenance and protec-

[1] Didier, *Droit des fiefs*, p. 68, n. 36; Gislebert of Mons, *Chronique*, c. 41 (p. 74).
[2] See above, pp. 80–81, 93–94, 119–120, and 152.

tion which he expected to receive from his lord, but (and this was a deduction from the general contemporary practice) the grant of the fief and the protection to which his lord had bound himself. From this point of view, it was easy to conclude that a contract of vassalage which did not include the grant of a fief created an obligation which lacked a 'cause' and which was consequently null and void. If it was not the existence of this danger which gave rise to the custom of regularly inserting a mention of the fief in the rite of homage, it certainly contributed to making it more frequent. Following in the steps of the Italian glossator Martinus de Fano, the illustrious French post-glossator Gulielmus Durandus in the thirteenth century recommended that the text of the act of homage should declare formally that the grant of the fief was the 'cause' of the vassal's undertakings: 'I promise this because you have granted to me and to my heirs such and such a property, as long as we shall remain your vassals, and also because you have promised to defend me and mine against every man' (*hoc ideo promitto quia talem rem mihi et heredibus meis concessisti, donec sub tuo dominio steterimus et insuper me ac mea defendere contra omnem hominem promisisti*).[1]

VII. Other Phenomena of 'Realization'

The study of vassalage and fiefs has provided us with numerous manifestations of the growing 'realization' of feudal relationships: the seizure or confiscation of the fief as the normal sanction for the failure of the vassal to perform his services, the heritability of the fief, the alienability of the fief, the multiplicity of liege homages, and so on. One may go so far as to say that during the thirteenth century the property element became the principal element in feudal relationships, though this evolution did not naturally take place everywhere at the same speed or to the same degree. It is also characteristic that terms describing the vassal in relation to the fief which he held were becoming increasingly common. If *homo feodalis* is already met with in the eleventh century,[2] the spread of expressions of this kind, such

---

[1] *Speculi Gulielmi Durandi . . . pars tertia et quarta*, [Lyons], 1532, fo. 119v.: Liber iv, particula iii, *De feudis*, 12.

[2] Douglas, 'A charter of enfeoffment . . .', E.H.R., xlii (1927), 247; this dates from 1066/87.

as *feodatarius, homme de fief*,[1] *Lehnsmann, leenman*, underline the fact that in the general view of contemporaries the essential element in the status of a vassal was the fact that he was the holder of the fief. And, as we have seen, legal theory was in substantial agreement with them on this point.

VIII. *Homage and Fealty as Necessary Preliminaries to Obtaining a Fief*

Under these conditions, it is clear that the personal engagements of the vassal were becoming mainly the preliminary and necessary formalities required for obtaining a fief. The importance attached to these personal engagements was consequently greatly reduced. No doubt, during the whole of the period with which we are dealing, the loyalty of vassals, and particularly that of the more important vassals, was never entirely to be relied upon. But at least in theory it was a personal obligation of the strictest sort, and the honour of the vassal suffered if it was not maintained. When it became attached to alienable property, however, instead of to property which could be alienated only with great difficulty and which had been simply intended to facilitate the service of the vassal, it virtually ceased to be a personal obligation and became no more than a commodity which might be sold to the highest bidder.[2] It lost in consequence all its stability and perhaps even the very reason for its existence.

---

[1] Already in Beaumanoir, *Coutumes de Beauvaisis*, i, no. 23 (p. 27).
[2] As Marc Bloch pointedly expressed it, it was 'mise dans le commerce' (*Société féodale*, i. 324).

Chapter Four

FEUDALISM AND THE STATE

1. Fief and 'Justice'

Before we can form a clear picture of the place held by feudal relationships in the structure of the State between the tenth and thirteenth centuries, there is one essential question that must be answered. Did the grant of a fief necessarily carry with it the grant of the right of 'justice'?

The difficulty of giving a single answer to this question is apparent when we remember that *justicia* included far more than we mean by the word 'justice' today. It involved police and other functions which we would regard as purely administrative in character, such as the right to levy tolls on the circulation of articles of commerce (Lat. *teloneum*; Fr. *tonlieu*), the right to authorize maikets and tax the transactions which took place in them, and so on.

With a remarkable understanding of the real essence of feudal institutions, the majority of jurists who in the course of the last centuries of the *Ancien Régime* in France put themselves this question, answered it in the negative. At the beginning of the seventeenth century, Antoine Loisel declared that 'fief, jurisdiction and "justice" have nothing in common',[1] and this phrase, repeated after him by other lawyers, became in time an accepted legal maxim.

This was true not only for France. There was nothing in the relationships of feudalism, whether considered from the personal or from the property standpoint, which required that a vassal receiving investiture of a fief should necessarily have the profits of jurisdiction within it, nor even that he should exercise such jurisdiction on behalf of the lord or of a higher authority. It might and frequently did happen that, in addition to an estate,

[1] *Institutes coutumières*, II, ii. 42 (ed. M. Reulos, Paris, 1935, no. 257, p. 47): 'Fief, ressort et justice n'ont rien de commun ensemble'.

a person was invested with rights of a public character, and notably 'rights of justice' within the limits of the estate or even outside. In thirteenth-century Germany, a distinction was made between the enfeoffment of land and the enfeoffment of *justicia*, at least where 'high justice' was concerned, 'high justice' including criminal jurisdiction where the heaviest penalties were involved and civil jurisdiction over actions which affected personal status and landed property. At the beginning of the century, the *Sachsenspiegel* still found it necessary to state that in order to exercise 'high justice', counts and high-advocates had to receive a special grant (*Bannleihe*) from the king.[1] It is even more remarkable when we find that in Lotharingia, the part of Germany which was most strongly feudalized, a distinction was still being made in Hainault in the last decade of the twelfth century between fiefs consisting of landed property and 'justice' held as a fief. Gislebert of Mons, when describing the events which in 1071 had made the county of Hainault a feudal dependency of the church of Liége, took pains to distinguish the former allodial property of the counts, which was now held in fief, and the public offices which were also held in fief; these last he enumerates as the lay abbacy and advocateship of Sainte-Waudru of Mons and the 'justice' of the county of Hainault (*abbatiam et advocatiam Montensis ecclesie et justiciam comitatus Hanoniensis*).[2] In France, on the other hand, this distinction must have disappeared very early, for it has scarcely left any traces in the texts. There sometimes 'justice' belonged also to lords when they were allodists; at other times vassals did not have the right of 'justice' in their own fiefs; and cases are not rare in which 'justice' within the boundaries of a fief belonged neither to the vassal holding it nor to the lord from whom it was held but to the prince or to some other third party. This shows that in France the right of justice, which was a public office, underwent perhaps less disintegration than property and certainly was often divided in a different fashion. It is true that there were certain regions—e.g. Beauvaisis in the thirteenth century[3]—in which every fief carried with it the exercise

---

[1] *Landrecht*, i. 59, 1; ii. 12, 6 (ed. K. A. Eckhardt, 2nd ed., Göttingen, 1955, pp. 114, 138).

[2] Gislebert of Mons, *Chronique*, c. 8 (pp. 11–12).

[3] Beaumanoir, *Coutumes de Beauvaisis*, i, no. 295 (pp. 146–7); ii, no. 1641 (p. 340).

of 'justice', and these justified the legal maxim subsequently locally
admitted in certain custumals on the identity of the two ('fief et
justice c'est tout un'). But these are not typical, and are to be
explained by particular circumstances; such as the rapid and
general disappearance of allodial property and allodists and by
the accident that in these regions the territorial fief and the
exercise of 'justice' did as a general rule happen to coincide with
one another.

II. Feudal Jurisdiction

Powers of jurisdiction were none the less very closely bound up
with feudal relationships. This was the case in particular with
what one normally calls feudal jurisdiction, meaning by it cases
arising out of the contract of vassalage and concerning its terms
or affecting the fief itself. This jurisdiction normally belonged
to the lord, who exercised it over his vassals and over the fiefs held
from him.

The duty of acting as a judge made no part of the essence of
feudal relations, for during the greater part of the Carolingian
period the lord did not act as judge of his vassals. This power
must have been acquired during the troubled and obscure years
of the end of the ninth and the first third of the tenth century.
Possibly the lord himself was at first the sole judge of failures or
conflicts in the fields of vassal and feudal relationships, but from
a quite early time we find such disputes being decided by a court.
This development did not come about everywhere in the same
fashion. In most parts of France, the territorial princes who at
that time were building up their power, and the counts who,
though under them, none the less succeeded in retaining a certain
autonomy, each set out to create for themselves a *curia*, a court,
either a new institution imitated from the royal 'court' or one
deriving from the Carolingian county court, furnished with
'échevins' (*scabini*) or judges (*judices*). This court was presided
over by the prince or the count, while his vassals assumed the
duty of assessors. They probably united at an early date to induce
the prince or count to allow cases which affected their relations
with him or between themselves and cases affecting the fiefs
which they held of him to be submitted to the court in the

same way as cases of a more strictly public character. The vassals of other lords who constituted courts in imitation of those of princes and counts naturally tended to copy the procedure of these, and even lords who exercised no other type of jurisdiction began in their turn to create courts attended by their vassals to judge cases in which vassals and fiefs were involved. Most of these developments were taking place in the tenth century. These courts varied greatly in their composition, their procedure, and their place in the judicial organization of the country or principality, and in the course of centuries they underwent considerable transformations. In Flanders, for example, where there existed tribunals of the count in each châtellenie where cases of common law came up for judgment, the count created side by side with these, and at latest by the early years of the thirteenth century, territorial feudal courts in each châtellenie. These courts extended their jurisdiction to embrace a large proportion of cases involving feudal law which would otherwise have gone to the *curia* of the count.

In the principalities of Lotharingia, courts of a type resembling those of France came into existence. But in the greater part of Germany things went very differently. Only the royal court was competent both in matters of common law and in matters of feudal law where royal vassals and fiefs held of the king were involved. Over most of Germany a system of public tribunals, deriving from those of Carolingian times, continued to exist. Lords had to constitute special tribunals to give judgment in cases concerning their vassals and fiefs, and a distinct system of law was applied in them: *Lehnrecht* and *Lehnsgericht*, the feudal law and the feudal court, were opposed to *Landrecht* and *Landgericht*, the territorial law and the territorial tribunal. The *Lehnsgericht* was composed of the vassals of a lord, and they gave judgment under his presidency.

England after the Norman Conquest followed the French pattern. Great lords holding 'honours', and no doubt many less important lords, had each a court, attended by their vassals, which exercised jurisdiction over questions of vassalage and fiefs and certainly over other matters as well. But from the second half of the twelfth century onwards the policy of the Crown was steadily expanding the sphere of action of royal justice, to the detriment of the feudal courts, which consequently lost much of their importance.

All these tribunals, attended by the lord's vassals and exercising each in its own sphere jurisdiction over matters of feudal law, had one feature in common. They were not simply concerned with breaches of the criminal law and the unravelling of civil issues. They also, and perhaps one might almost say principally, exercised a *juridiction gracieuse*, for it was before them that fealty and homage, investiture, the resignation and transfer of fiefs, and so on were carried out. One example of this may be given. In 1119 or 1120, Dirk Rufus, a vassal of the count of Flanders, wished to give the abbey of St. Nicolas of Furnes 60 measures of land which he held as a fief of the count, and it was in the latter's court, in the presence of his vassals, that Dirk divested himself of his fief and the count gave it as an allod to the church. The proceeding is described in a charter of Charles the Good: *sexaginta mensuras terre quas a me Theodericus Ruphus . . . jure feodi tenuerat, coram optimatibus et principibus meis publice michi ab ipso redditas, ecclesie Furnensi Sancti Nicolai . . . manu propria donavi.*[1]

III. *Feudal Relationships within the Framework of the State*

Having dealt with the relationship between feudalism and the exercise of justice, it only remains for us to deal with the use that kings and princes made of feudalism in the government of the State. This is a matter that must be examined separately for France, Germany and England, for while in each country feudal law played an essential part in the government, the way in which it did so differed greatly in each case.

IV. *France*

It is no exaggeration to say that until late in the twelfth century the French king could exercise power outside the royal domain only in a feudal capacity. It is true that the Capetians never renounced their royal title, or the claim that in virtue of it they exercised a supreme authority answerable to none, but this pre-

---

[1] Vercauteren, *Actes*, no. 98 (pp. 223–5).

tension was for long of a purely theoretical character. When Louis VI undertook an expedition in 1126 against the count of Auvergne, who had been causing the bishop of Clermont trouble, Duke William VIII of Aquitaine, who was both vassal of the king of France and overlord of the count of Auvergne, intervened on the latter's behalf. He demanded that the count of Auvergne should be summoned, through him, before the royal court, and he undertook that on the appointed day he would ensure the presence of his vassal and give him his support. The king was constrained to abandon the expedition and content himself with the process of feudal law.[1] When he intervened in Flanders after the murder of Count Charles the Good in the following year he showed that he had learned his lesson. Though he designated a new count in the person of William Clito, son of Duke Robert of Normandy, directed the military operations against the murderers and their supporters, and carried out a whole series of political measures in Flanders, he was careful throughout to conform in everything to the requirements of feudal law. Up to the reign of Philip Augustus and perhaps even later, the idea of monarchical sovereignty was only clearly appreciated and recognized by a small proportion of the educated classes, nearly all of them clergy. On a smaller scale, within the great territorial principalities, it was only in virtue of the feudal authority claimed by the lord over his vassals that many of the princes could exercise authority over large portions of their territory. This is clear in the cases of the dukes of Aquitaine and Burgundy and the counts of Toulouse, for a large part of the territory feudally subject to these princes was in fact ruled by counts or viscounts who enjoyed a large measure of independence. It was also true, though in smaller measure, of territorial principalities as strong and closely knit as Normandy and Flanders; in the eleventh and twelfth centuries the count of Flanders, for example, could exercise no authority over the counts of Boulogne, Guines, Saint-Pol and Hesdin except in his capacity of their feudal lord. Even within territory directly subject to their authority, the king and many princes, and not necessarily the weaker of the latter—for example the counts of Anjou—could control the actions of the

[1] Suger, *Vie de Louis VI le Gros*, c. 29 (ed. H. Waquet, Paris, 1929, pp. 238, 240).

lesser lords, those holding perhaps one or very few castles, only in virtue of the obedience which these lords owed them as vassals.

The kings of France made constant use of rights deriving from the contract of vassalage. They did this at first, in the tenth and eleventh centuries and in most of the twelfth, only in a small way, and only when, rightly or wrongly, they judged the circumstances to be in their favour. From the majority of the territorial princes they contented themselves with exacting fealty and homage, by which the princes recognized themselves as their vassals or, when the doctrine of liegeancy came into existence, as their liege vassals. Later, as their strength increased, the kings grew bolder, and made more vigorous use of this power, even against the strongest princes. The most famous case was the condemnation of King John to the loss of all his French fiefs for failing in his duties as a vassal. The process is described by a contemporary chronicler: 'Then when the court of the king of France had met, it judged that the king of England should be deprived of all the land which up to then he and all his ancestors had held of the kings of France, because for a long time they had refused to furnish nearly all the services due for these lands and they were not willing to obey their lord in anything' (*Tandem vero curia regis Franciae adunata adjudicavit regem Angliae tota terra sua privandum quam hactenus de regibus Franciae ipse et progenitores sui tenuerant, eo quod fere omnia servitia eisdem terris debita per longum tempus facere contempserant nec domino suo in aliquibus obtemperare volebant*).[1]

When in the thirteenth century the successors of Philip Augustus began to build up an administrative machine disposing of a reasonably efficient system of finance and served by a body of paid officials, the kings insisted more than ever upon their feudal rights. Although by the beginning of the fourteenth century they had not succeeded in their endeavours to secure the insertion into every feudal contract of a clause reserving the fealty due to the king, the Capetians tried to systematize all feudal relationships in France so that these derived ultimately from themselves; in this way the king would become 'le souverain fieffeux du royaume', as he is termed by the 'feudists', the exponents of the theory of

[1] Ralph of Coggeshall, *Chronicon Anglicanum*, ed. J. Stevenson (London, 1875), p. 136.

feudal law under the *Ancien Régime*. They exploited systematically every occasion offered them by feudal law of taking action against the more powerful feudatories, whose autonomy they hoped to diminish by securing their condemnation in the royal *curia*. The history of the relations between the county of Flanders and the Crown in the thirteenth century consists largely of repeated attempts of this kind. While feudal law ceased to be in reality the essential basis of royal authority, it remained and indeed became more and more an instrument of royal policy and a means of government.

V. *Germany*

In Germany the evolution of the relations between feudalism and the state followed quite a different pattern. As we have seen, feudal relations had some part in the structure of the German state under the Saxon and Franconian dynasties from the tenth to the beginning of the twelfth century. The dukes, the majority of the bishops and margraves, the counts palatine and a number of the other counts were bound to the Crown by the link of vassalage. But this link did not constitute the basis of royal power. The authority of the Crown rested on two things: on the one hand, what had survived of the organization of the Carolingian state; and on the other, the use it could make of the Church. But when the struggle of Papacy and Empire in the second half of the eleventh century and in the early twelfth deprived the Crown of much of its authority over the bishops and impaired the whole structure of the Imperial Church, at the same time giving the margraves and counts the opportunity of transforming themselves into autonomous princes whose public character had almost disappeared, some other basis for royal authority had to be found. It was Frederick Barbarossa who, in the second half of the twelfth century, drew the logical conclusion from this state of things and attempted to reorganize the kingdom on a new basis, and that a feudal one.

His opportunity came in 1180, when Henry the Lion, duke of Saxony and Bavaria, was condemned to the loss of his imperial fiefs, the charge being the grave dereliction of his duty as a vassal which he had committed in failing to appear before the royal court sitting in its feudal capacity as the emperor's *Lehnsgericht*.

The princes who gave their support to their king on this occasion naturally expected their reward, so the new organization of the state was to a large extent a compromise between the wishes of the sovereign and the interests of the princes. Henceforward the royal power was to be largely based on the new class of imperial-princes (*Reichsfürsten*), those tenants-in-chief of the Crown who were themselves lords of at least two counties either directly controlled by them or held of them in fief. This meant that with few exceptions the new order of princes of the empire (*Reichsfürstenstand*) was limited, among the lay princes, to those who were dukes or margraves. In addition, there was established a strict hierarchy of lord and vassal, with the king at the top and the class of serf-knights at the bottom (*Heerschild*). The princes of the empire were recognized as enjoying a specially privileged position, and the holding by a vassal of a fief of a lord not belonging to a class superior to his own was forbidden, the penalty for breach of this regulation being the vassal's own descent into an inferior class. Germany rapidly became entirely feudalized. Although one can scarcely speak of an absolute obligation on the king to re-grant within a year and a day such fiefs of the Crown as became vacant (*Leihezwang*), these fiefs tended less and less to remain in his hands. The extension, in practice if not in law, of claims to inheritance by collaterals, the succession pacts concluded by members of the same family between themselves, and the possibility of extracting the royal consent more or less willingly to such arrangements, all played their part, along with other considerations, in building up a custom in the matter. It thus became virtually impossible to create or develop a royal domain. The Hohenstaufen and their successors failed to retain their control of public institutions which had been radically transformed. It was the great territorial principalities, from which the chief modern German states—Austria, Bavaria, Prussia. etc.—emerged.

VI. *England*

The development of the relations between feudalism and the State in England exhibits a number of peculiar features. It was almost the converse of what took place in Germany and, although in many respects it resembled the development in France, there were none the less some striking contrasts.

English society before the Norman Conquest had been familiar with a relationship of personal dependence known as thegnage, which had many points of contact with vassalage; the thegn who depended on the king and undertook to serve him was a person closely resembling a vassal. But while on the Continent the distinction between vassals and other free men who owed service to a lord had already developed by the eleventh century, the class of thegns in England still included, in addition to the great royal thegns, many free but quite inferior servants of the ecclesiastical and secular magnates. In addition, the thegn who received from the king a grant of land, received it in full ownership and not on conditional tenure, so that such a holding was quite different from the continental fief. The existence of thegnage may have facilitated the introduction of feudalism into England, but there was no true continuity between the two institutions, any more than the tenements which existed before 1066 had anything in common with the later fief.

English feudalism was a creation of the Norman Conquest. The system of feudal relations which existed in the duchy of Normandy was introduced into England by William the Conqueror; English feudalism however differed greatly from Norman feudal institutions. It was developed by William's successors in the fullest possible manner, though always in such a way as to minister to the needs of the Crown. From the point of view of English law, the whole country became the property of the Crown, and allodial estates, over which the proprietor exercised full and unrestricted ownership, did not exist. A tenure by frankalmoign ('free alms'), which in other countries was regarded as a privileged form of allodial holding, was in England regarded as a feudal tenement carrying with it an obligation of prayer. Every estate was regarded as a tenement held directly or indirectly of the king, and no form of holding could be ultimately independent of him. In order to diminish the danger of sub-vassals being employed by tenants-in-chief against the Crown, William the Conqueror imposed on all free men occupying a tenement an oath of fealty or 'allegiance' to the king (Oath of Salisbury, 1086). Similar oaths were taken in 1087 to William Rufus and in 1100 to Henry I. The idea behind these oaths was subsequently influenced by the conception of liegeancy, and one came to term all those who had taken them the liegemen of the king. In the reign of

Henry I, the Crown insisted that a reservation of fealty to the king should form part of the ordinary oath of vassalage. The military obligations of vassals, more particularly in respect of the number of knights they were required to furnish, were fixed in relation to the needs of the royal army. Finally, with the exception of feudal justice and 'low justice', no holder of a normal fief enjoyed the full powers of jurisdiction or the administrative functions which were comprised in the medieval concept of *justicia* or was able to keep them for a long time if he had got hold of them; exceptions to this rule were those barons who held the great 'honours' and chiefly the palatinates on the Scottish and Welsh borders— an example is the county palatine of Durham between the Tees and the Tyne—and the Channel coast. From the reign of Henry I onwards, but especially under the Plantagenets and more particularly during the reign of Henry II, the policy of the Crown was directed, on the one hand, to restricting still further the place reserved to feudal relationships in the State and, on the other, to developing new methods of using these relations in the interests of the royal administration. The advance of royal justice gradually restricted the judicial functions of the holders of 'honours' and made substantial inroads on the competence of feudal courts; the development of scutage, the replacement of the military service of the vassal by a money payment, rendered the Crown more independent of the feudal levy and at the same time placed it in a position to pay for troops of its own. The feudal reaction which lay behind the conspiracy of the barons under King John and produced the grant of Magna Charta in 1215 was impotent to check this evolution.

VII. Conclusion

This brief sketch of the relations between feudalism and the State in the three chief countries of western Europe between the tenth and thirteenth centuries justifies us in drawing one conclusion, which is that feudal institutions were not of necessity a source of weakness in the state. As M. Olivier-Martin has very justly put it, 'vassalage and monarchy were far from being incompatible institutions'.[1] There were elements in feudal law which made possible the development of royal authority. The monarchy

[1] F. Olivier-Martin, 'Les liens de vassalité dans la France médiévale', in *Société Jean Bodin. I. Les liens de vassalité et les immunités* (Brussels, 2nd ed., 1958), p. 217; cf. also H. Mitteis, *Lehnrecht und Staatsgewalt*, pp. 4–5.

in France and England succeeded in turning them to their advantage; in Germany, on the other hand, different circumstances resulted in an abnormal development of the rights of vassals as opposed to those of the Crown. It was the accidents of history which determined the direction and fashion in which the same system of institutions developed in each country and within each society.

CONCLUSION

I. *Feudalism after the Thirteenth Century*

Feudal institutions lasted in western Europe to the end of the *Ancien Régime*, and in some countries elements of them survived into the nineteenth and even the twentieth centuries. But from the end of the thirteenth century they ceased in western Europe to be the most fundamental element in the structure of society, lying behind and influencing every aspect of its life and thought.

The survival of feudal institutions was most complete in the case of fiefs, even when from the point of view of private law these came to be regarded as nothing more than a particular type of estate. Their transmission was accompanied by certain legal forms and had to take place in accordance with certain specific rules, and their occupants, from the time when the service of military vassals was no longer or only infrequently required, were bound to certain payments sometimes in kind on specified occasions. The personal element in feudal relationships became something purely accessory: homage and fealty were no more than formalities which had to be undertaken within a certain time in order that one could enter into the legal possession of one's fief. The effective rights attached to the possession of the latter and the dues which it entitled its holder to collect resulted in the development of written documents regarding it, such as *aveux* and *dénombrements*, and records in *livres de fiefs* or *livres de feudataires*. The litigation which changes of holding involved, and the legal disputes provoked by conflicts over the rights of the different parties over fiefs, led to an increase in the importance of the feudal courts attended by the vassals, the tribunals competent in such matters.

Side by side with these changes, a transformation was taking place in the personnel of the holders of fiefs. From the thirteenth century onwards, and no doubt even before that date, men of bourgeois origin were acquiring fiefs side by side with the nobility; they became so numerous that in France an unusually heavy form of payment known as *droit de franc-fief* was customarily exacted on such occasions. The acquisition of a fief was a regular way in which a man of the middle or lower classes could hope to rise in the social scale. This was a consequence of the fact that very frequently, and in some regions invariably, a fief constituted a lordship, and gave to the person acquiring it the exercise of certain powers of jurisdiction and a number of positive rights and honorary prerogatives.

In relation to public law, feudal institutions long continued to enjoy a certain importance. They were to the end of the Middle Ages a favourite means of creating a link between a State and some territory which the ruler of this State wished to acquire, or a means of maintaining a bond between a State and a territory which threatened to become independent of it. A good example of this is provided by the relations of Flanders and Artois with the French Crown from the reign of Philip the Good to that of Charles V. In Germany, feudal law played a considerable part in the later Middle Ages and early modern times in determining the legal relations between many of the smaller princes and even the knights of the empire (*Reichsritter*), and the Empire, a political organization whose substance was becoming more and more unreal. Immediate dependence on the Empire (*Reichsunmittelbarkeit*) was often a good protection against absorption by the larger German states which were being built up by such families as the Luxemburgs, Hapsburgs, Wittelsbachs and Hohenzollern, and conflicts over the status of these petty rulers gave rise between the sixteenth and eighteenth centuries to interminable litigation before the supreme tribunal of the Empire (*Reichskammergericht*). On the other hand, the existence of feudal relationships provided the Great Powers on more than one occasion with suitable pretexts for wars of conquest; under Louis XIV, for example, their examination with a view to political profit was one of the main activities of the 'Chambres de Réunion'.

Finally, the obligation laid on the vassal of giving counsel to his lord gave rise, as we have seen, to the courts of justice, attended by vassals, some of which developed into the supreme or judicial tribunals of many countries: the 'Parlement de Paris' and several other French 'parlements', the Council of Flanders (*Raad van Vlaanderen*) and so on. The same duty of giving counsel, and the custom which required that a lord should consult his vassals before making any important decision, played an essential part in the formation of 'estates' (Fr. "les Etats") and other organizations representing particular classes of society in the course of the three last centuries of the Middle Ages. The origins of the English parliament itself derive in part from this feudal practice. There are even survivals of actual feudal ceremonies: in the Channel Islands today the tenants-in-chief still swear fealty and do homage to their lord.

II. The Legacy of Feudalism

In addition to some great institutions which, in the modern world, still exist, in however changed a shape, feudalism has left behind it many legacies—vestigial remains, one might almost call them—in our methods of behaviour and thought and feeling, in the ways in which we express our ideas. We are scarcely conscious of this inheritance, but it is none the less there. When a Frenchman presents 'ses hommages' to a lady, he is in effect declaring himself her vassal. When a Dutchman or a Fleming says that he will support a person or a cause 'met raad en daad', he is undertaking the same duties as those of a vassal, *consilium et auxilium*. It is from feudalism that the prestige of the military profession, the belief in the binding force of engagements freely entered into, the idea that one is not bound to obey an order incompatible with one's dignity as a free man, are ultimately derived. It is to the sacredness formerly attached to the 'foi' which bound together lord and vassal, that the high importance still attached in western Europe to the virtue of fidelity directly goes back.